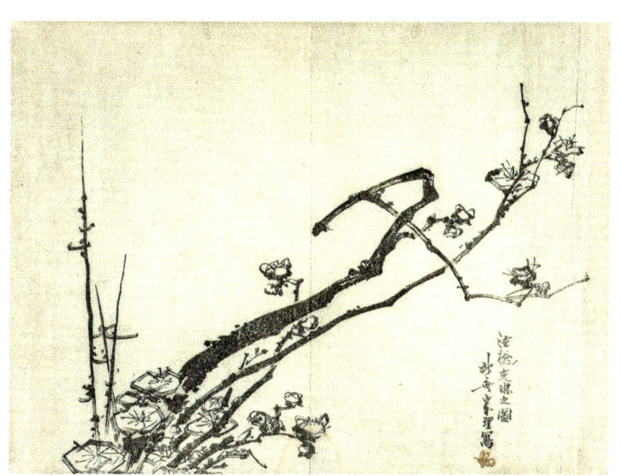

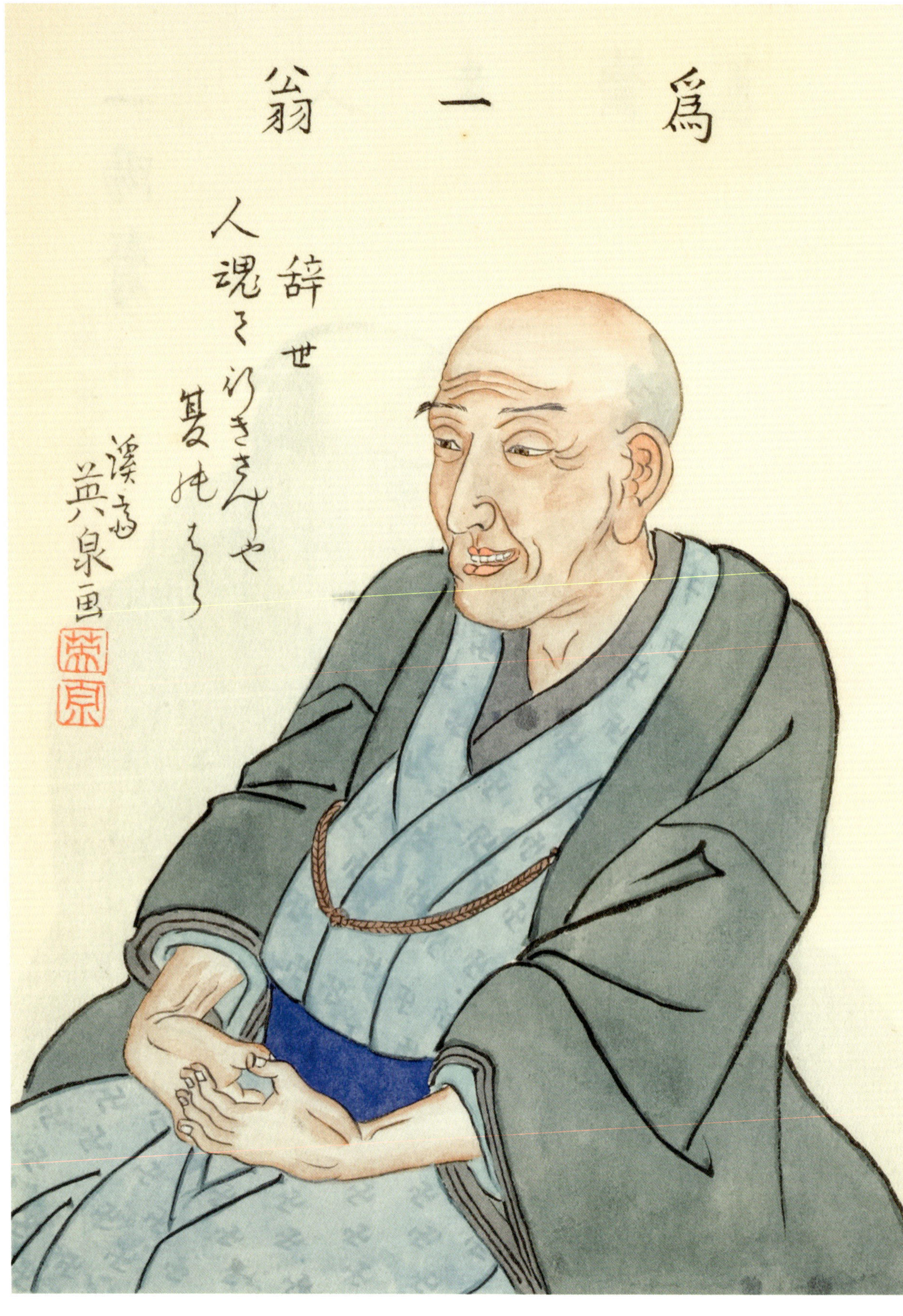
爲一翁
辞世
人魂で行きさんせや夏の原
渓斎
英泉画

Rhiannon Paget

Hokusai

1760–1849

TASCHEN

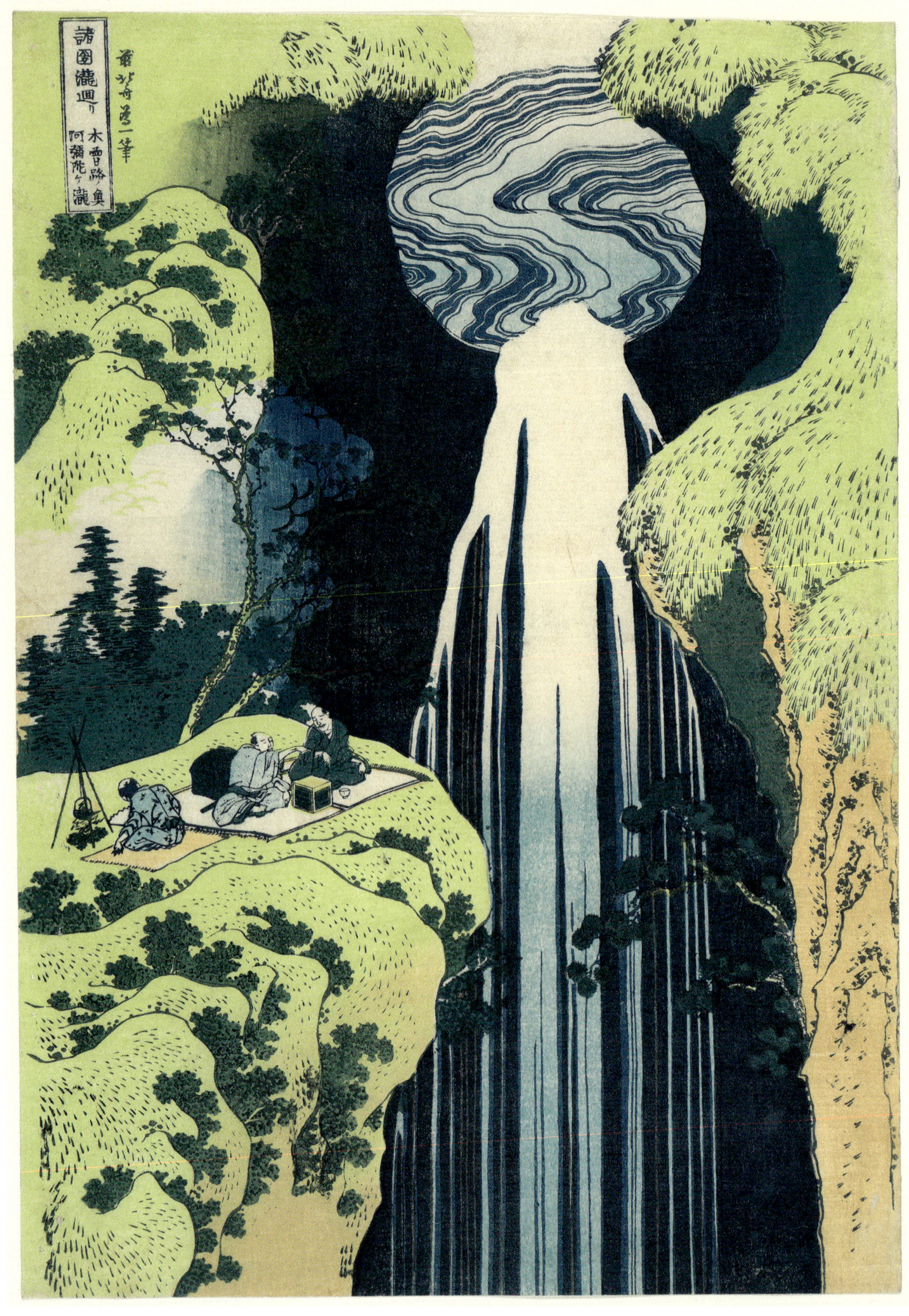

諸國瀧廻り　木曽路ノ奥　阿弥陀ヶ瀧
前北斎為一筆

Contents

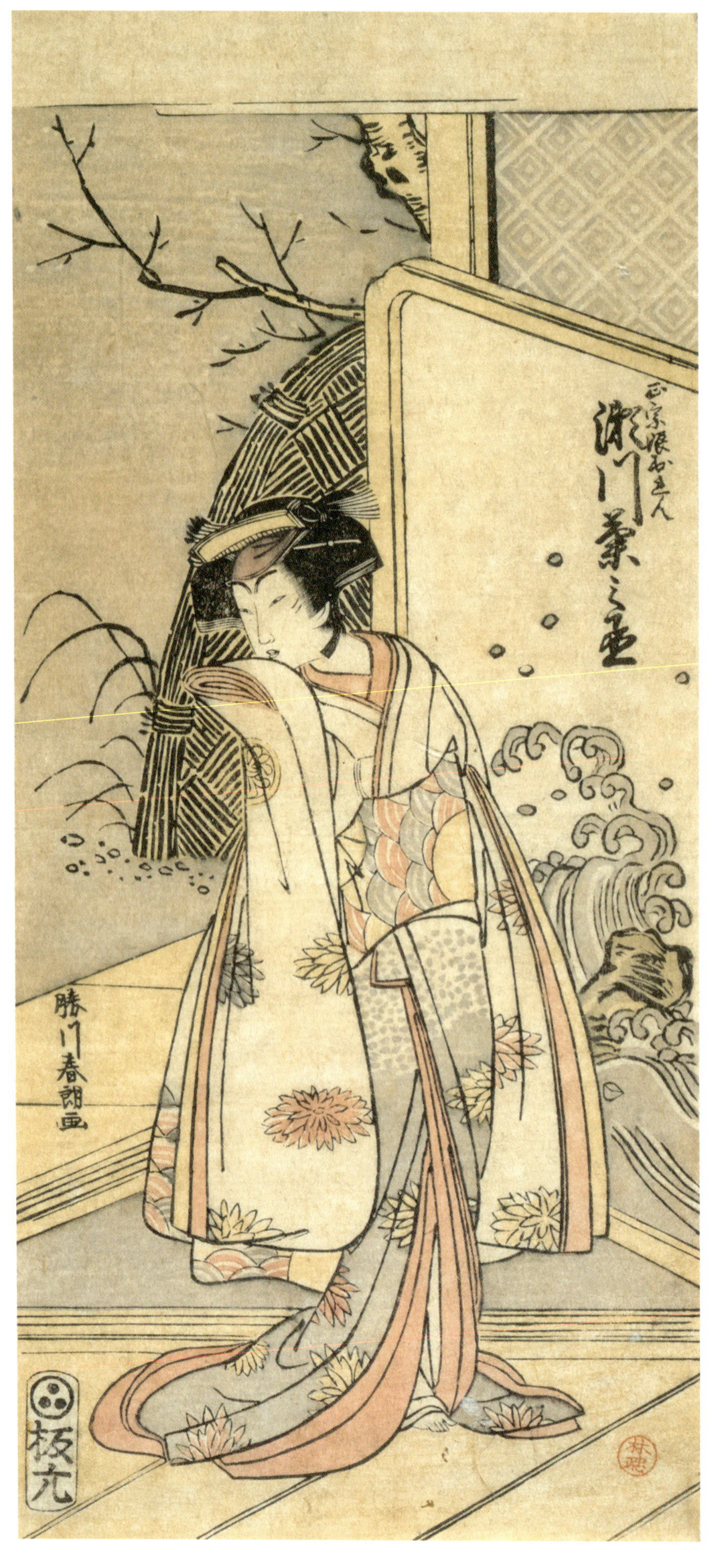

江戸娘おせん
瀬川菊之丞
勝川春朗画

Capturing the Floating World

The artist known as Hokusai (1760–1849) created some of Japan's most celebrated and influential masterpieces. So far-reaching was his appeal that his prints, paintings and illustrated books were collected by foreign visitors to Japan and both exhibited and reproduced in Europe within his own lifetime. Later, his designs captivated a generation of French painters, thereby launching *Japonisme*, a stylistic movement that shaped the development of modern art. An icon of Japanese art, Hokusai's *Under the Wave off Kanagawa* (*c.* 1830/31; ill. p. 64), also known as *The Great Wave*, has been endlessly imitated, parodied and abstracted into corporate logos and consumer goods – yet his restless genius extended far beyond the wave's unfurling mass of brilliant blue. Hokusai's indelible mark across time and continents continues to set him aside as the most eminent Japanese artist, not only in Japan, but also throughout the Western world.

A late bloomer, Hokusai's best work was completed in his senior years. Although his early designs are pale in comparison to his later masterpieces, they show how his ideas, often borrowed from other designers, gradually came to life over years of experimentation. Hokusai's genius lies in equal parts in his flawless technique, keen instinct for composition and his witty sense of humour, intelligence and vivid imagination. Over his long career, he remained a highly sensitive observer of urban life, fellow creatures and nature. Led by his curiosity, he broke new ground in the adaptation of Western pictorial techniques, which he used freely in combination with local aesthetic conventions.

Hokusai created an estimated 30,000 designs over his lifetime. His works belong to the category of *ukiyo-e*, "pictures of the floating world", which sought to depict the hedonistic pleasures of the mortal world – from kabuki actors and landscapes to beautiful women and erotic scenes. This new genre flourished among the sophisticated and increasingly wealthy inhabitants of the city of Edo (present-day Tokyo), the seat of the military government (or shogunate) which held power from 1603 to 1868. *Ukiyo-e* generally refers to mass-produced woodblock-printed images which could be issued as loose sheets or as illustrated books, but can also include paintings on paper or silk.

Commercial prints were not produced by an individual artist, but rather by a team of individuals working in specialized roles. A publisher, anticipating market preferences, would commission an artist to create one or more designs which would then be realized by a block carver and a printer. Prints

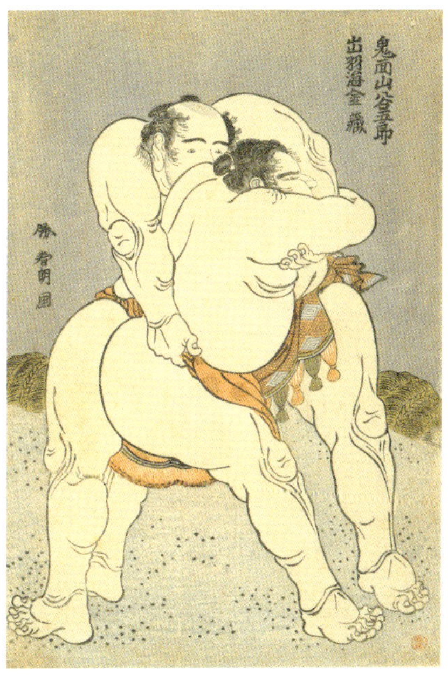

***The Sumo Wrestlers Kimenzan Tanigorō
and Dewanoumi Kinzō***, mid–late 1780s
Colour woodblock print, *aiban*,
32.5 x 22.2 cm (12⅞ x 8¾ in.)
Tokyo National Museum

***Segawa Kikunojō III as Oren,
Masamune's Daughter***, 1779
Published by Iseya Kinbei
Colour woodblock print, *hosoban*,
approx. 33 x 15 cm (13 x 6 in.)
Tokyo National Museum

PAGE 1
Flowering Plum Tree, 1789
From *Nightingale Deep in the Mountains*
Woodblock-printed book, ink and colour
on paper
London, British Museum

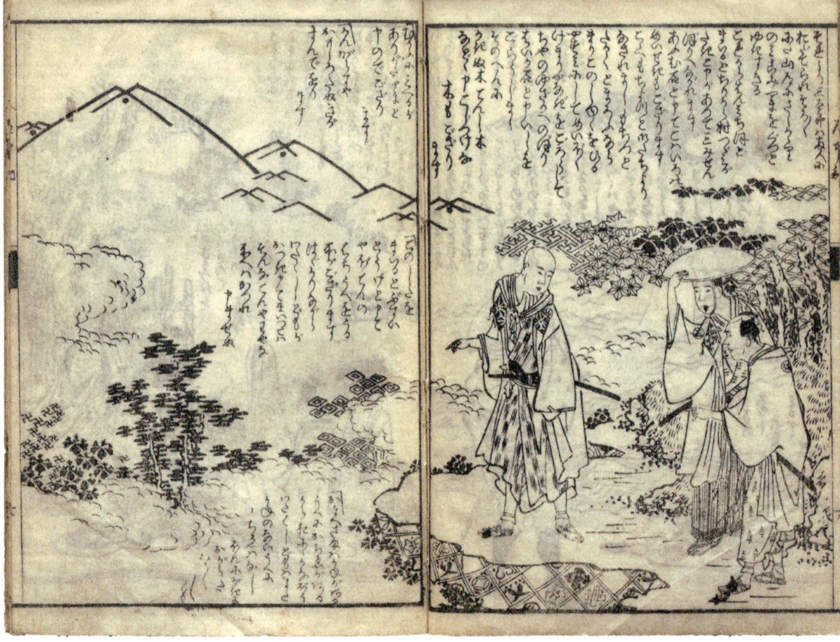

and printed books ranged from the cheaply made and affordable for the common man, to the deluxe and costly.

Many of Hokusai's prints and paintings are undated; however, artist's signatures and seals make it possible for scholars to determine when certain pieces were created. Over the course of his career Hokusai used more than 30 different names to sign his work. This was common practice in Japan; once an artist was deemed to have reached a certain level of proficiency, he (for they were largely male) would typically receive a new name that included one character from his master, carrying on his teacher's legacy in his very identity. In Hokusai's case, his teacher Shunshō bestowed upon him the name Shunrō. Later, he would adopt new names to signal a new direction in his work. It is thanks to Hokusai's multiple names that scholars are able to estimate an interval of years when a print was likely designed.

For the shogunate, *ukiyo-e* presented a threat to public morals and a rigid social order that placed the samurai (military class) at the upper tier of the social hierarchy and the increasingly prosperous *chōnin* (townsmen) at the bottom, by and for whom commercial prints were largely produced. Between 1791 and 1876, print designs had to be inspected by official censors prior to publication. Once approved, works were impressed with the censors' seals, which were then reproduced as part of the composition. These seals were often dated, and thus became invaluable tools when determining when a print was published.

Advertisements for upcoming products, included in books as well as publishers' colophons, also help in dating certain works. In some cases, the subject matter itself is sufficient when estimating a date; for example, the publication date of a print commemorating the performance of an actor in a specific role can be inferred with the help of kabuki playbills.

Hokusai's first biographer was Iijima Kyoshin (1841–1901). His writings have passed down colourful tales that unveil Hokusai's personality with some purporting to come directly from his contemporaries. However, it is important to

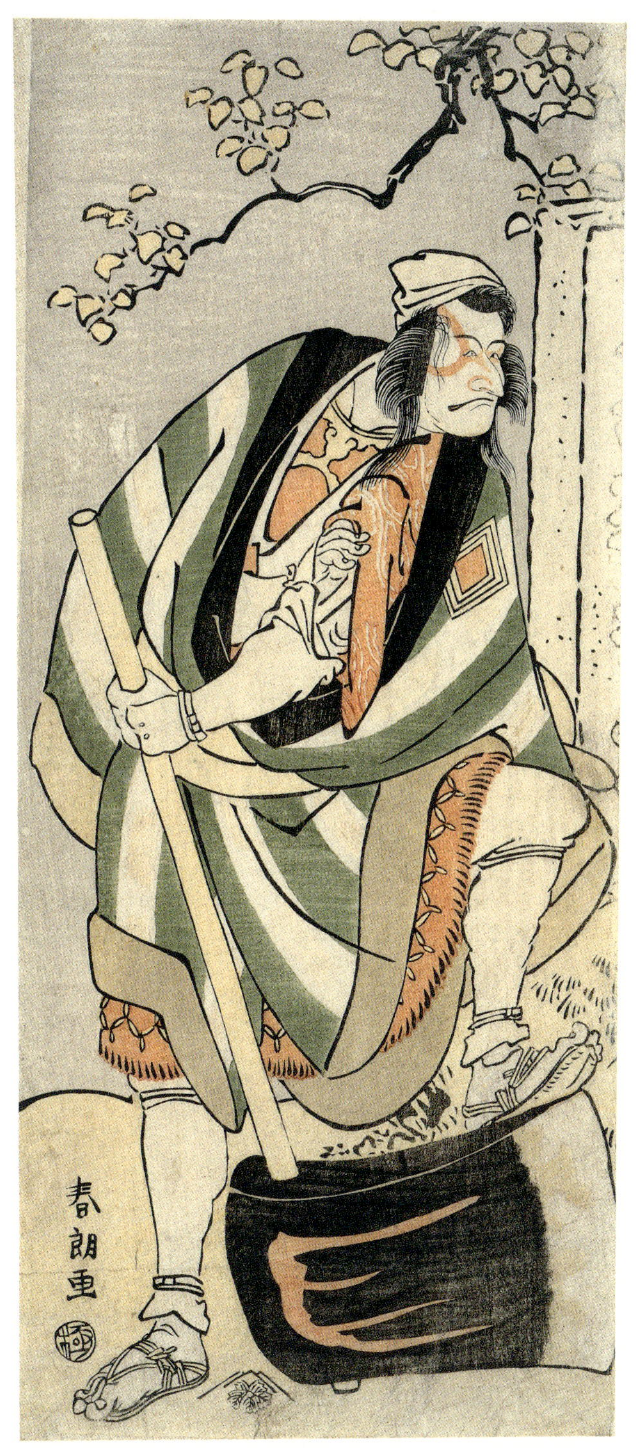
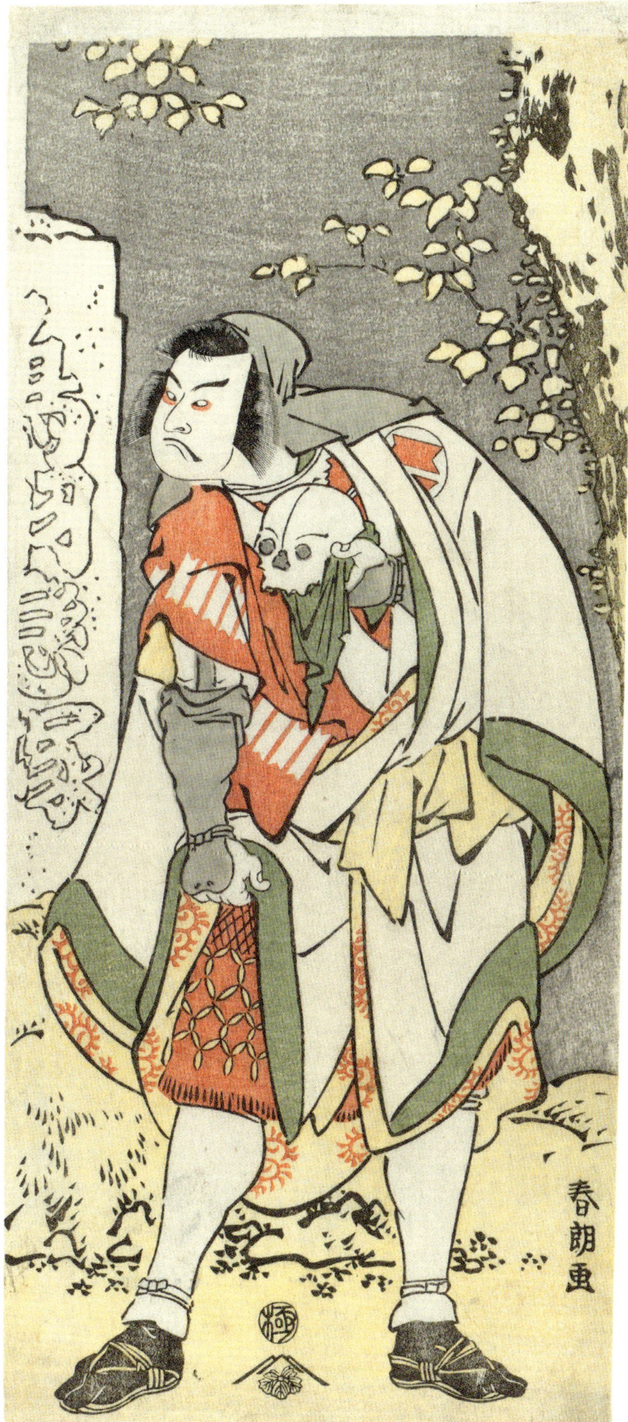

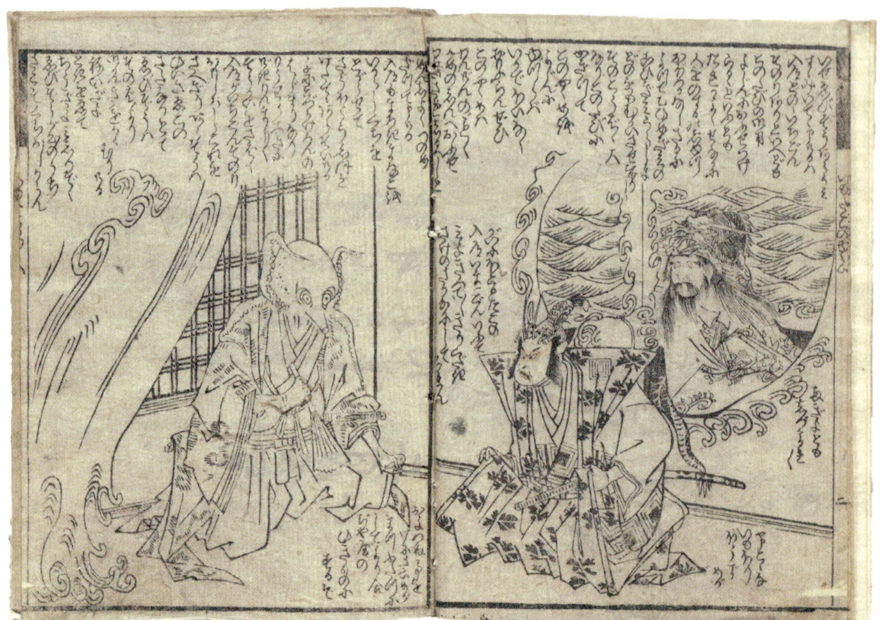

note that Hokusai and several of Iijima's sources died when the writer was still a child. Iijima completed Hokusai's biography in 1893, more than 40 years after the artist's death. Much like other biographies passed down to us from these times, we must treat Iijima's text with caution.

The artist we know today as Hokusai is believed to have been born Kawamura Tokitarō, son of Kawamura Ichiroemon, on the 23rd day of the ninth month in 1760 (dates given follow the lunar calendar used in Japan until 1873), in Honjō, on the eastern fringes of Edo. As a young child, Tokitarō was adopted by his uncle Nakajima Ise, a mirror smith working for the shogunate, presumably with the intention that he would be trained in the same craft and succeed him. It seems these plans were abandoned. Upon joining the Nakajima household, he was given the name Tetsuzō. As he would recall in his *Picture Book: The Essence of Colouring* (*Ehon saishiki tsū*), Hokusai began painting at the age of six years.

Hokusai began learning to carve wood blocks for printing in around 1774. His task was to first create a key block for the artist's design, typically comprising the outlines and areas to be printed in black. He would paste a copy of the design face down onto prepared cherrywood blocks and carve through the paper itself. To the corners of the block he would add L-shaped registration marks (*kentō*), which allowed each sheet of paper printed from the block to be positioned in precisely. A set of impressions in monochrome were then printed from the key block which were used to create the colour blocks, usually one for every colour that appeared in the design. Learning this demanding process himself gave Hokusai a lifelong appreciation for the importance of working with skilled block carvers.

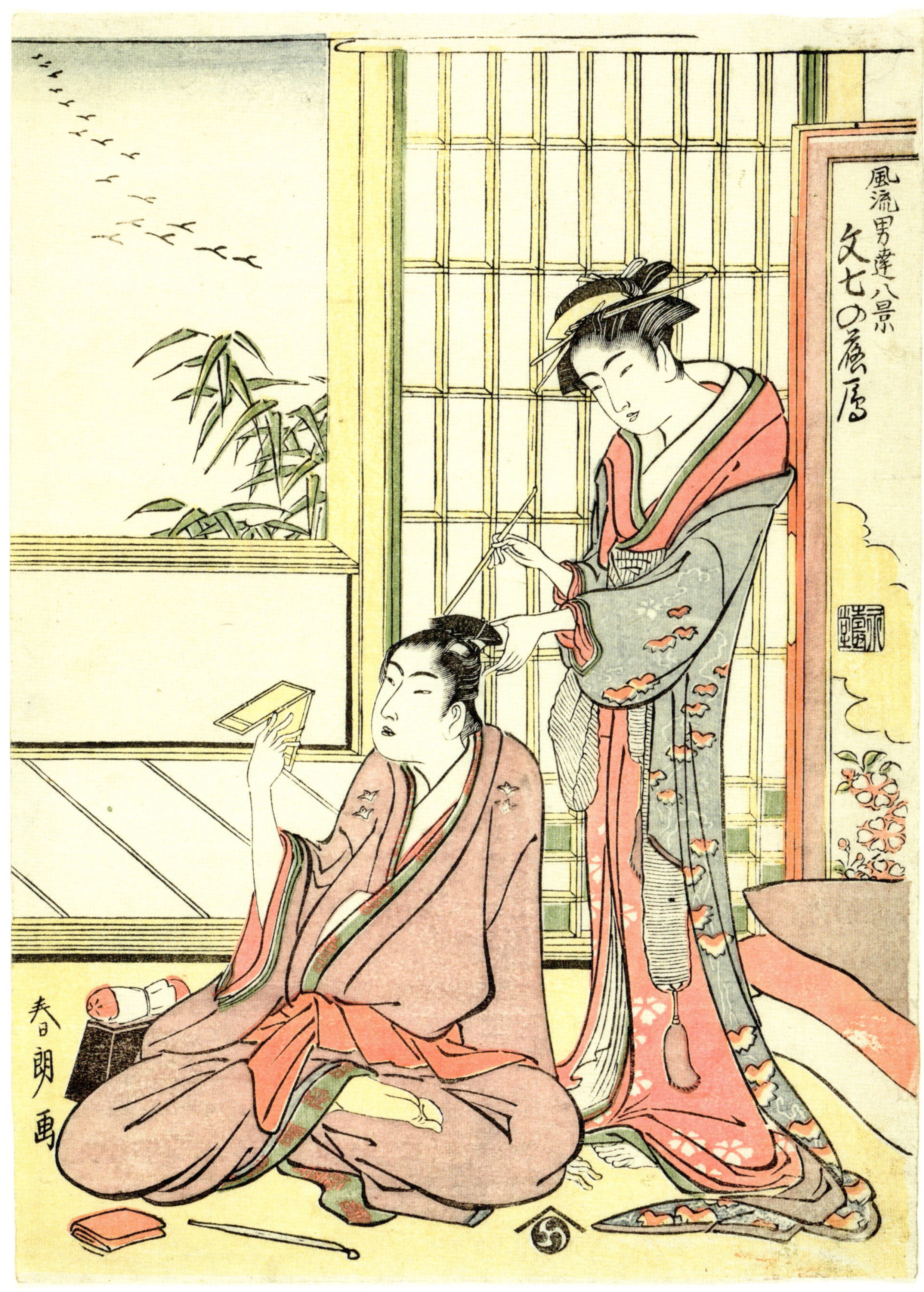

風流男達八景
文七の夜雨
春朗画

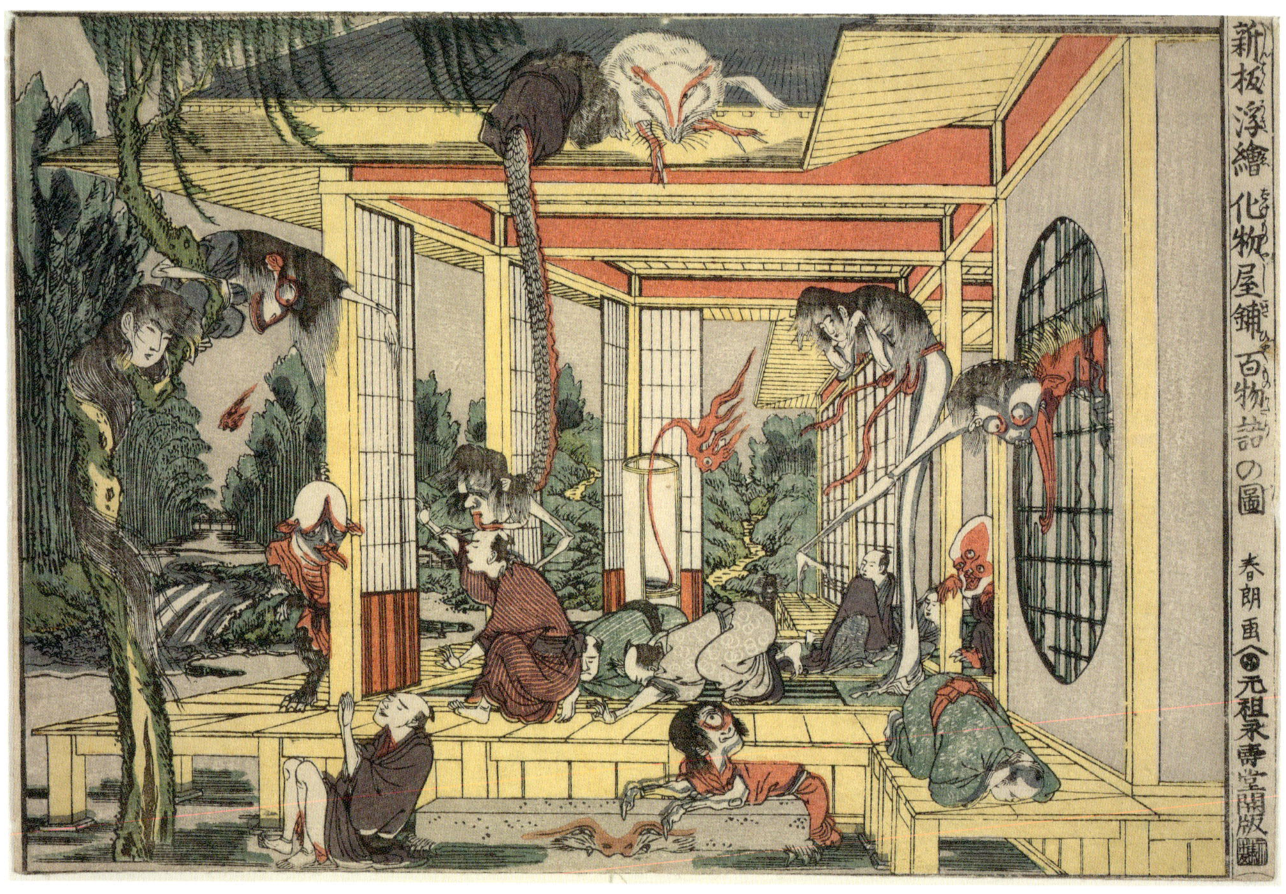

*One Hundred Ghost Stories in
a Haunted House*, *c.* 1790
From the series *Newly Published
Perspective Pictures*
Published by Nishimuraya Yohachi
Colour woodblock print, *ōban*,
23.7 x 35.4 cm (9⅜ x 14 in.)
Boston, Museum of Fine Arts,
Gift of C. Adrian Rübel

Katsukawa Shunrō

Hokusai left his job as a block carver and in around 1779, entered the atelier of Katsukawa Shunshō (1726–1793), one of the foremost *ukiyo-e* artists of his generation and progenitor of the Katsukawa school that dominated the genre of actor prints in the late 18th century. Shunshō was the student of painter Miyagawa Shunsui (active 1740s–early 1760s), the son of Miyagawa Chōshun (1683–1753) and was especially known for his skilfully individualized portraits of the kabuki actors he depicted. Shunshō's designs starkly challenged the genre's Torii school stronghold and its more stylized portraits. Kabuki theatre was one of the most popular Edo-period amusements, and the exclusively male actors garnered a broad and devoted fanbase eager to collect prints of their favourites in their various roles. Shunshō also designed prints of tall, slender beauties, principally courtesans from the pleasure quarters, and realistic full-length portraits of sumo wrestlers.

During his tenure in Shunshō's studio, Hokusai learnt to replicate his teacher's repertoire and style. It is under the name of Katsukawa Shunrō that Hokusai created his earliest known prints: 82 designs of kabuki actors. All in the tall, narrow *hosoban* format, these would comprise the bulk of his output within this school.

Segawa Kikunojō III as Oren, Masamune's Daughter is one of his first four designs, released in the eighth month of 1779, the year he joined the Shunshō studio. The subject of the print is a celebrated female-role actor as the virtuous

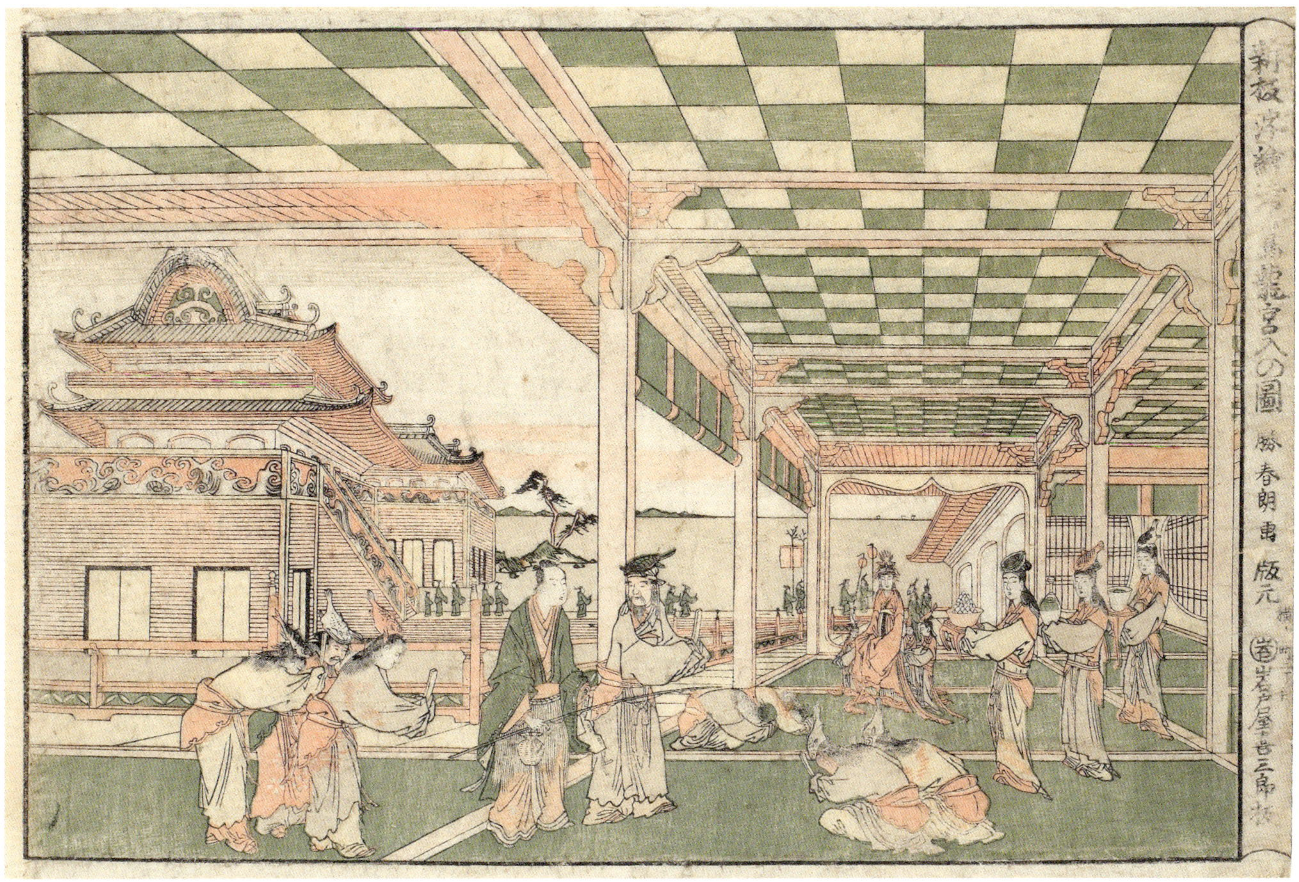

*Urashima Enters the Palace of
the Dragon King*, c. 1790
From the series *Newly Published
Perspective Pictures*
Published by Iwatoya Kisaburō
Colour woodblock print, *ōban*,
24.9 x 37.3 cm (9⅞ x 14¾ in.)
Honolulu Museum of Art,
Gift of James A. Michener, 1991

heroine from the play *New Tale of Usuyuki* (*Shin Usuyuki monogatari*). Hokusai
depicted Kikunojō posing before a standing screen with a motif of waves
crashing against rocks (ill. p. 6). The design follows the formula developed by
Shunshō for actor prints: a single standing figure represented in full length,
turning and/or leaning to one side.

As a low-ranking artist within the atelier, and by various accounts not one
of Shunshō's most favoured students, Hokusai's role in the Katsukawa enterprise
was to design prints for the middle market. He was seldom given the opportunity to design prints for important kabuki productions, which were reserved for
artists of higher standing within the atelier. As *ukiyo-e* scholar Matthi Forrer
has observed, most of his early actor prints commemorate "off season" perfor-
mances, and were printed on cheap paper using poor-quality pigments, with
little care for execution.

Gradually, however, Hokusai was given more prestigious actor print
commissions, including the diptych *Ichikawa Ebizō as Sanzoku, Actually
Mongaku Shōnin* and *Sakata Hangorō III as a Traveling Priest, Actually Chinzei
Hachirō Tametomo* (ills. p. 9). The prints commemorate a production of
the play *The Golden Hilt Ornament and Square Swordguard of the Minamoto
Family* (*Kin menuki genke no kaku tsuba*) at the Ichimura theatre, in the 11th
month of 1791. This marked the debut performance of the veteran star Ichikawa
Ebizō (1741–1806), previously known as Ichikawa Danjūrō V, under his
new name.

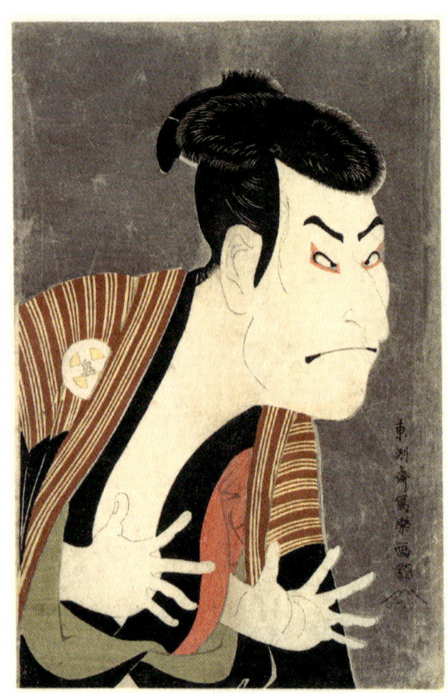

Tōshūsai Sharaku
The Actor Ōtani Oniji III as Edobei, 1794
Colour woodblock print, *ōban*,
37.9 x 25 cm (15 x 9⅞ in.)
New York, The Metropolitan Museum of Art,
Henry L. Phillips Collection,
Bequest of Henry L. Phillips, 1939

Shunrō's beauties, with their oval faces, small narrow foreheads and statu-esque figures wrapped in heavily layered robes surprisingly owe more stylistical-ly to Torii Kiyonaga (1752–1815) than to Shunshō. One of his more elegantly conceived undertakings within this genre is the *chūban* series *Eight Views of Elegant Gallants* (*Fūryū otokodate hakkei*, 1781–1789). The title of the series parodies the classical Chinese painting theme of the Eight Views of the Xiao and Xiang Rivers. In each of the five known designs, Hokusai paired an *otokodate*, a Robin Hood–like figure in Edo popular culture, with an irreverent take on one of the original eight views. *Descending Geese for Bunshichi* alludes to "returning geese at Yongzhou", and depicts Karigane Bunshichi, probably because the first character of the name Karigane means "goose". Bunshichi led a gang of outlaws in Osaka during the Genroku era (1688–1704) and was ultimately executed by the authorities, but in death became a people's hero immortalized in several plays. Hokusai's print shows Bunshichi's lover binding his hair with white cord. A flock of geese in formation is visible through the open window (ill. p. 11).

As well as actors and beauties, Hokusai made five known portraits of sumo wrestlers in the realistic style of the Katsukawa school between 1784 and 1790. *The Sumo Wrestlers Kimenzan Tanigorō and Dewanoumi Kinzō* shows two celebrated wrestlers clashing in the ring. Tanigorō, famous for his prominent buttocks, is presumably the foremost figure (ill. p. 7). As he squints in concentra-tion, his opponent Kinzō's eyes open wide with exertion or surprise. The lifelike depiction of the wrestlers' formidable bulk using only outlines and a few contour lines demonstrates Hokusai's growing competence in the Katsukawa style.

In the late 1780s, Hokusai began designing *uki-e* or "floating pictures", prints of landscape and architectural subjects employing the Western linear perspec-tive. *Uki-e* were initially copies of Dutch copperplate prints but artists soon began representing local scenery and kabuki theatres. The illusion of depth and volume offered by *uki-e* could be enhanced by viewing them through an optical device fitted with a lens and mirror, in which case they might be called *megane-e*, or "glasses pictures". With his foray into this genre, Hokusai ventured outside the standard repertoire of the Katsukawa atelier and into that of the Utagawa school founder Utagawa Toyoharu (1735–1814), who dominated *uki-e* design during the 1770s and 1780s. Toyoharu's designs were inspired by Dutch engravings, directly or indirectly through prints produced in Suzhou, China, from the mid-18th century. As Toyoharu's production of *uki-e* trickled off in the mid- to late 1780s, Hokusai began picking up commissions for new designs.

One Hundred Ghost Stories in a Haunted House is one of a group of prints commissioned by Nishimuraya Yohachi. None of the prints in this series is dated but the time of publication can be estimated from the depiction of a perfor-mance that took place at the Kiri Theatre in 1787, in one of the designs of this group. This datable image is a close reworking of a print by Toyoharu; however, Hokusai's haunted house design gives the *uki-e* genre a new twist. The theme of "one hundred stories" derives from a parlour game played on summer eve-nings. Participants light a hundred candles or lanterns, then take turns terrifying one another telling *kaidan* or "strange tales", a term usually translated into English as "ghost stories". With the completion of each tale, one light would be extinguished, leaving the room progressively darker. In Hokusai's print, a comic take on the *uki-e* genre, the final light has been extinguished, unleashing pan-demonium upon the elegant mansion. A party of young men cower from the torments of ghosts and demons (ill. p. 12). Here, Hokusai creates two vanishing

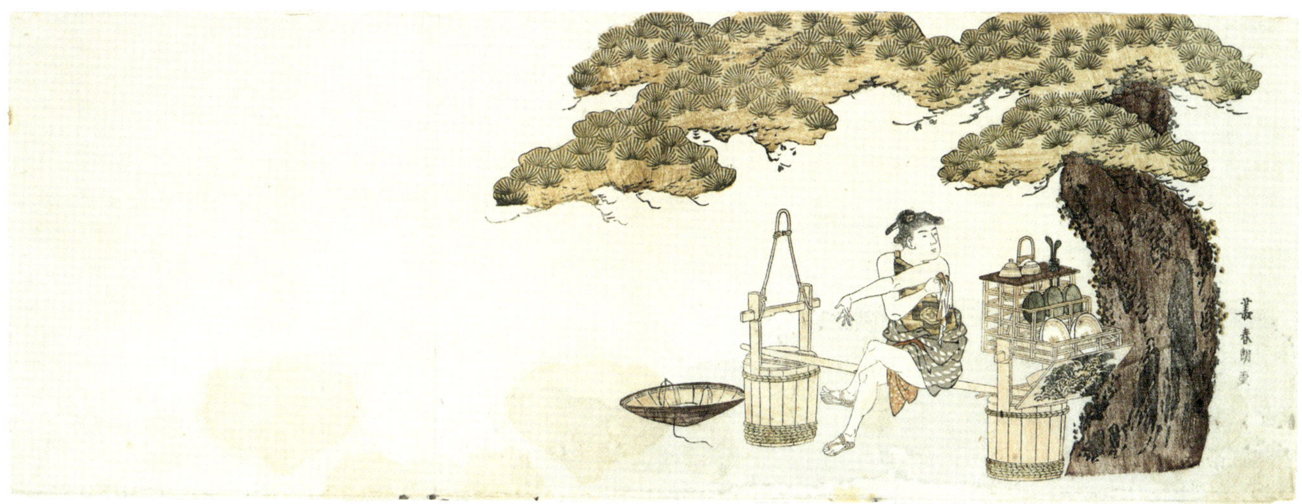

points: the first leading through the avenue at the left of the composition;
the second to the right through the house's open doors.

Published around the same time by Iwatoya Kisaburō was *Urashima Enters the Palace of the Dragon King* from the series *Newly Published Perspective Pictures* (*c.* 1790; ill. p. 13). It depicts the folkloric hero holding his fishing rod as he receives a princely welcome in the underwater palace – a fittingly exotic subject for a novelty print. Costumes and architecture vaguely evoking Ming dynasty provenance signify the otherworldly setting. The geometry of the architecture, especially the chequerboard patterned ceiling and the grid of exposed beams, emphasizes the illusion of depth. Vanishing lines converge around the figure of the princess who would soon become Urashima's bride.

In 1780, a year after creating his first single-sheet prints, Hokusai's first book illustrations were published. Illustrating books was less prestigious work than designing prints, and although Katsukawa school artists mostly avoided such commissions, several of his contemporaries including Kitagawa Utamaro (1753–1806) and Utagawa Toyokuni (1769–1825) began their careers with illustration work. During his tenure as Katsukawa Shunrō, Hokusai created illustrations for 30 *kibyōshi* or "yellow covers", illustrated works of popular fiction (ills. pp. 8, 10), three *hanashibon,* anthologies of humorous short stories, and three *sharebon* – "witty books" whose narrative revolved around the pleasure quarters. In addition to illustrating books, Hokusai also wrote a handful of popular novellas in the 1780s.

Hokusai's time in Shunshō's studio was not without its challenges. According to one anecdote cited by Iijima, Hokusai was forbidden to use the Katsukawa name after Shunshō discovered that his student had been disloyally receiving lessons from a Kanō school painter. For a time, Hokusai called himself Kusamura Shunrō instead. Another source attributes Hokusai's departure to bad blood between him and Shunkō I (1743–1812), a senior student of Shunshō. As a student, Hokusai undertook a commission for a sign from an *ezōshi* shop, a business selling books and other printed materials in Ryōgoku. The shop owner was delighted by his work and hung the sign proudly at the entrance. When Shunkō discovered the commission he declared the work a disgrace to the Katsukawa name and destroyed it. Hokusai later credited the incident as

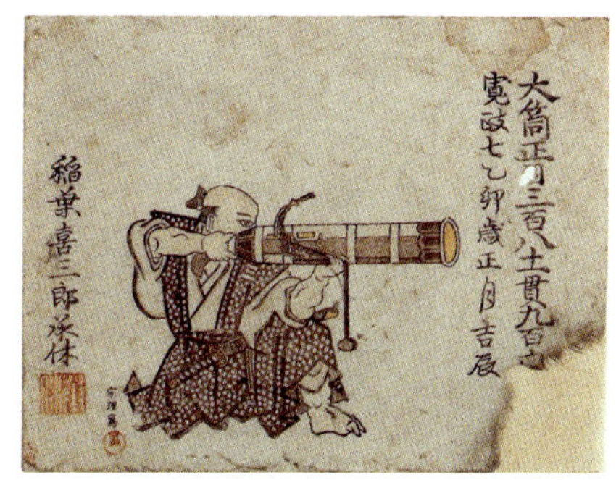

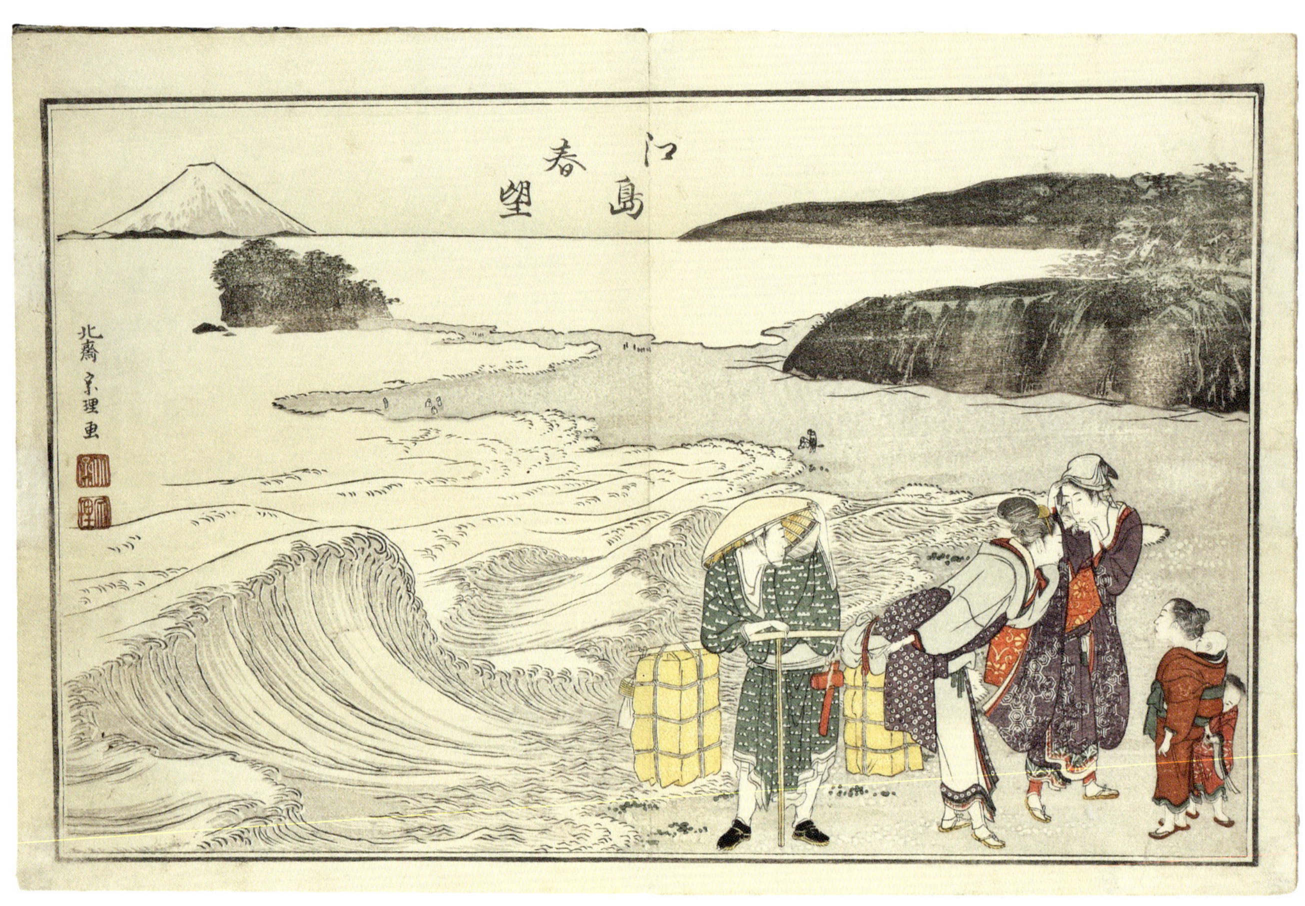

Spring View of Enoshima, 1797
From *Willow Silk*
Published by Tsutaya Jūzaburō
Printed folding album with poems
and illustrations by various artists
London, British Museum

The Toilet, 1795/96
Colour woodblock print,
yatsugiriban, 14.2 x 10.6 cm
(5⅝ x 4¼ in.)
London, British Museum

a source of impulsion that motivated him to become a great artist. During the years 1785 and 1786, he provided illustrations for at least three *kibyōshi* under the name Gunbatei (or Gunmatei) suggesting he had, temporarily at least, parted with Shunshō.

Towards the end of 1792, around the time of Shunshō's death, Hokusai began to seek instruction outside the Katsukawa school. He studied with the minor academic painter Kanō Yūsen (1778–1815), the Sumiyoshi school painter Sumiyoshi Hiroyuki (1755–1811), and Tsutsumi Tōrin III (active 1790s–1830s), who envisaged himself as an heir to the traditions of the great ink painter Sesshū Tōyō (1420–1506) and dabbled in the Chinese styles of the Nanpin school and literati painting. Although Hokusai continued to use the name Shunrō for another year or so, that summer marked a departure both in style and in the type of work he produced. In contrast to commercial prints featuring actors and beauties he had designed as a member of the Katsukawa atelier, Hokusai began creating designs for *surimono*, literally "printed things", high-end productions released for private circulation. Issued in small print runs with no imperative to yield a profit, *surimono* were produced more painstakingly and with finer materials than commercially published prints, often with luxurious effects like embossing and embellishments of metallic powders.

Surimono encompassed invitations to exclusive events, programmes for poetry readings, and New Year's greeting cards commissioned by members of the prosperous merchant class, who, with their increased wealth and leisure,

16

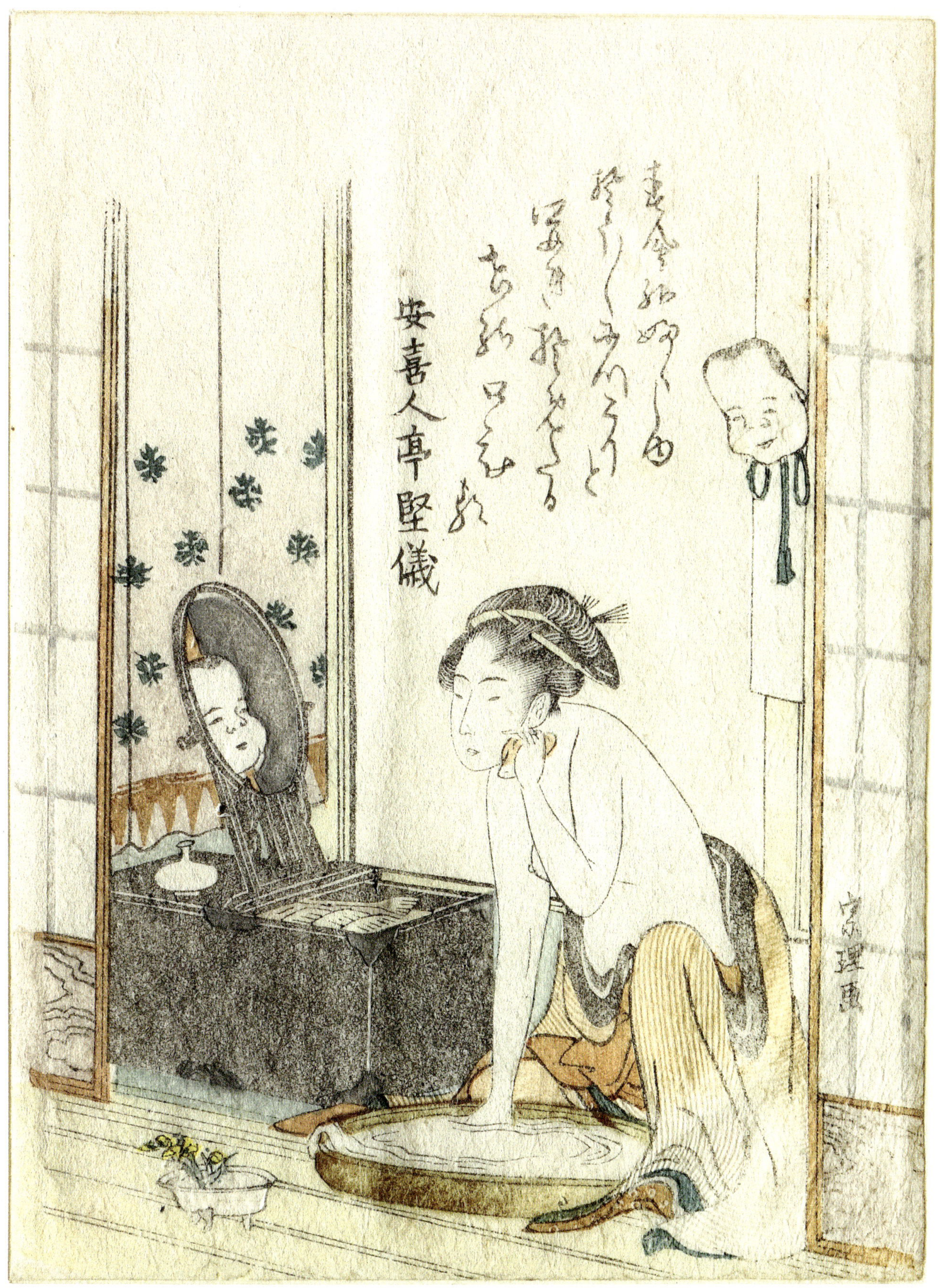

まきかねのぬぐへとも
をりしみひそうと
ほどきをかへなる
あらひ口も
あり

安喜人亭
堅儀

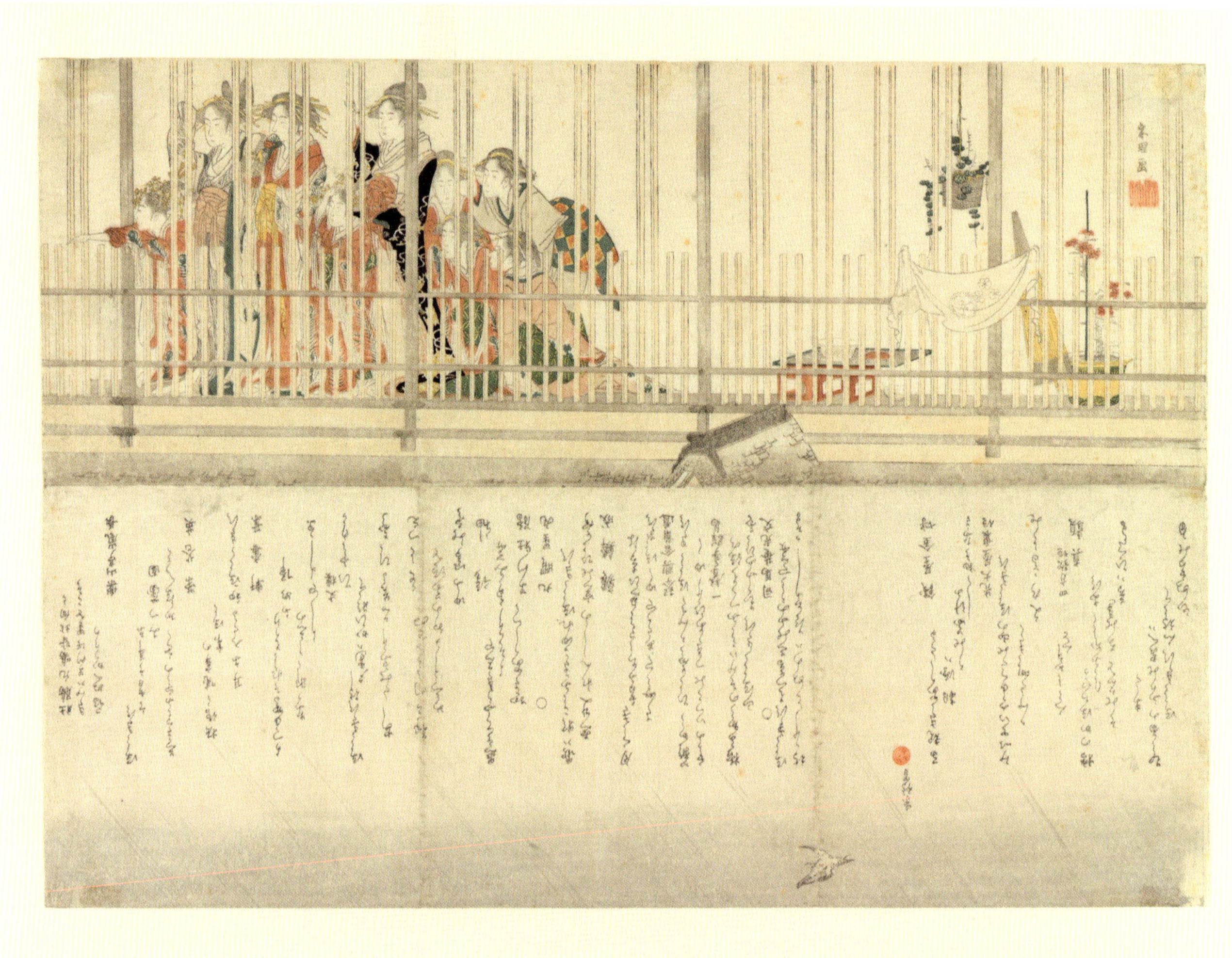

Courtesans and Attendants Watching a Cuckoo, late 1790s
Colour woodblock print,
39.6 x 55.9 cm (15⅝ x 22 in.)
Dublin, Chester Beatty Library

began to enjoy creative pursuits such as writing poetry. They formed literati coteries and held poetry gatherings, which required invitations, programmes, anthologies and other kinds of printed materials. A subset of *surimono* are *egoyomi* or "calendar prints". During the Edo period, the shogunate divided each year into a sequence of long months lasting 30 days and short months of 29 days. The order of long and short months altered annually to avoid repetition. Print artists devised ingenious compositions into designs, encoding the order of long and short months.

Among Hokusai's earliest *surimono* is the *Water Seller* (1793/94), depicting a young vendor of cold water resting on his buckets' carrying pole in the shade of a spreading pine tree (ill. p. 15 top). A dragon painted on the boy's sign suspended from the rack of crockery announces the vendor's business (dragons being associated with water in East Asian lore). The motif on the boy's garment is the emblem of the *tokiwazu-bushi*, musicians who perform songs accompanied by the shamisen; the *surimono* may have been printed as part of a *tokiwazu* programme.

Over a period of ten months between 1794 and 1795, 164 prints, mostly actor portraits, bearing the signature Tōshūsai Sharaku appeared on the market (ill. p. 14). Stylistic similarities between prints by Sharaku and prints by Hokusai,

the abrupt emergence and disappearance of Sharaku during an apparent break
in Hokusai's career, and Hokusai's habit of regularly changing his name have
led some to believe that Hokusai and Sharaku were, in fact, the same artist.
Other candidates, credible or otherwise, proposed for Sharaku's identity include
the painter Maruyama Ōkyo (1733–1795), the writer Jippensha Ikku (1765–1831),
Sharaku's publisher Tsutaya Jūzaburō (1750–1797), and the noh actor Saitō
Jūrōbei (1763–1820).

Sōri

Sometime in 1794, Hokusai definitely abandoned the name Shunrō, indicating
that he had officially left the Katsukawa school. In the same year Hokusai found
a new creative identity within the ranks of a branch of the Tawaraya lineage of
artists, originating with Tawaraya Sōtatsu (d. 1643) who is now credited as being
the father of the nativist Rinpa school. There Hokusai produced designs for
surimono and *egoyomi*, illustrations for poetry books and albums, and paintings
marked by a whimsical, decorative sensibility and elegantly conceived compositions. He adopted the name Sōri in honour of the now-obscure artist Tawaraya
Sōri (active late 1760s–1770s). The earliest known works bearing this new name
are two calendar prints or *egoyomi* and a volume of *kyōka* or "mad poetry", a
popular genre that humorously parodies classical Japanese poetry, issued during
the New Year of 1795. For these designs to be ready in time for release Hokusai
must have designed them under his new name at least several weeks prior to publication. He continued using the name Sōri until around 1798 when he bequeathed
it to his student Sōji. This has today created a degree of uncertainty about the
attribution of some designs bearing this name.

One of the two calendar prints mentioned depicted a samurai taking aim
with a large matchlock rifle, a type of firearm introduced by the Portuguese in
1543 and manufactured locally with improvements thereafter (ill. p. 15 bottom).
The inscription marks the dates as the first month of 1795. The text, purporting
to list the specifications of the weapon, called an *ōzutsu* or "large pipe", actually
records the long months for the year ahead.

More representative of the lyrical sensibility and sophisticated design for
which the Sōri period is known is a collaborative design, the *surimono*
Courtesans and Attendants Watching a Cuckoo (late 1790s; ill. p. 18). To the
left of the composition, a group of prostitutes and their attendants are shown
peering through the barred window of the Daimonjiya brothel. In a major
break from the round-jawed, dark-browed beauties of his Shunrō period, the
women here have angular, even pinched features and high foreheads. Below,
to the right, is a single cuckoo in free flight, drawn not by Hokusai but rather
by the writer Santō Kyōden (1761–1816), who began his career creating book
illustrations under the pseudonym Kitao Masanobu. The print was designed
to be folded along the horizontal centre line and then folded concertina-style
such that the rightmost third of the upper half is visible. When this flap is open,
the bird appears to be flying just past the women to the left. The cuckoo appeared
in visual imagery and literature as a symbol of early summer, as its beautiful
call announced the arrival of the season. The bird also evoked a melancholy
awareness of the fleeting nature of time and loss; here, no sooner have the
women heard the bird has it vanished from view.

A *surimono* from around the same time, *The Toilet*, demonstrates Hokusai's
impish sense of humour. A slender beauty, naked to the waist, bathes herself before a mirror (ill. p. 17). Peering back at her from the glass is a grotesque face,

the reflection of a Otafuku mask hanging from a post behind her. A plump, homely but jolly figure, Otafuku, also known as Okame and Ofuku, is the goddess of mirth and is associated with happiness, fertility and bawdy humour. Such a mask might be hung to bring good fortune into a home or business. Hokusai's design offers a witty twist on the device of a mirror, used frequently in *ukiyo-e* to emphasize a figure's beauty or add a voyeuristic dimension to images of beautiful women. An inscription by the poet Anki Jintei Katagi reads, "At the breath of the spring breeze, smilingly the blossoms of the lucky plant begin to part their lips."

In 1796, Hokusai began signing his designs as Hokusai Sōri, thus introducing the name by which he is best known today. In 1797, he contributed the illustration *Spring View of Enoshima* to the *kyōka* poetry anthology *Willow Silk* (*Yanagi no ito*; ill. p. 16). The design depicting a large wave approaching a group of figures on a beach is one of Hokusai's earliest explorations of a theme that would culminate with his masterpiece *Under the Wave off Kanagawa*. The book was finely printed and bound as a concertina-style folding album, a single volume with one illustration each by Hokusai and some of his contemporaries, published by Tsutaya Jūzaburō. Commissions for illustrations in similarly lavish publications followed, such as *The Stamping Song of Men* (*Otokodōka*, 1798), also published by Tsutaya.

During this period, Hokusai increased his output of paintings. Approximately 20 works firmly attributed to him survive from this period. The best known is a diptych of hanging scrolls, *Chinese Immortal Yuzhi and Her Dragon* (ills. p. 21). The subject of the painting is Yuzhi (Jap. Gyokushi), the daughter of the Queen Mother of the West and a member of the Daoist pantheon. According to legend, Yuzhi was a musician of such sublime skill that a hundred birds flocked around her, mesmerized as she played her *kin* (Ch. *qin*). So compelling was her music that a white dragon was tamed just by the sound of it. Rather than depicting Yuzhi riding on the back of a dragon as is typical in Japanese imagery, Hokusai has her standing apart from the mythical beast. The composition may be derived from an illustration by the Kanō school artist Tachibana Morikuni (1679–1748), in which Yuzhi is shown playing the *kin* to the dragon. However, Hokusai modified the scene and narrative: here the dragon presents her with the instrument as if to state that her creative gift was bestowed upon her by a divine muse. To Hokusai the dragon was of personal significance, as the first character of his given name means "dragon" and he was born in the Year of the Dragon. Hence, this and the impression of a seal on the painting reading "creativity is my master" have led Hokusai authority Roger Keyes to suggest that the painting may have been a statement about the artist's own formidable creativity.

*Chinese Immortal Yuzhi and
Her Dragon*, c. 1798
Pair of hanging scrolls, ink and colour on paper,
each about 125.4 x 56.5 cm (49⅜ x 22¼ in.)
Private collection

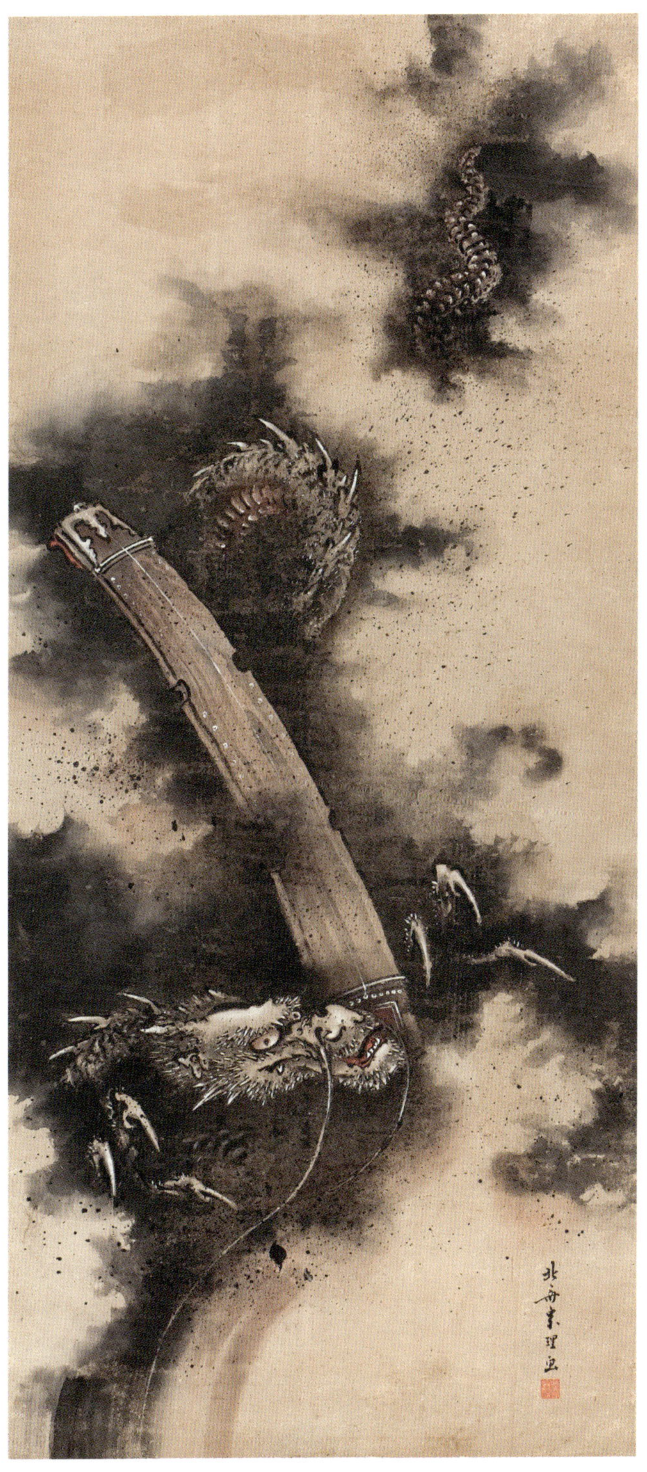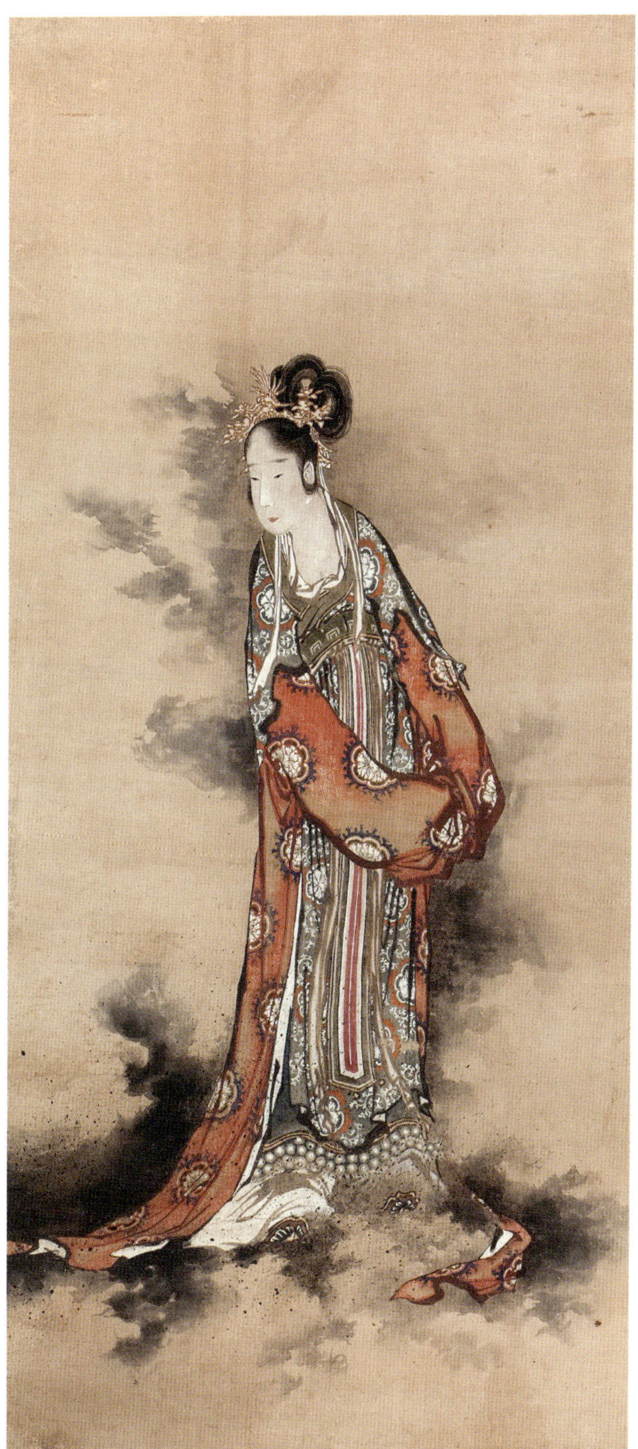

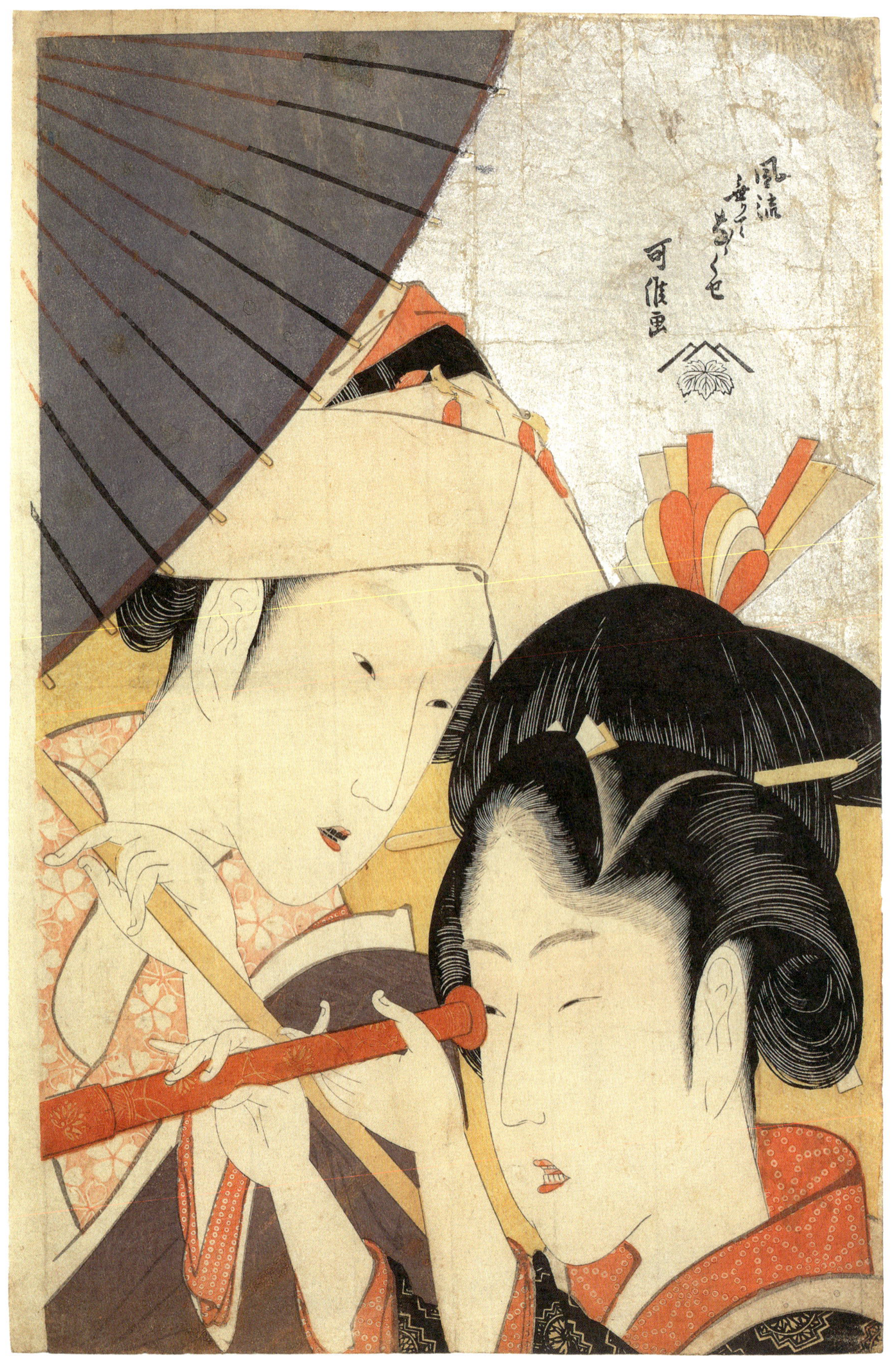

風流
五つく
さ〜も
可候画

The Fellow Mad about Painting

In 1798, Hokusai started using the name by which he is known around the world today. He began signing his work as "Sōri aratame Hokusai", meaning "Hokusai, the artist formerly known as Sōri". The name Sōri was bequeathed to his student Sōju and a new appellation, "Hokusai Tatsumasa", made its appearance. The Chinese characters for "Hokusai" mean "northern studio", a reference to the Buddhist deification of the North Star, Myōken. The characters for Tatsumasa are conventionally read "Tokimasa"; however, art historian Roger Keyes has pointed out that Hokusai sometimes signed works with this character alone, which can only be read "Tatsu", therefore suggesting that the correct reading is Hokusai Tatsumasa.

As mentioned above, this character, meaning "dragon", held special significance to Hokusai, who was born in the Year of the Dragon in the Chinese zodiac. This mythical beast was also the symbol of the North Star and associated with Myōken. Around 1800, he began signing works as "Gakyōjin Hokusai", meaning "Hokusai, the fellow mad about painting". It was in 1805 that he added the name Katsushika, drawn from his native district of Katsushika.

He continued to produce *surimono* under the name of Hokusai Tatsumasa, but what distinguishes this period is a series of *kyōka* albums illustrated in the elegant, whimsical style that characterized his earlier Sōri phase. The single volume *Picture Book of Amusements in the Eastern Capital (Ehon azuma asobi)* was the first of such titles. Like several that followed, it was a visual celebration of the city of Edo, depicting people at work and play in and around its various landmarks. Pictorial books showcasing the capital's attractions became popular in the late 18th century with illustrated volumes by Kitagawa Utamaro and Kitao Shigemasa (1739–1820). First published as an anthology of *kyōka* in 1799 by Tsutaya, a second version comprising three volumes was printed in colour in 1802 without the accompanying poems (ill. p. 26 bottom). Hokusai included an image of the Tsutaya publishing house storefront that had issued this book. Among the customers are a samurai, identified by the two swords tucked into his sash, and a traveller with a carrying-pole heavy with bundles, presumably purchasing prints to take home as souvenirs. The publisher's crest, an ivy leaf under Mount Fuji, appears on a lantern at the entrance and above the doorway. To the right, signboards announce available titles.

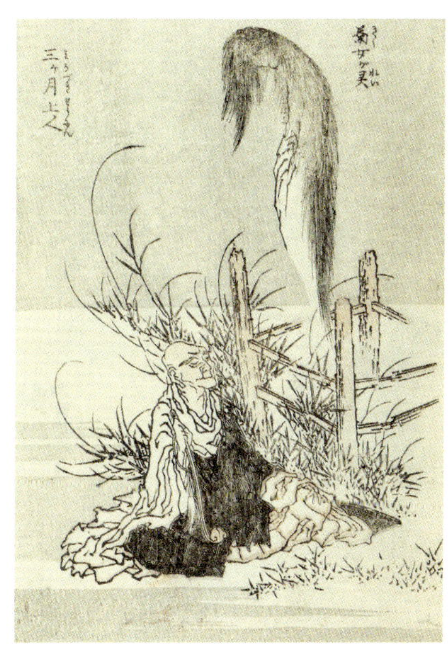

High Priest of Yūten and Kasane (I), 1819
From volume ten of *Hokusai manga*
Published by Eirakuya Tōshirō and others
Woodblock-printed books, 15 volumes
London, British Museum

The Telescope, late 1790s
From the series *Seven Stylish Foibles*
Colour woodblock print, *ōban*,
approx. 25.4 x 38 cm (10 x 15 in.)
Hagi, Uragami Museum

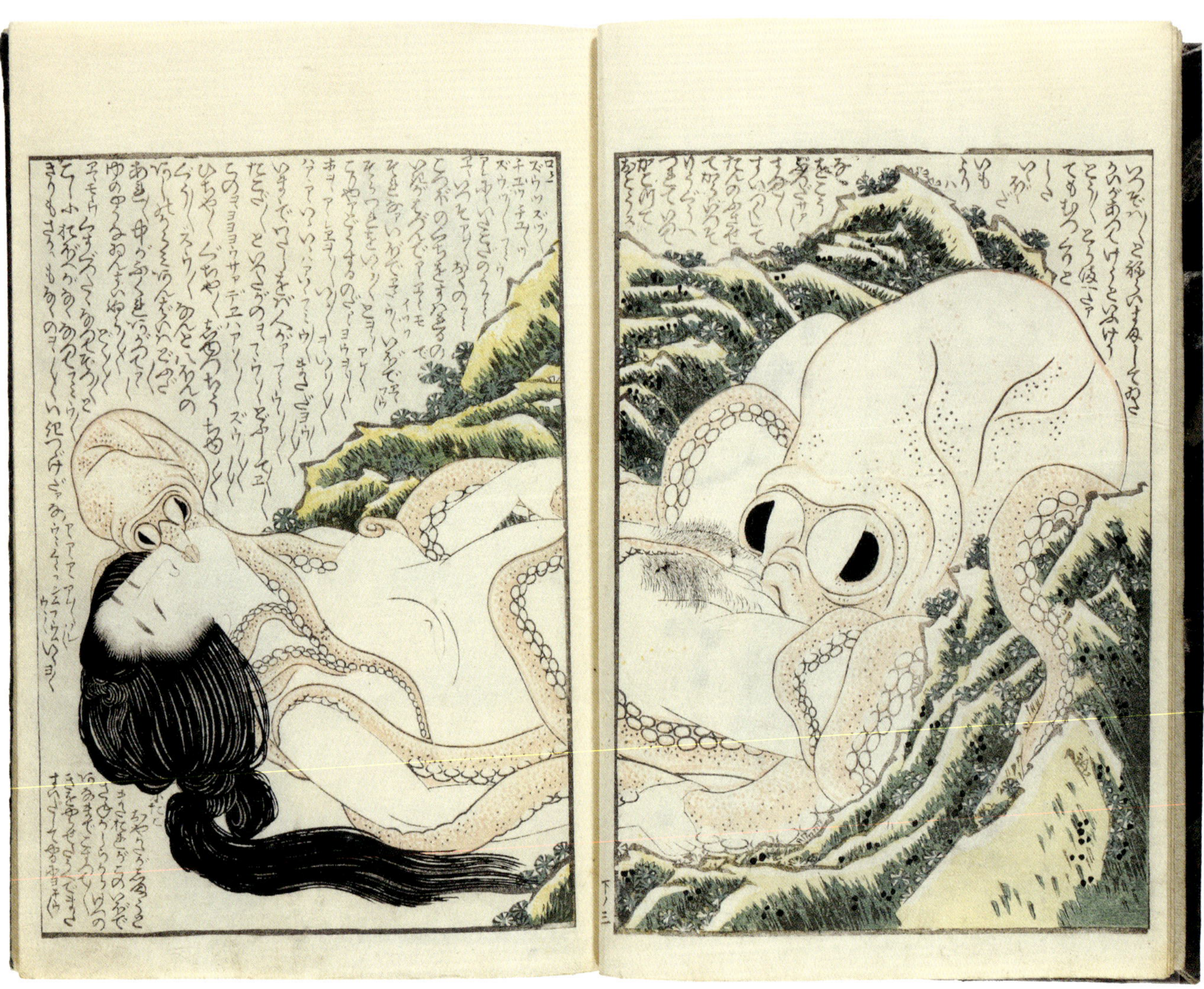

Two Amorous Octopuses and
a Fisherwoman, *c.* 1814
From volume three of *Pine Seedlings*
on the First Rat Day
Woodblock-printed books, three volumes
Washington, D.C., Freer Gallery of Art
and Arthur M. Sackler Gallery,
Smithsonian Institute, Freer Study Collection

High Priest of Yūten and Kasane (II), 1819
From volume ten of *Hokusai manga*
Published by Eirakuya Tōshirō and others
Woodblock-printed books, 15 volumes
London, British Museum

This was followed by the two-volume *kyōka* anthology *Fine Views of the Eastern Capital at a Glance* (*Tōto shōkei ichiran*) in 1800. The two volumes encompass a standard inventory of Edo's famous sights depicted at optimal times of the seasonal calendar, but rather than simply depicting scenic views Hokusai's designs capture the essence of Edo as a bustling metropolis dominated by prosperous townsmen and women. Indeed, during the artist's lifetime, it was one of the largest cities in the world. His image of Shiba Shinmei Shrine (now known as Shiba Daijingu Shrine) in the second volume shows the grounds crowded with throngs of people during the ginger market, held for 11 days during the ninth month, as if the viewer was looking down from a neighbouring balcony (ill. p. 26 top).

In *Kyōka Picture Book: Mountains upon Mountains* (*Ehon kyōka yama mata yama*, 1804), the "mountains" refer to the Yamanote district, hilly areas to the west of Edo where the samurai settled, and the Yamanote Poetry Circle for which the three volumes were made. While the books represent yet another ode to Edo, the activities of the figures take precedent over the locales, which are sometimes only vaguely referred to in the text. An illustration in the first

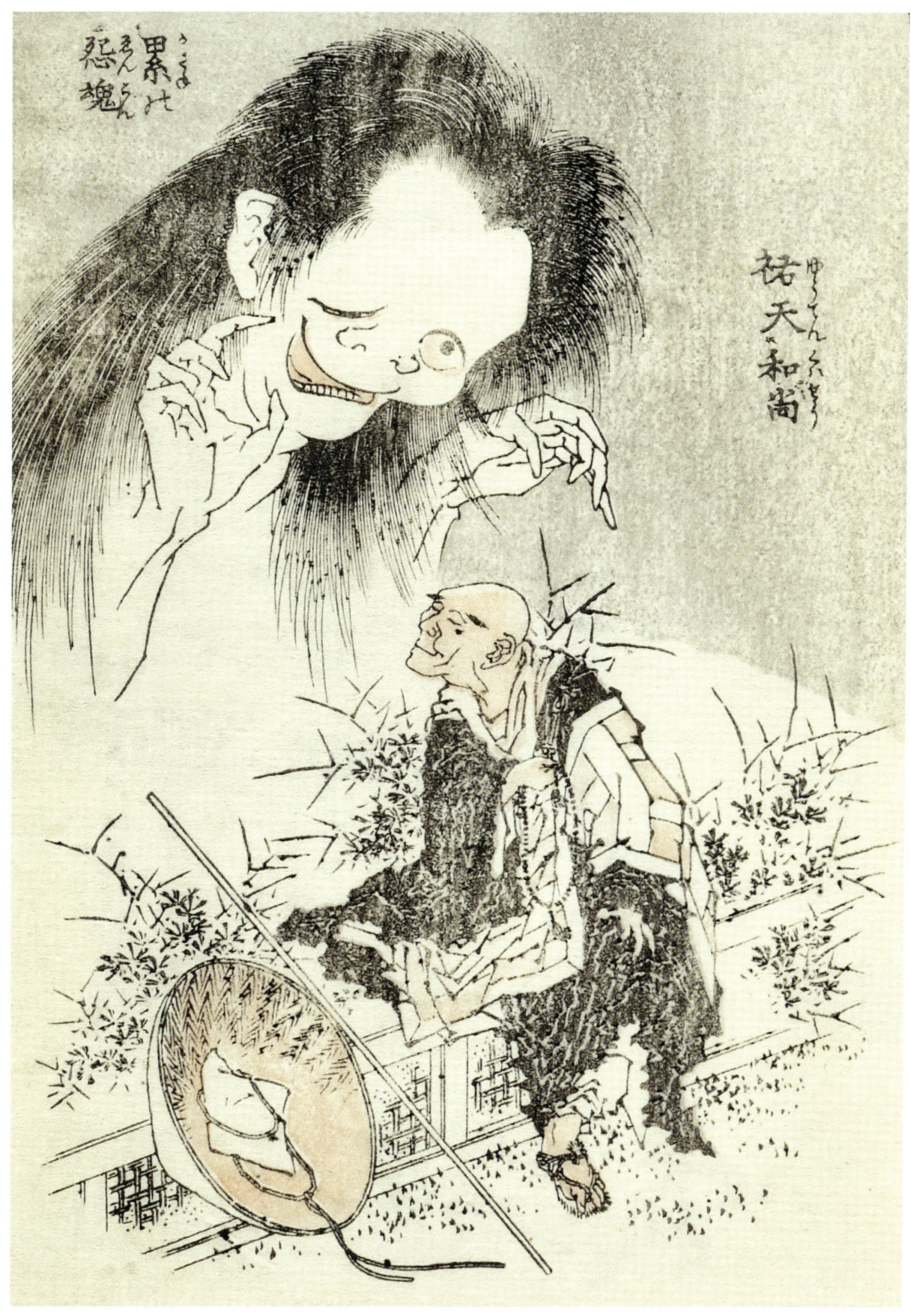
累の怨魂
祐天和尚

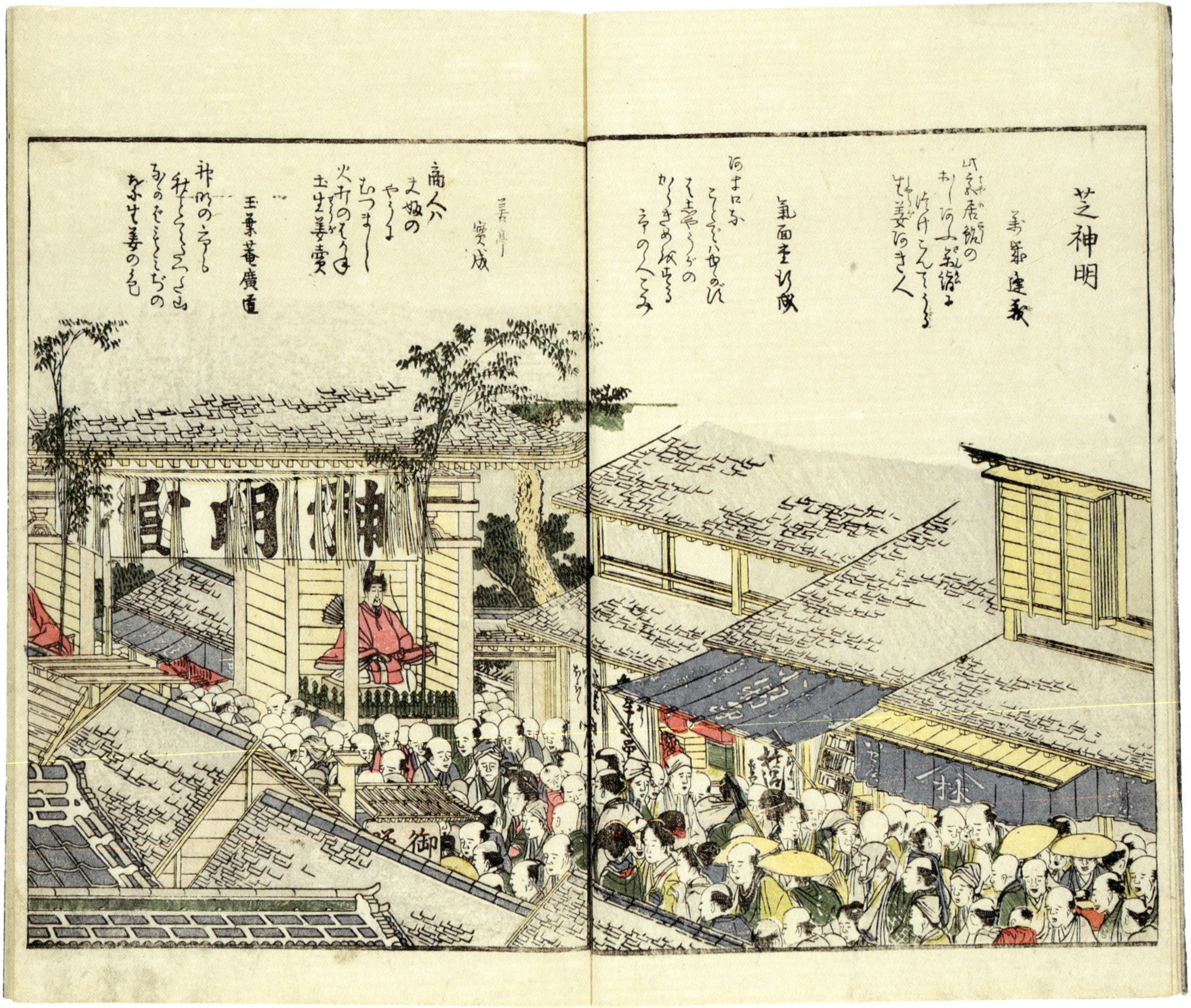

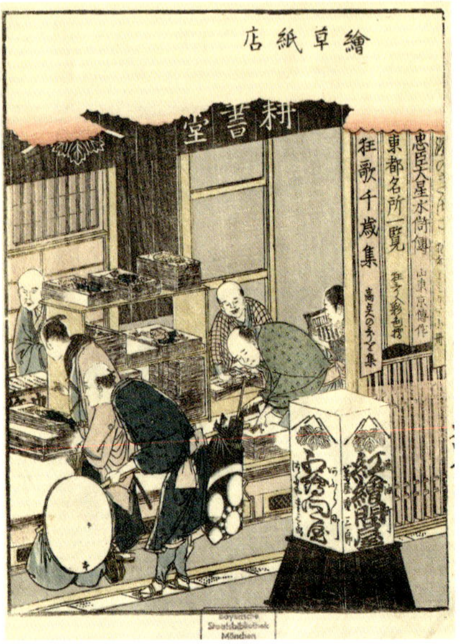

volume, for example, shows three women picnicking at Takadanobaba, a horse-riding ground for samurai, with Mount Fuji in the distance (ill. p. 27). The narrative of the scene, however, centres not on the site itself but rather on a red-and-gold lacquered telescope, pointed at some unseen, distant target. One of the women offers her friend a glimpse through the device, but she seems somewhat reluctant; perhaps some impropriety is taking place. The women each wear an *agabōshi*, a headdress of folded white fabric worn to protect women's hair from dust on outings.

The masterpiece of this period, however, is *Picture Book: Both Banks of the Sumida River at a Glance* (*Ehon Sumidagawa ryōgan ichiran*, *c.* 1805), published by Maekawa Zenbei. The illustrations in the three volumes form a continuous panoramic composition as one would find in a handscroll, although due to the binding, only two facing images may be viewed at once. These depict daily life over the four seasons along Edo's arterial waterway and masterfully fuse human and landscape elements. Volume one opens with Mount Fuji rising over Edo Bay

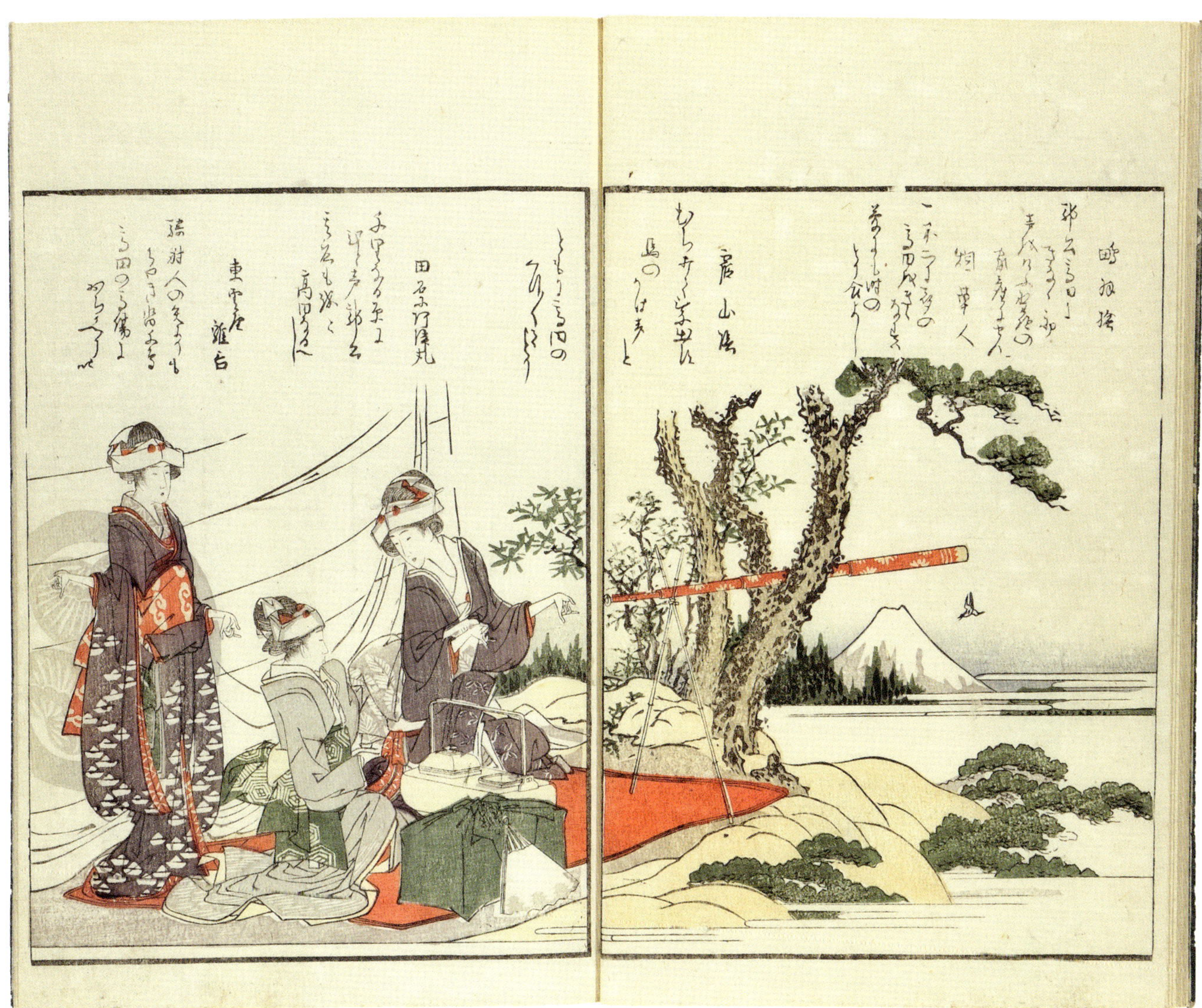

on New Year's Day, which would take place in early spring according to the lunar calendar; while volume three concludes at the end of the year with the Yoshiwara pleasure district. The middle volume holds a scene captioned *Sudden Rain at the New Yanagi Bridge, Rainbow at Otakegura*, where an assortment of figures crossing a wooden bridge shield themselves against the squall with paper umbrellas, a woven mat, and a tie-dyed garment that flies in the wind (ill. p. 28). The rainbow referred to in the caption points us to the visual pun of the arched Okura Bridge on the east side of the river at Otakegura, a wooded area that supplied timber for official use in Edo.

A little further on is *The High Votive Lantern of the Kaya Temple, the Ferry from the Shore of Onmaya* (ill. p. 29). Among the seven passengers on the boat headed for Honjō on the east bank are a young woman, a farmer with two baskets of eggs, two pilgrims, and a member of the Shintō clergy carrying what appear to be a purification wand and a lantern. The votive lantern of the temple is suspended on a pole on the left-hand side, breaching the image frame. Hokusai

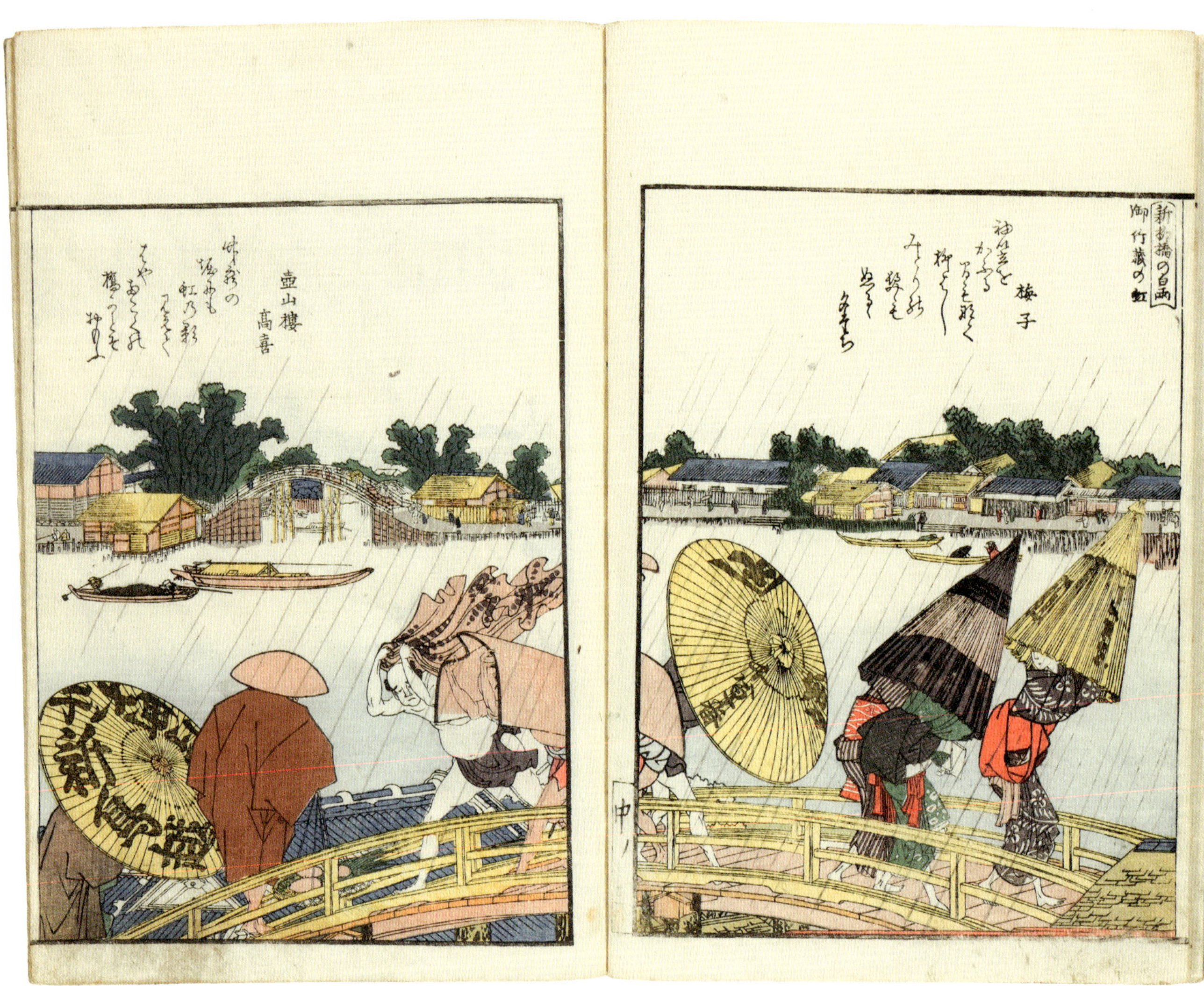

***Sudden Rain at the New Yanagi Bridge,
Rainbow at Otakegura***, *c.* 1805
From volume two of *Picture Book:
Both Banks of the Sumida River at a Glance*
Published by Maekawa Zenbei
Woodblock-printed books, three volumes
Washington, D.C., Freer Gallery of Art
and Arthur M. Sackler Gallery,
Smithsonian Institute, Freer Study Collection

PAGE 27
Takadanobaba, 1804
From volume one of *Kyōka Picture Book:
Mountains upon Mountains*
Published by Tsutaya Jūzaburō
Woodblock-printed books, three volumes
London, British Museum

revisited the composition in *Viewing Sunset over Ryōgoku Bridge from the Onmaya Embankment* (*c.* 1830/31) from the series *Thirty-six Views of Mount Fuji* (*Fugaku sanjūrokkei*). In this later image, he simplified the landscape elements and reversed the vantage point, positioning the viewer on the east bank, with Ryōgoku Bridge and Mount Fuji in the background.

Between 1800 and 1810 generally, Hokusai produced at least five small series of prints in different formats. These depict landscapes around Edo and other regions, mimicking copperplate engravings in their handling of line, shading and perspective, and the inclusion of Western-style, trompe-l'œil frames. One series bears the title *The Dutch Picture Lens: Eight Views of Edo* (*Oranda gakyō, Edo hakkei*; ill. p. 33) but the other three are unnamed (ills. pp. 30, 31). In two of these series, inscriptions in looped Japanese writing imitate the appearance of Roman cursive script. Larges waves in Sagami Bay were also a regular motif in these images and can be regarded as early experiments that would culminate in Hokusai's most famous design *Under the Wave off Kanagawa* (*c.* 1830/31; ill. p. 64). His general interest in Western pictorial techniques would strongly inform his more sophisticated landscape works in the 1820s and 1830s.

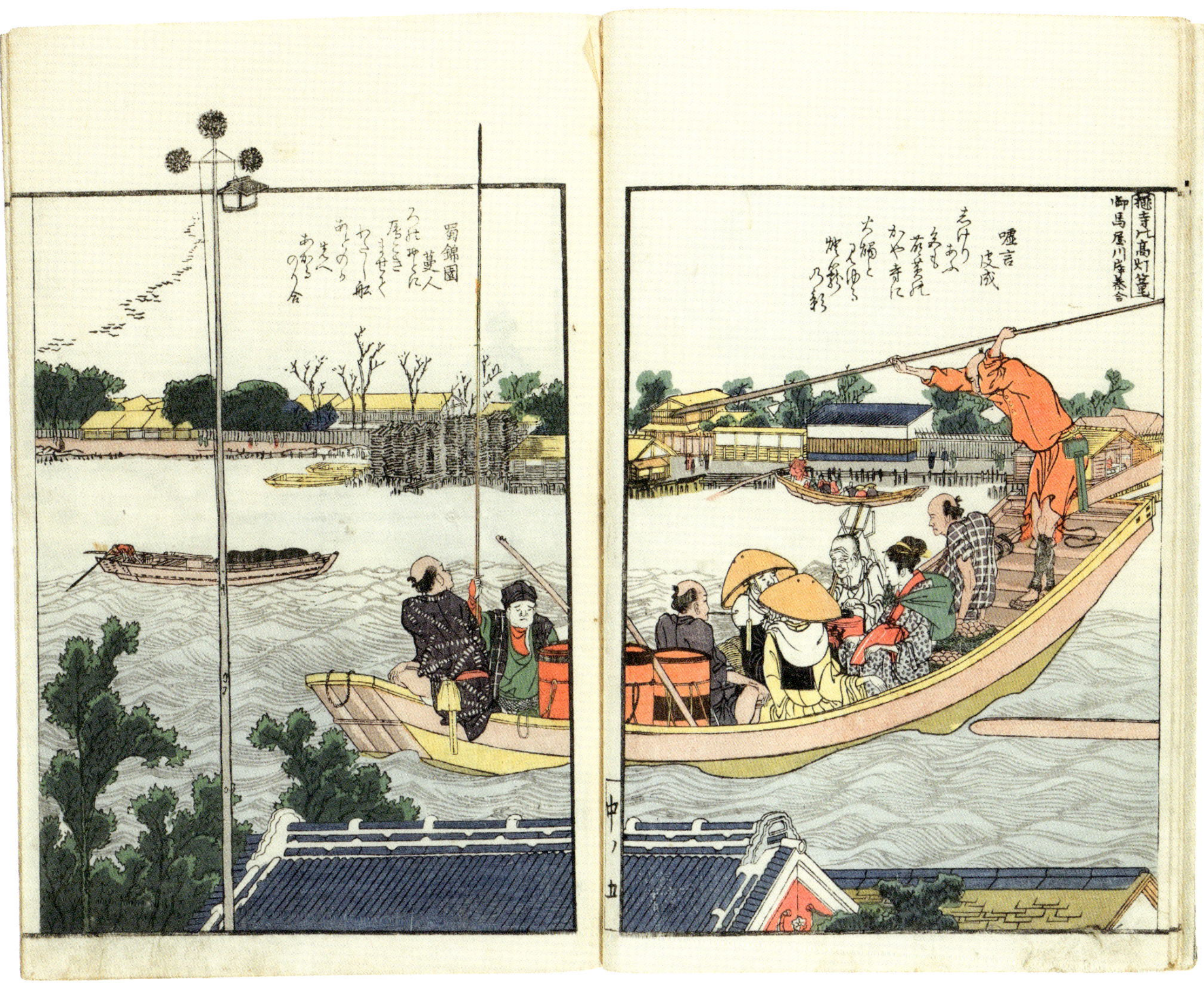

An early landmark of Hokusai's experimentation with Western techniques is the painting *Gathering Shellfish at Low Tide* (*c*. 1806–1811; ill. p. 32). Against a backdrop depicting a sandy beach, perhaps along Edo Bay with Mount Fuji rising at the horizon (a composition he revisited sporadically over his career), Hokusai painted women, children and a few men collecting clams. The blending of colours in the sky, the low horizon line and the diminishing scale of the figures, boats and landscape elements, and the subtle use of tonal modelling to give volume to the figures in the foreground are all techniques foreign to conventional Japanese imagery of the time. Hokusai would probably have learnt these from studying European images or the work of local Western-style artists such as Shiba Kōkan (1747–1818).

Hokusai maintained a distinct brand for his alter egos of Sōri and Hokusai Tatsumasa, reserving these names almost exclusively for private commissions. For his commercial work in the late 1790s and early 1800s he used the name Kakō. Among the works produced under this name is the masterful series *Seven Stylish Foibles* (*Fūryū nakute nana kuse*). Originally conceived as a group of seven designs, only two are extant today (a third was lost in the Great Kantō

The High Votive Lantern of the Kaya Temple,
the Ferry from the Shore of Onmaya, *c*. 1805
From volume two of *Picture Book: Both Banks*
of the Sumida River at a Glance
Published by Maekawa Zenbei
Woodblock-printed books, three volumes
Washington, D.C., Freer Gallery of Art
and Arthur M. Sackler Gallery,
Smithsonian Institute, Freer Study Collection

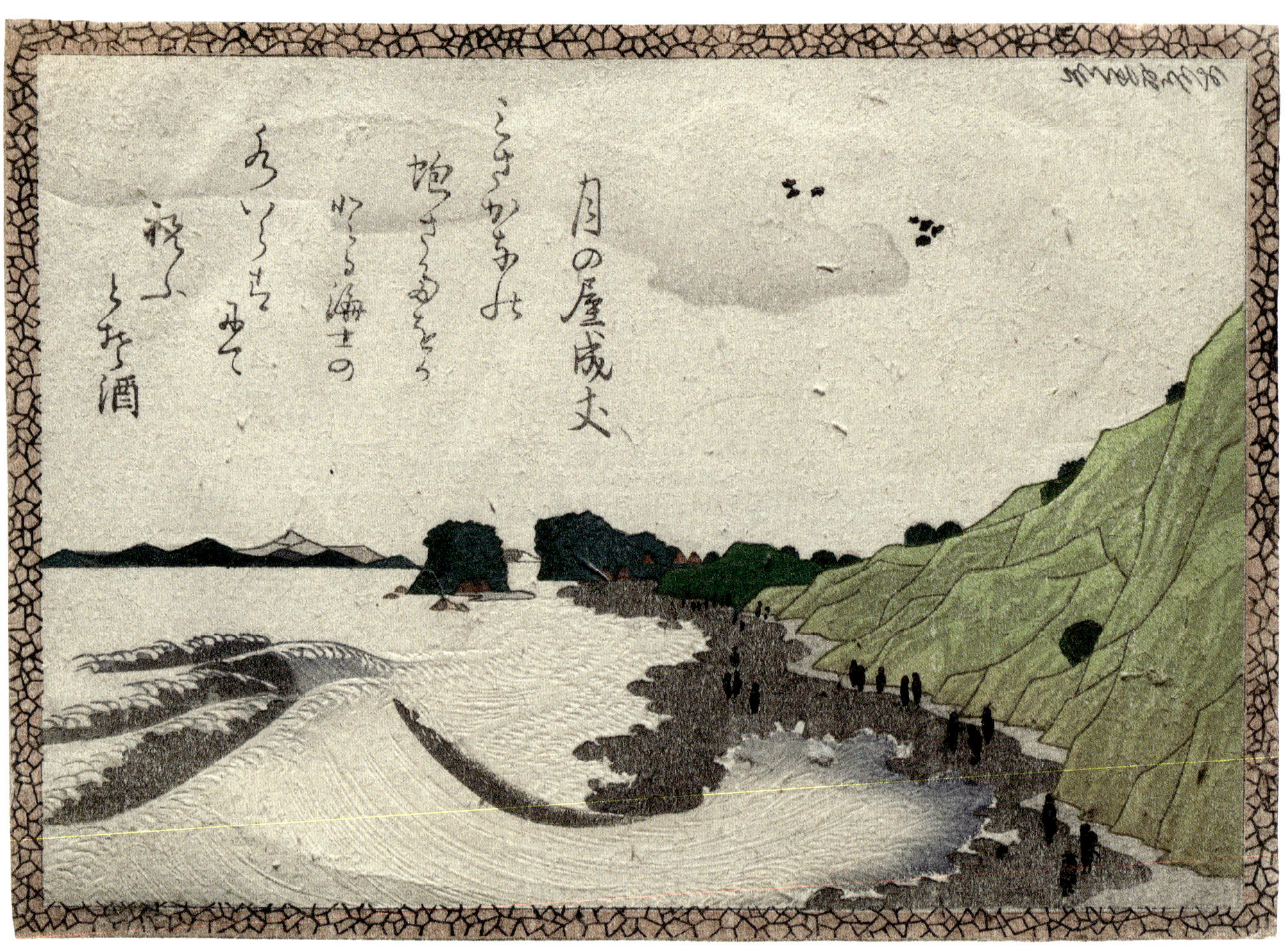

Panoramic View of Enoshima, *c.* 1804–1810
From an untitled series of
Western-style landscapes
Colour woodblock print, *kokonotsugiriban*,
13.5 x 19.1 cm (5⅜ x 7⅝ in.)
Boston, Museum of Fine Arts,
William Sturgis Bigelow Collection

Earthquake of 1923). The surviving designs each feature a pair of women
depicted close up, a composition style called *ōkubi-e* or "large head pictures".
Hokusai gave the figures exaggerated, elongated features, lending the designs
an air reminiscent of 16th-century European Mannerism. Both backgrounds
are made of shimmering mica or powdered silicate minerals. In *The Telescope*
a young woman squints through a lacquered spyglass, teeth bared grotesquely
(ill. p. 22). Behind her a second woman, eyebrows shaved and teeth blackened
to indicate her married status, tilts her parasol to obscure her young companion
from view of her quarry. Viewing devices such as telescopes, microscopes or
peep-boxes would recur sporadically in Hokusai's work, reflecting the diffusion
of Western technologies imported by Dutch traders into Japanese popular
culture in the 18th and 19th centuries.

Also remarkable is *Evening Glow for Date no Yosaku and Seki no Koman*
from an vertical *chūban* series of four known designs, passed down to us with
no title but known today as *Eight Views of Tragic Lovers* (*Michiyuki hakkei*). The
"eight views" allude to, as mentioned earlier, the canonical Chinese painting
theme, the Eight Views of the Xiao and Xiang Rivers. The term *michiyuki* is a
reference to travel sequences in Japanese theatre, where two or more characters
advance along a road together dancing or engaging in dialogue. However, it
could also implicitly refer to a journey undertaken by doomed lovers, culminat-
ing in double suicide. In the play by Chikamatsu Monzaemon (1653–1725),

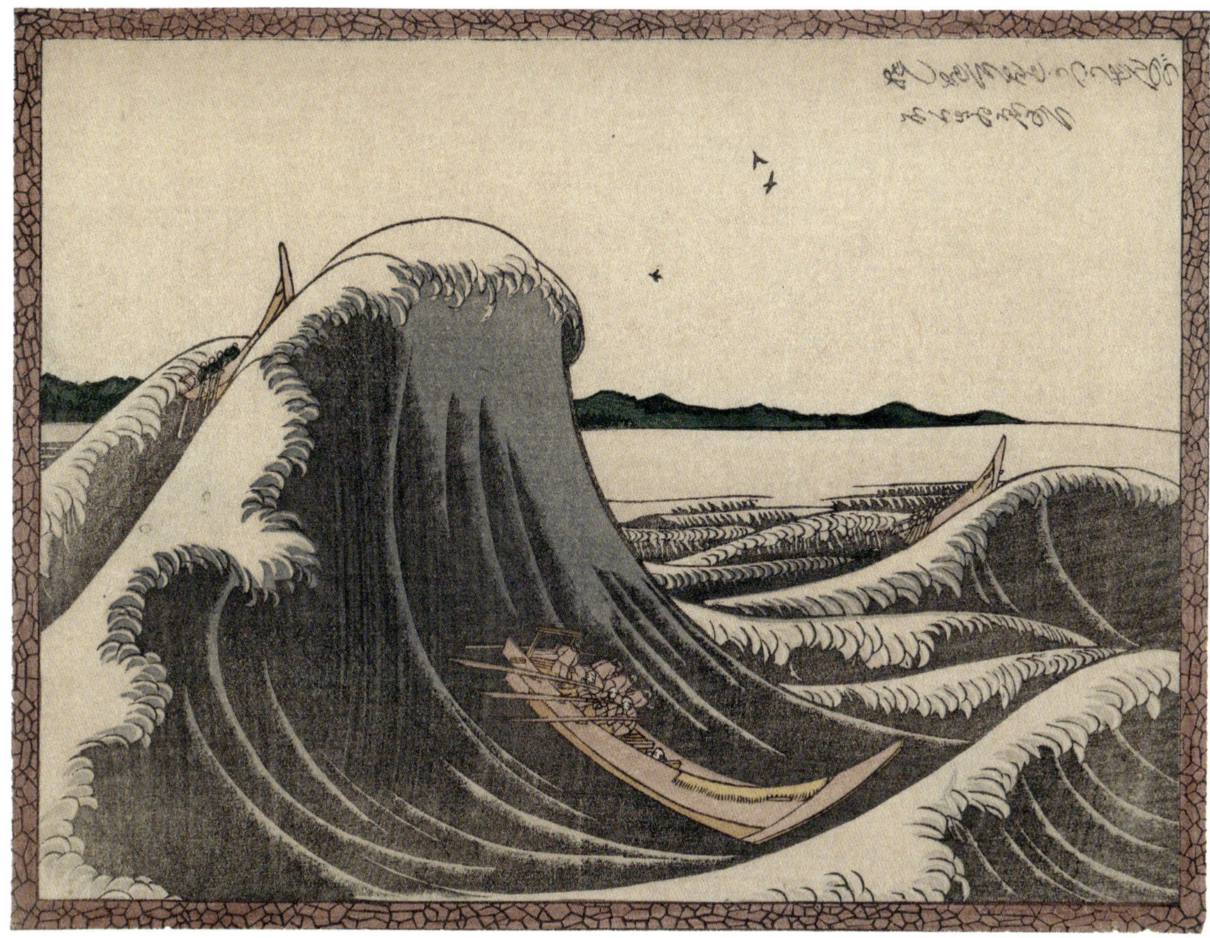

Yosaku, a disgraced retainer of the Yurugi family, falls in love with Koman, his lord's mistress. The lovers seek redemption in double suicide but are pardoned for their transgressions at the last minute and persuaded to return to court. In reference to a line from Chikamatsu's script, Hokusai depicted the lovers sharing a light to smoke their pipes at a roadside teahouse. Yosaku affectionately rests his elbow on Koman's bent knee, thus conveying the warmth between the two despite the bleak journey (ill. p. 37).

One of the best-known works from his Kakō period is the aiban series *Newly Published Perspective Pictures of the Chūshingura* (*Shinpan uki-e Chūshingura*, c. 1801–1804), published by Iseya Rihei (ill. p. 41). This marked a return to the genre of perspective pictures that he had previously undertaken as Shunrō in the 1780s. *The Treasury of Loyal Retainers*, or *Chūshingura*, launched with the puppet play *Kanadehon Chūshingura* (1748), refers to theatrical productions or literary texts loosely based on the historical Akō Incident (1701–1703), where 47 masterless samurai or *rōnin* avenged the death of their lord.

Hokusai's series presents 11 designs, one for each act in the original play. His composition for act five contains three vignettes taking place on a rainy night in a single landscape setting. In the foreground, the highwayman Sadakurō is poised to slay an elderly man from whom he has just stolen a pouch of gold coins. The money is from the old man selling his daughter into prostitution to help his son-in-law Kanpei, one of the masterless samurai. Meanwhile, Kanpei

Express Delivery Boats Rowing through Waves, c. 1800–1805
From an untitled series of Western-style landscapes
Colour woodblock print, *chūban*, 18.5 x 24.5 cm (7⅜ x 9¾ in.)
Boston, Museum of Fine Arts, William Sturgis Bigelow Collection

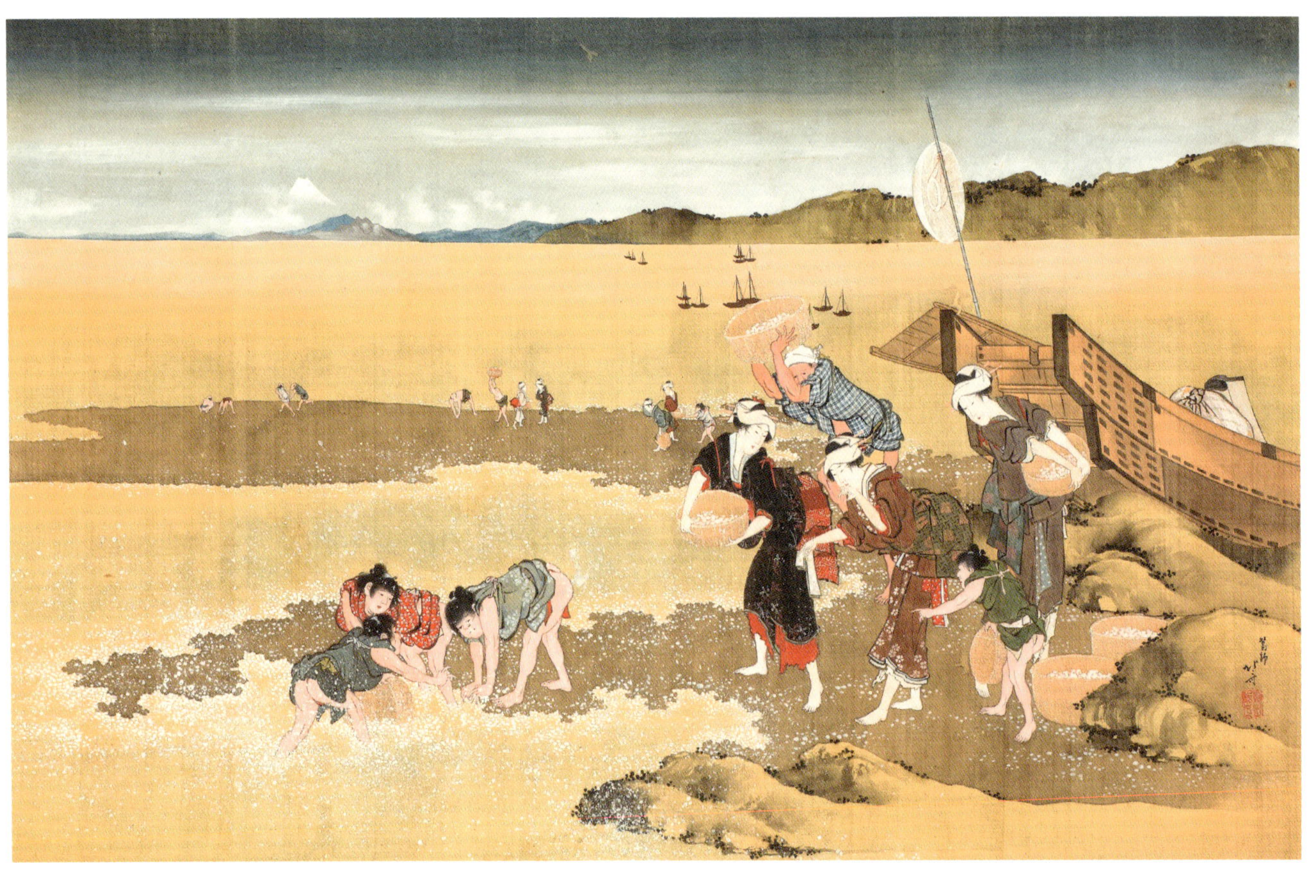

Gathering Shellfish at Low Tide, *c.* 1806–1811
Hanging scroll, colour on silk,
54.3 x 86.3 cm (21½ x 34 in.)
Osaka City Museum of Fine Arts,
Important Cultural Property

and a fellow *rōnin*, depicted in the distance, meet on the road. Shortly after, Kanpei, who had been supporting himself as a hunter since his master's death, accidentally shoots Sadakurō, mistaking him for a wild boar. Alluding to this tragic development, a boar charges down an embankment on the left.

Although Hokusai had yet to attain the full brilliance and artistic genius we know him to be capable of today, his reputation was growing. In the fourth month of 1804, he was to complete a *sekiga*, a painting executed before a gathering at Edo's Gokokuji Temple. The painting was a half-length portrait of Bodhidharma (known in Japan as Daruma), the Central Asian monk credited with transmitting Zen Buddhism to China in the fifth or sixth century. The work was brushed on a quilt of paper covering an area of 120 *tatami* mats, almost 200 square metres. In 1817, he repeated the performance at Honganji Betsuin Temple in Nagoya.

Iijima recorded another act of showmanship that allegedly took place in 1807. Hearing of Hokusai's unusual skill, the 11th shogun Tokugawa Ienari (1773–1841) invited him to compete against Tani Bunchō (1763–1841) in a painting duel at Sensōji Temple in Asakusa. During the competition Hokusai first painted a landscape and a bird-and-flowers composition, received with great admiration from his audience. He then drew an undulating line in blue along a ream of paper and, to everyone's astonishment, took a chicken from a basket, dipped its feet in red paint, and set it loose on the freshly-completed painting. He proclaimed the artwork represented "Maple Leaves on the Tatsu River". According to Iijima, Bunchō watched on, wringing sweat from his hands.

Between 1806 and 1815, Hokusai's work focused on illustrating a new type of novel called *yomihon* or "reading books" typically made up of a single narrative, bound in multiple volumes. Often adapted from Chinese tales, *yomihon* were written in a literary, sometimes didactic style that made them more demanding on the reader than the popular *kibyōshi*. First produced in the mid-18th century, rising education levels and the emergence of skilled writer-illustrator partnerships, such as that of Hokusai and Takizawa Bakin (1767–1848), helped the genre to proliferate in the early 19th century. *Yomihon* were sparsely illustrated compared to other fiction works of the time and were typically produced only in monochrome, sometimes with halftone overprinting. However, the fact that established artists like Hokusai, Utagawa Toyokuni, Utagawa Toyohiro (1773–1828) and Keisai Eisen (1790–1848) all produced images for such books indicates that publishers considered skilfully designed illustrations to be crucial to the success of their products.

Yomihon became an important source of income for Hokusai. His first title, *Ancient Curious Tales Left by Fishermen* (*Kokon kidan ama no sutegusa*), was published in 1803, and he continued to work in the genre over his entire life, contributing illustrations to 49 known titles. Despite limitations of the *yomihon* format Hokusai created many compelling designs, especially those depicting the strange or grotesque. Among the most memorable is a double-page image from the first of the six-volume *yomihon* entitled *Snow in the Garden* (*Sono no yuki*, 1807), a historical warrior novel by Bakin. Hokusai presented the samurai Sonobe Saemon Yoritane, armed with a pole weapon and flaming torch, confronting a monstrous spider wearing the skulls of its victims strung from its legs (ill. p. 34). It is a prime example of Hokusai's keen sense of realism and vivid imagination working together: here the artist depicted the spider as if it genuinely existed in the phenomenal world rather than just in the realm of fantasy.

In the following year, Ryūtei Tanehiko's (1783–1842) five-volume ghost story *The Stars on a Frosty Night* (*Shimoyo no hoshi*, 1808) gave Hokusai ample scope

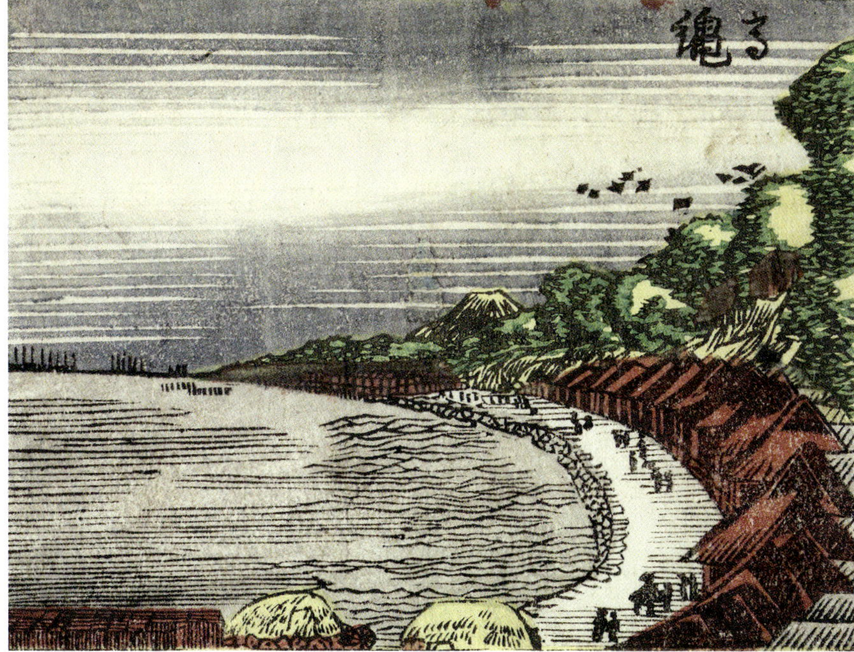

Takanawa, c. 1802
From the series *The Dutch Picture Lens:
Eight Views of Edo*
Colour woodblock print, *yatsugiriban*,
8.6 x 11.4 cm (3½ x 4½ in.)
Boston, Museum of Fine Arts,
William Sturgis Bigelow Collection

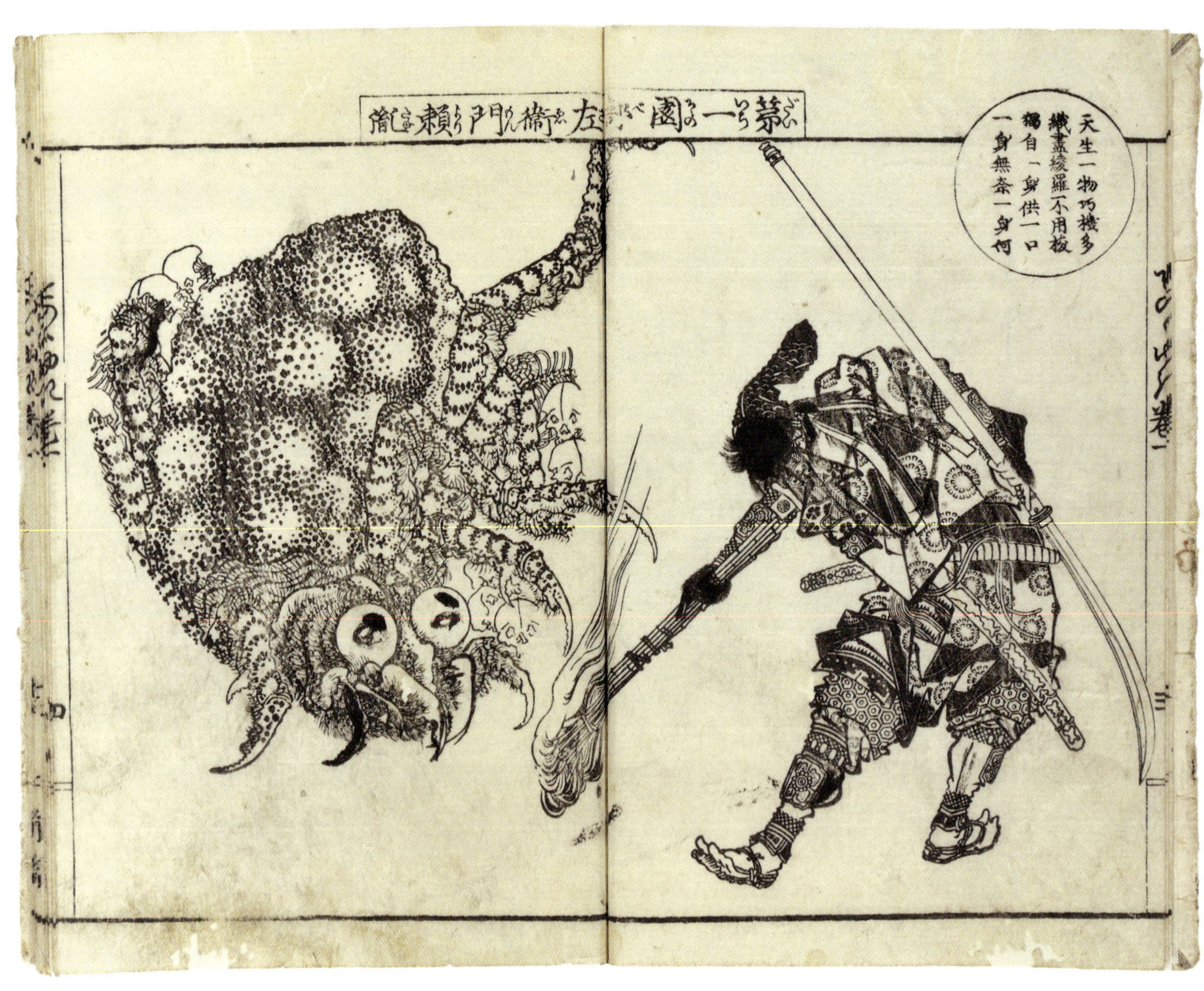

Number One: Sonobe Saemon Yoritane, 1807
From volume one of *Snow in the Garden*
Woodblock-printed books, six volumes
London, British Museum

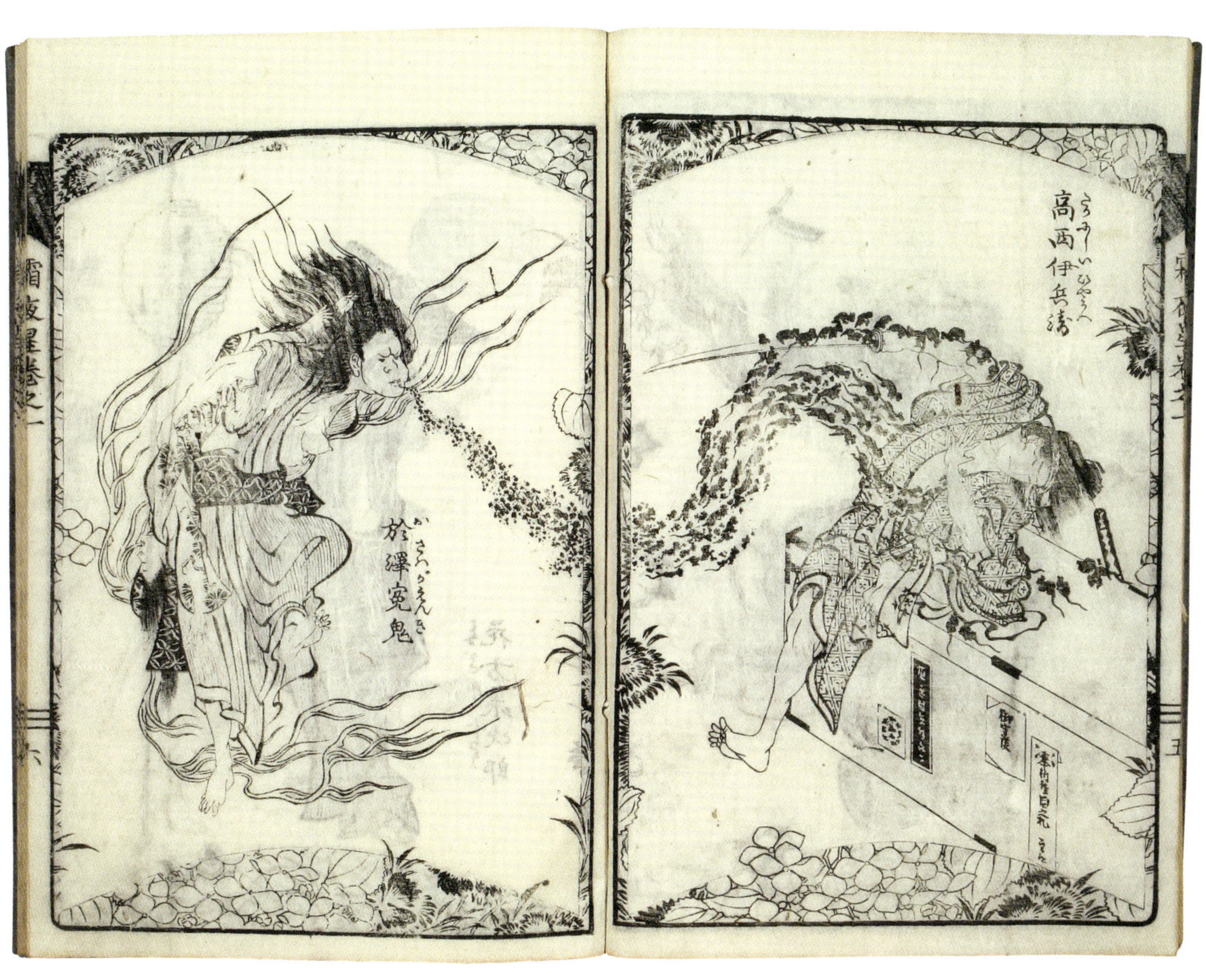

Takanishi Ihei and the Vengeful Spirit
of Osawa, 1808
From volume one of *The Stars on a Frosty Night*
Published by Gunhōdō
Woodblock-printed books, five volumes
Tokyo, Waseda University Library

*Evening Glow for Date no Yosaku
and Seki no Koman*, 1801–1804
From the untitled series known as
Eight Views of Tragic Lovers
Colour woodblock print, *chūban*,
23.1 x 17.5 cm (9 x 7 in.)
Art Institute of Chicago,
Clarence Buckingham Collection

to test his fertile imagination. In Tanehiko's story, the antagonist Ihei abuses
his wife Osawa, whom he married for her wealth, until she eventually ends
her life. From the grave she then wages a relentless campaign of vengeance
upon her worthless husband. Hokusai introduced these two characters with
a grotesquely humorous image in which Osawa breathes a venomous cloud
that envelops Ihei and materializes into a swarm of rats (ill. p. 35).

Hokusai's longest-running *yomihon* illustration venture was Bakin's masterpiece *Strange Tales of the Crescent Moon* (*Chinsetsu yumiharizuki*, 1807–1811).
A saga of warrior virtue comprising 30 volumes, the book is a fictionalized
account of the life of Minamoto no Tametomo (1139–1170). Set partly in the
Ryūkyū Islands – an exotic, far-flung locale to the *yomihon* reader – the commission presented another opportunity for Hokusai to give free reign to his
sense of the marvellous.

Hokusai introduced Tametomo in a double-page illustration. He depicts
the fabled archer with two inhabitants of Demon Island (Onigashima) where
he had been exiled, attempting to draw the string on his weapon (ill. p. 36).
The publisher Hirabayashi Shōgorō commissioned Hokusai to create a painting
that celebrated the series' completion in 1811. The artist revisited the composition with brilliant coloured pigments, adding two more figures and landscape
elements to indicate the island setting, reversing the relationship between
Tametomo and the demons and finishing the work with lavish applications
of gold dust. Bakin added an inscription in the upper left (ill. pp. 38/39).

Taito

Around 1810, Hokusai was struck by lightning. This event brought about a new
phase in his life, which he marked by adopting the name Taito in 1813. This name,
meaning "receiving the Big Dipper", indicates that he saw this fearful incident as
a blessing from the North Star, the main object of his previous name. He would
use this new name for about ten years before passing it on to a student.

Hokusai's Taito era was distinguished by his prolific output of *edehon* or
drawing manuals. His first venture into this genre can be traced to 1810 when
the artist, despite his lasting, heavy engagement in illustrating *yomihon*, produced *Foolish Ono's Nonsense Picture Dictionary* (*Ono ga bakamura mudaji
ezukushi*), published by Tsutaya. These works parodied the famous poetry text-
book *Ono Takamura's Picture Dictionary* (*Ono Takamura utaji zukushi*, 1692),
which shows budding artists how to build forms from basic Chinese characters.

Edehon were produced by most painting schools in the 18th and 19th centuries
reflecting a growing population of people with both disposable income and time
to pursue leisurely interests. These works could also be used as training manuals
for professional artists. That Hokusai entered this market points to his growing
popularity, not only for consumers of woodblock-printed imagery but also among
those who aspired to produce designs of their own. Although Hokusai, unlike
his competitors in the Utagawa school, lacked a large atelier of students who
would perpetuate his style, drawing manuals proved a greater possibility of dis-
seminating his teaching much more widely and indiscriminately.

Hokusai's most ambitious *edehon* project was *Transmitting the Essence
and Enlightening the Hand: Random Drawings by Hokusai* (*Denshin kaishu
Hokusai manga*), better known simply as *Hokusai manga*. These comprised
15 volumes, released over a 64-year period from 1814 to 1878. The final three
volumes were published after Hokusai's death; within these, the first two
compiled some previously published work while the last is largely believed

*Inhabitants of Onigashima Testing
Minamoto no Tametomo's Bow*, 1807
From volume one of *Strange Tales of
the Crescent Moon*
Published by Hirabayashi Shōgorō
Woodblock-printed books, 30 volumes
London, British Museum

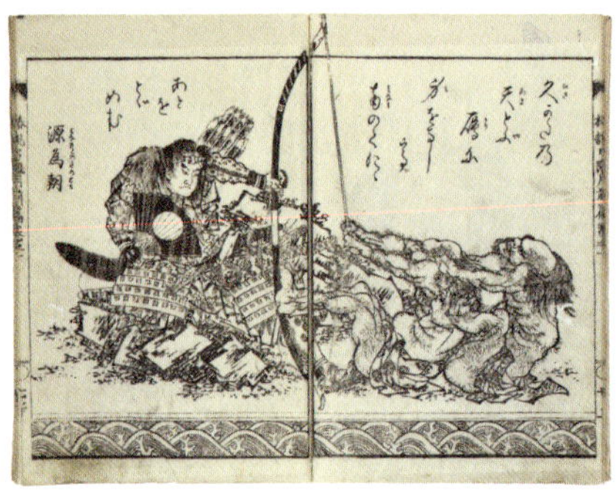

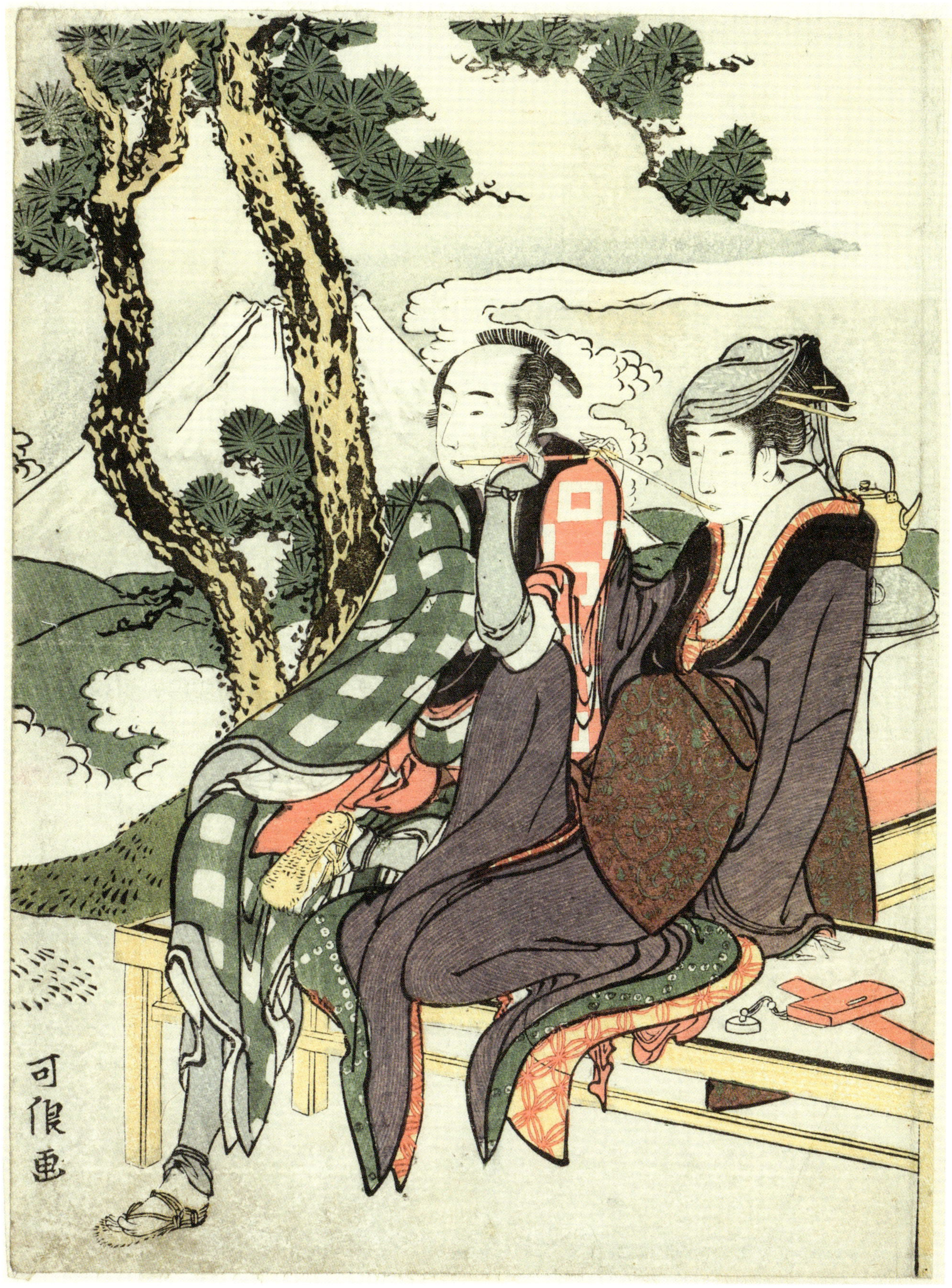

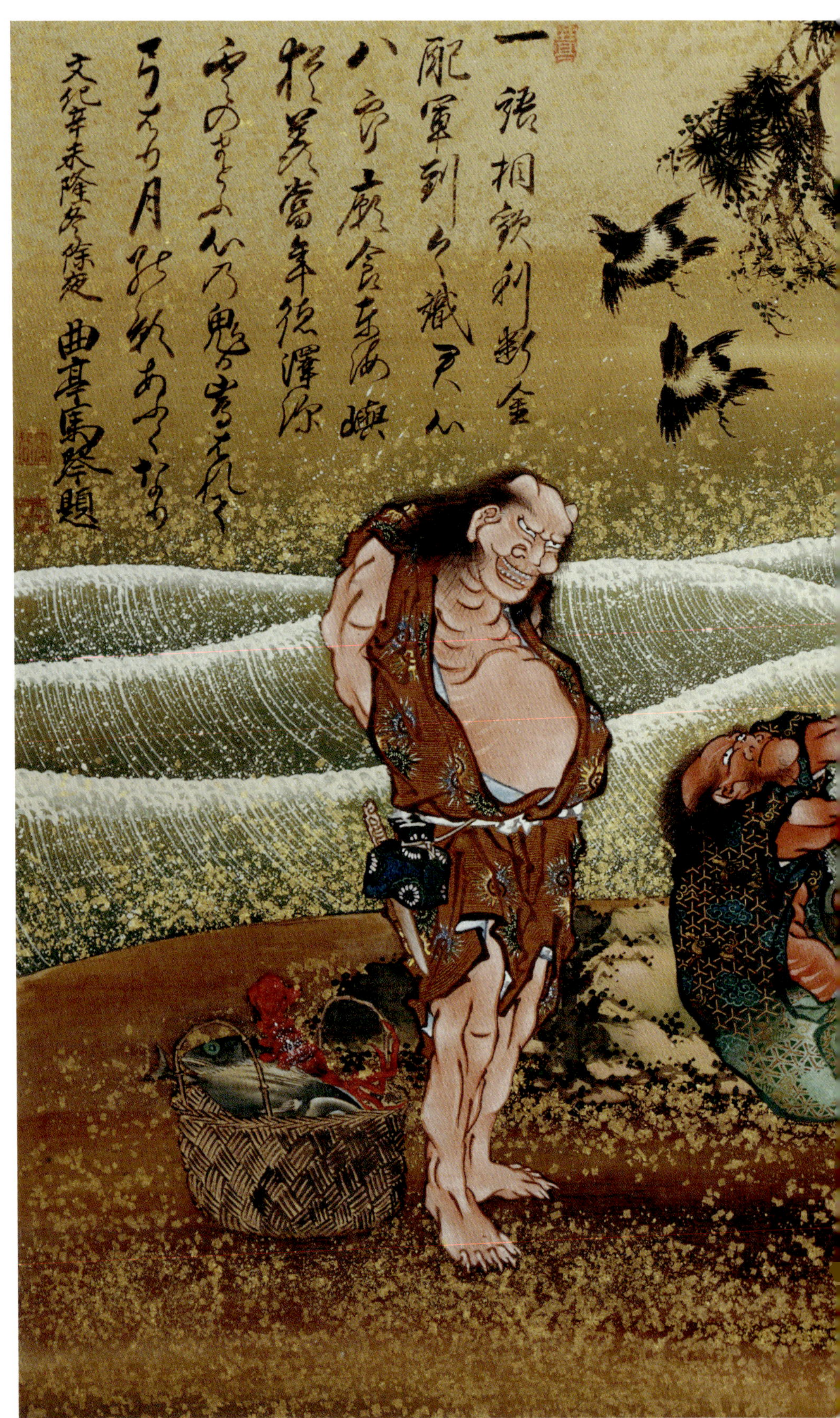

***Tametomo and the Inhabitants
of Onigashima Island***, 1811
Hanging scroll, ink, colour and gold
on silk, 54.9 x 82.1 cm (21⅝ x 32⅜ in.)
London, British Museum

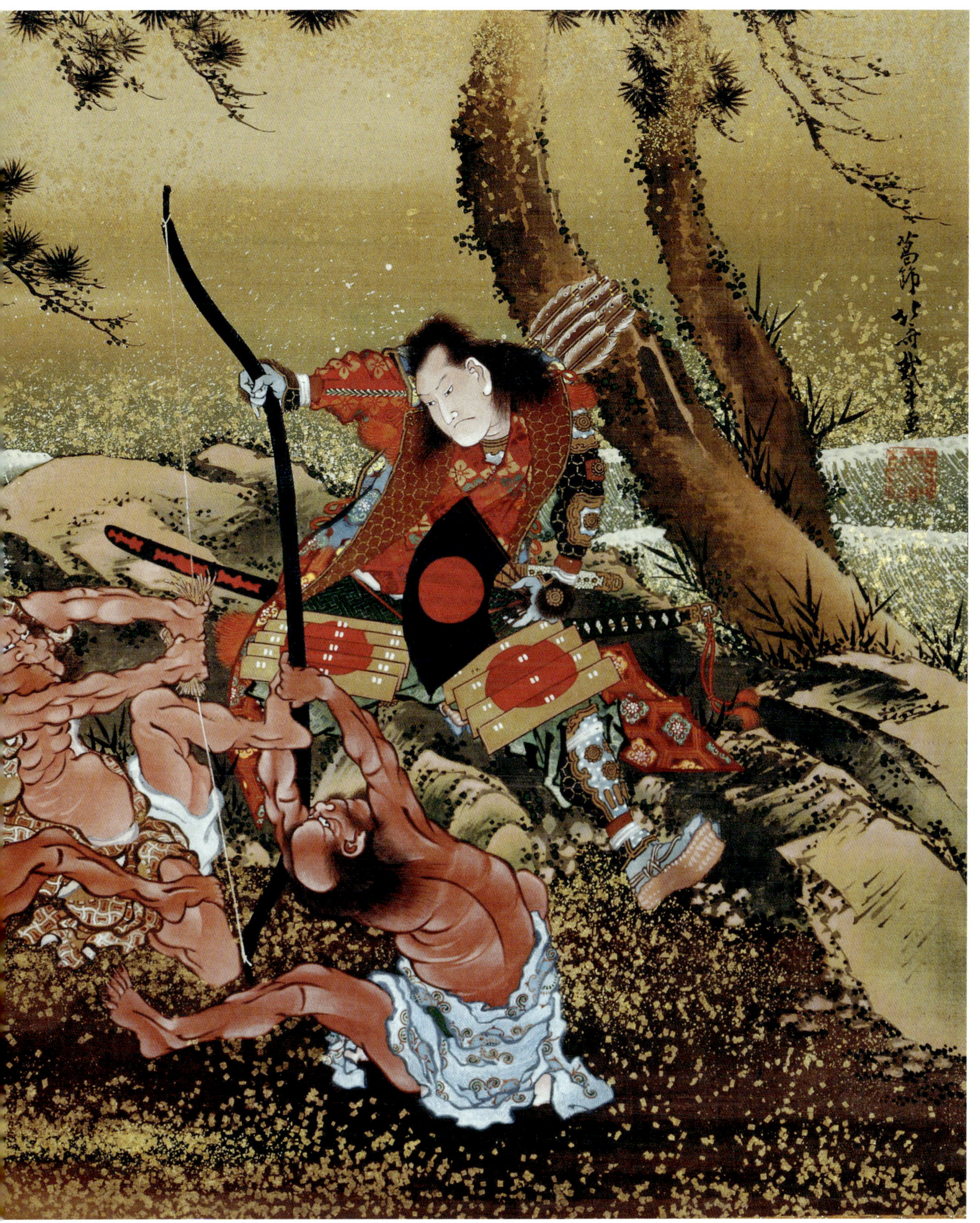

to be spurious, as it contains images by artists other than Hokusai. The word *manga* can be translated as "random pictures" or "whimsical pictures", but also carried the meaning, "pictures of all things".

According to the first volume's preface, the books began with around 300 drawings Hokusai penned while visiting his student Gekkōtei Bokusen (active 1809–1824) in Nagoya, and the first voumes were issued by a local publisher, Eirakuya Tōshirō, rather than one in Edo. With the assistance of Bokusen and other students, Katsushika Hokuun (active 1804–1844), Toenrō Hokusen (active 1815–1819), and Totoya Hokkei (1780–1850), this blossomed into about 4,000 drawings of an array of subjects. Several images anticipate future directions in his work – from terrifying ghosts to representations of Mount Fuji in various guises (ills. pp. 25, 40 left). We also encounter recurring figures such as the travellers buffeted by a gust of sudden wind in volume seven. These were revisited by Hokusai years later in the print *Ejiri in Suruga Province* from the series *Thirty-six Views of Mount Fuji* (ills. pp. 40 right, 42/43). Turning his sharp yet sympathetic eye to the daily lives of ordinary people and animals, and creating compositions of startling elegance and originality, Hokusai revealed his charming lyricism, gentle humour and sense of humanity.

Hokusai manga was a phenomenal success and was reprinted several times into the 1860s. These books were the principal source through which Europeans became acquainted not only with Hokusai and *ukiyo-e*, but with Japanese landscape and its peoples. The first ten volumes of *Hokusai manga* were among the illustrated books Philipp Franz von Siebold (1796–1866) and his colleagues brought back to Europe to be publicly exhibited at Siebold's museum from 1837. Several images from *manga*, including a dramatic image of a stone bridge spanning a ravine at Kume in Shinano, were reproduced as lithographs in Siebold's illustrated *Nippon: A Descriptive Archive of Japan* (*Nippon: Archiv zur Beschreibung von Japan*), published between 1832 and 1852 (ills. pp. 44, 45 top).

The European trend for *Japonisme* began, most improbably, when pages from a volume of *Hokusai manga*, allegedly used as packing material in a crate of porcelain, turned up in the workshop of the master printer August Delâtre between 1856 and 1859. Several designs from the discovered collection were adapted in

Untitled View of Mount Fuji, 1816
From volume five of *Hokusai manga*
Published by Eirakuya Tōshirō and others
Woodblock-printed books, 15 volumes
London, British Museum

Sudden Rainstorm at the Village of Sekiya in Shimōsa Province, 1817
From volume seven of *Hokusai manga*
Published by Eirakuya Tōshirō and others
Woodblock-printed books, 15 volumes
London, British Museum

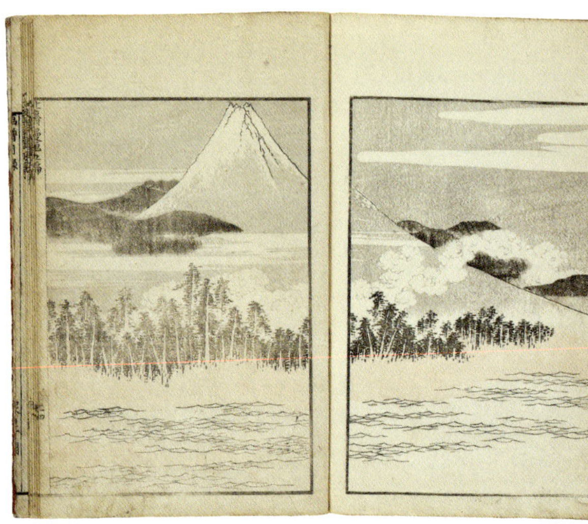

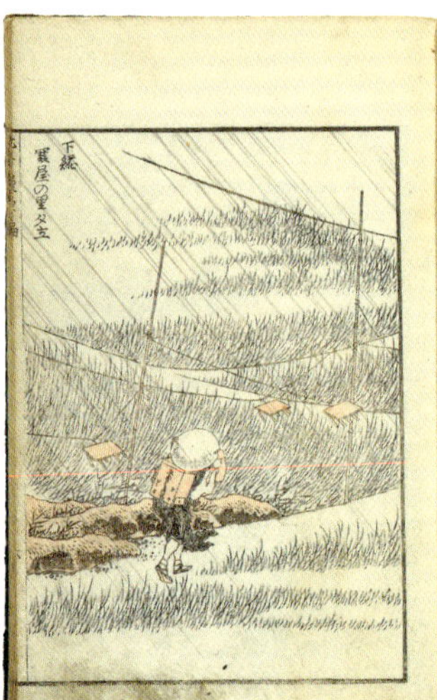

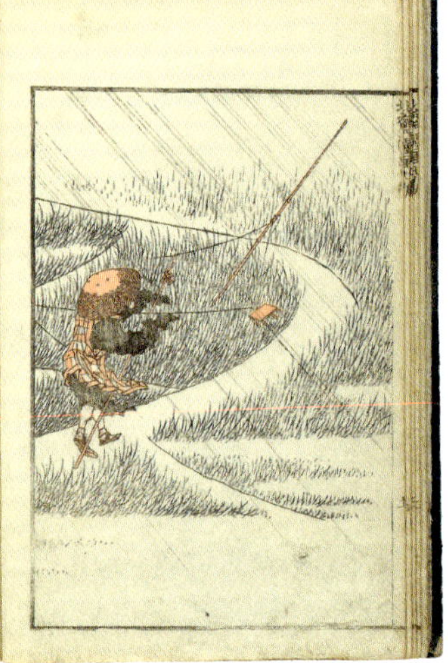

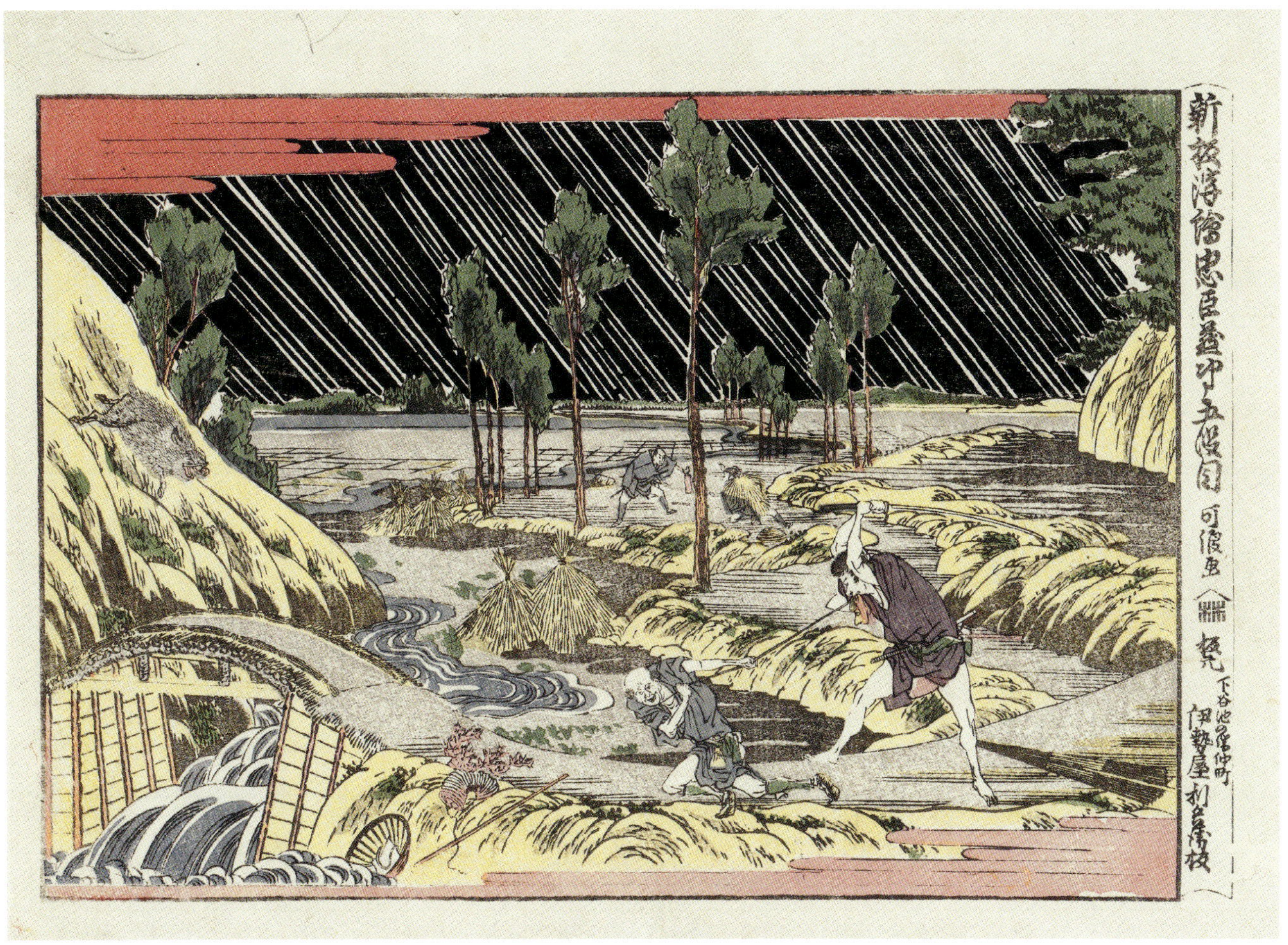

Act V, *c.* 1801–1804
From the series *Newly Published
Perspective Pictures of Chūshingura*
Published by Iseya Rihei
Colour woodblock print, *aiban*,
23.3 x 35.1 cm (9¼ x 13⅞ in.)
Boston, Museum of Fine Arts,
William Sturgis Bigelow Collection

the industrial design book *Recueil de dessins pour l'art et l'industrie* by Eugène V. Collinot and Adalbert de Beaumont, published in 1859. Highly interested in the book, artist Félix Bracquemond (1833–1914) was eventually able to buy it from Delâtre in around 1859 and began showing the images to his artist friends. Around the same time, Claude Monet (1840–1926) started his own collection of *ukiyo-e*, which ultimately grew to some 250 prints. Édouard Manet's (1832–1883) etching, *Line in Front of the Butcher Shop* (1870/71), is just one of many Western images to have been inspired by *Hokusai manga*, in this case a vignette from the very first volume (ill. p. 47 top right). This same composition was reintroduced back to Japan in a design by the Austrian artist Friedrich (Fritz) Capelari (1884–1950) in his print *Umbrellas* (ill. p. 47 bottom), published in 1915 by Watanabe Shōzaburō (1885–1962).

For the Illustrated Album of Three Styles of Painting (Santai gafu, 1816), Hokusai again collaborated with his students Hokkei, Hokusen, Bokusen and Hokuun. The book presented subjects as varied as Daoist immortals and crabs (ill. p. 47 top left). The title's "three styles" refers to the classification of painting and calligraphy into formal, semi-cursive, and cursive styles that represent a scale from the more deliberate to the more fluid and spontaneous. Some images are standard copybook models, but the brilliant, lifelike rendering of animal subjects reveals Hokusai's genuine sensitivity and curiosity towards his fellow creatures.

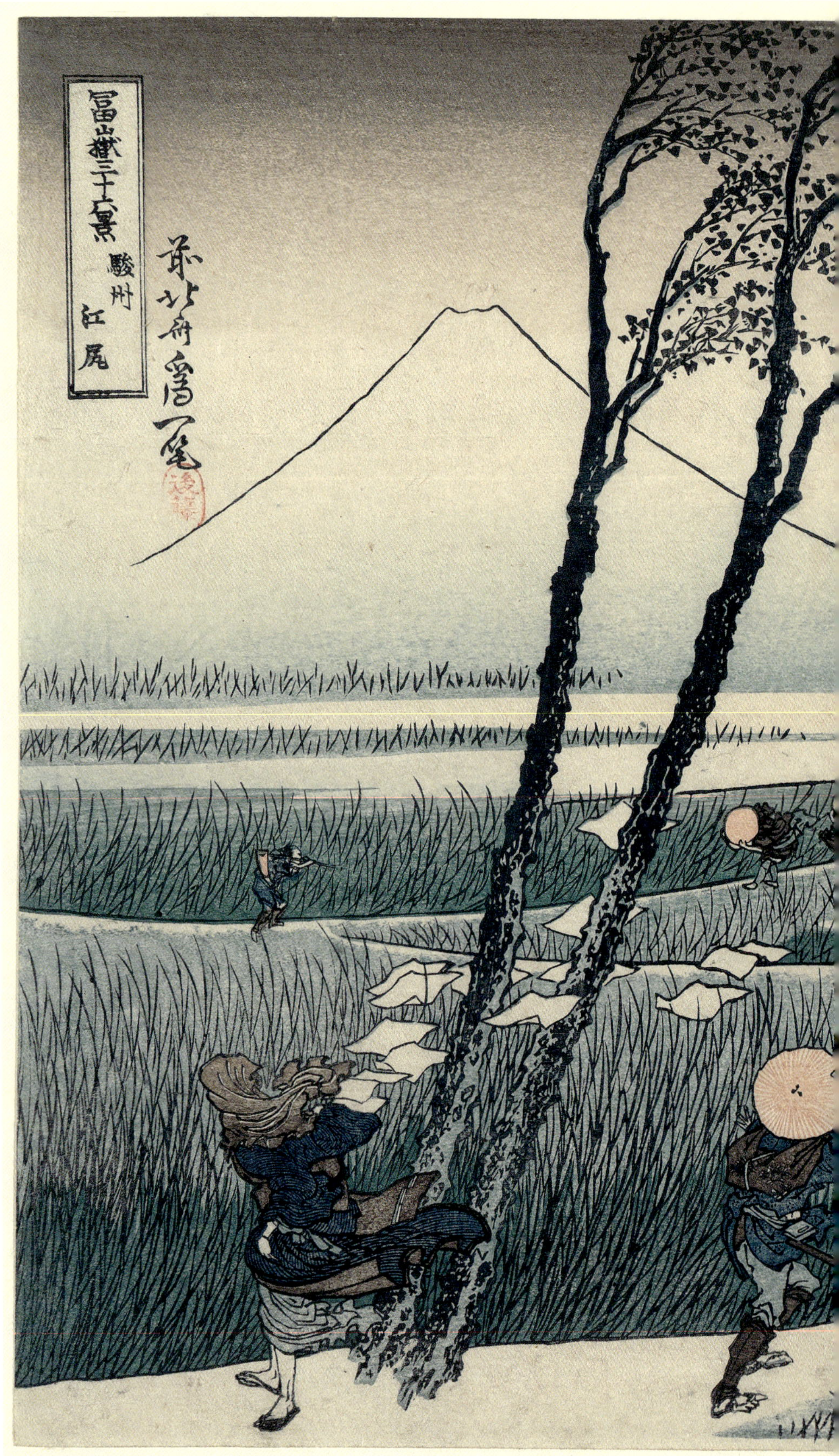

Ejiri in Suruga Province, *c.* 1830/31
From the series *Thirty-six
Views of Mount Fuji*
Published by Nishimuraya Yohachi
Colour woodblock print, *ōban*,
25.2 x 37.5 cm (10 x 14⅞ in.)
Boston, Museum of Fine Arts, William
S. and John T. Spaulding Collection

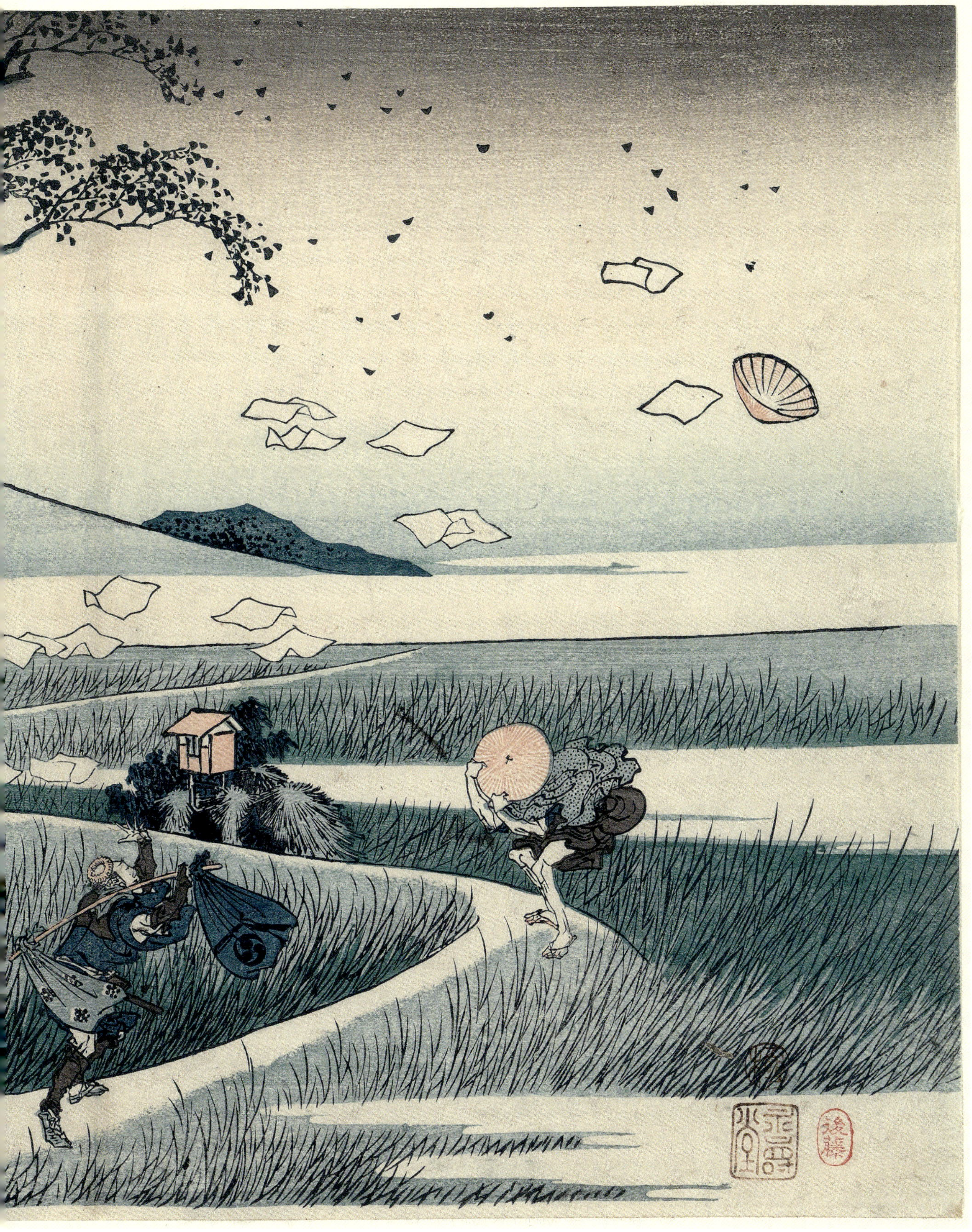

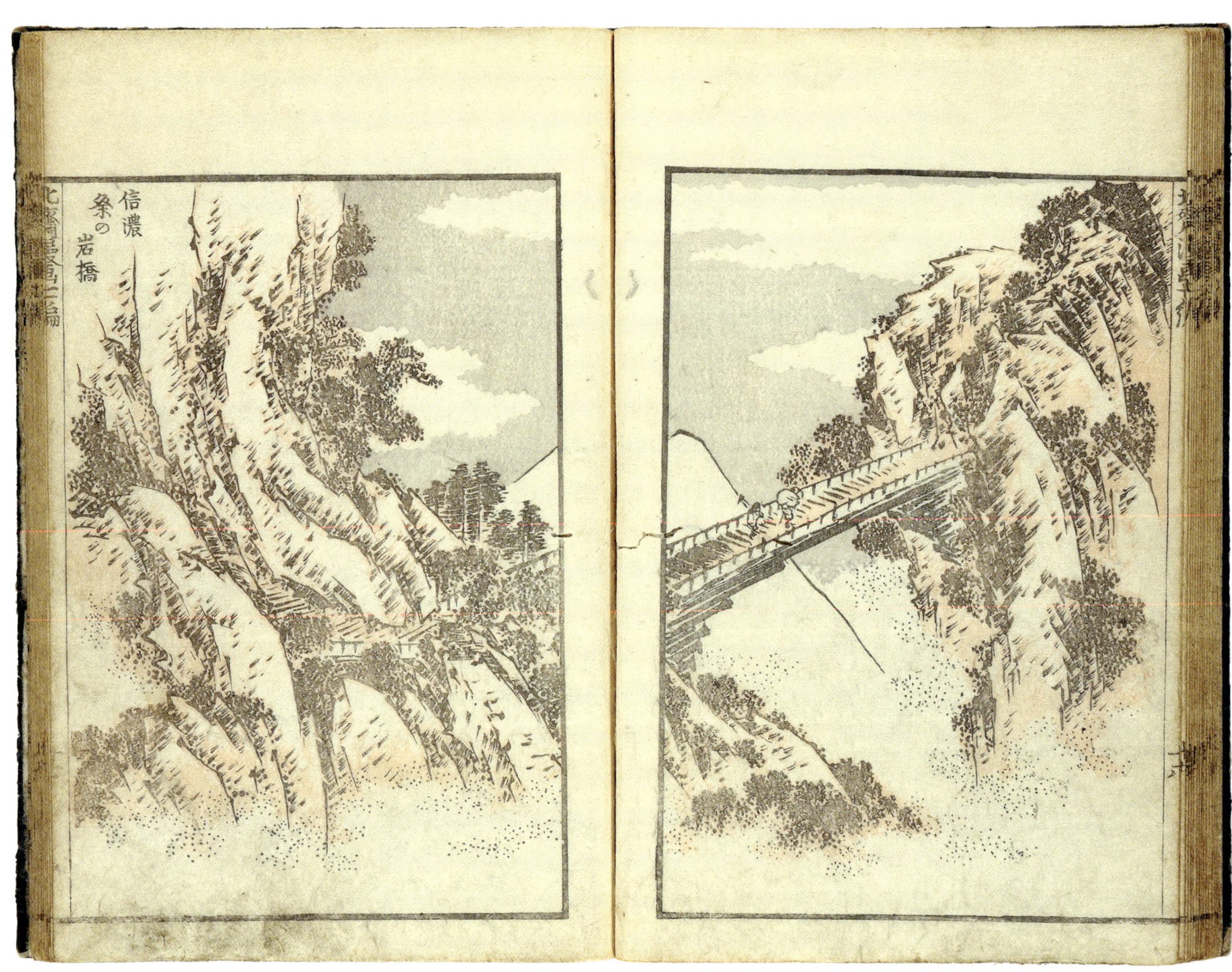
信濃
糸の岩橋

Hokusai's interest in drawing manuals seems to have waned by 1820, though he occasionally returned to this genre as well as to the related field of books on applied design, for example, with the *Illustrated Album of One-Brushstroke Drawings* (*Ippitsu gafu*, 1823). The premise of the book was to present a miscellany of line drawings executed with as few brushstrokes as possible. Hokusai seems to have particularly enjoyed drawing birds, as he dedicated several pages to waterfowl such as cormorants, geese and, above all, cranes, which occupy the first four pages following the frontispiece (ill. p. 46). Their elegant forms were ideally suited to the constraints of the exercise. Hokusai's models demonstrate how a single calligraphic line can materialize into a bird's beak, head, neck, abdomen, tail and wings, with one or two extra strokes to depict legs. His lines swell and thin with the weight of the brush, and sometimes cross over themselves playfully, veering into the decorative and toward the abstract.

In 1823, he created *Modern Designs for Combs and Tobacco Pipes* (*Imayō kushi kiseru hinagata*), a three-volume set of miniature sourcebooks for artisans that gathered over 400 designs of intimate personal items featuring landscapes, including different views of Mount Fuji in a variety of guises, narrative scenes, delicately rendered animals and plants and abstract patterns. In several cases, Hokusai created motifs of ocean waves; one pair of facing pages presents four designs for combs with waves depicted in different styles (ill. p. 45 bottom). We discover a range of tightly curled and undulating waves, naturalistic choppy waves and arabesque waves in the lineage of his later masterpiece *Under the Wave off Kanagawa*.

Like virtually all *ukiyo-e* artists, Hokusai also created erotic imagery or *shunga*, mostly in the form of illustrated books. The dozen or so titles attributed to him were all published between around 1782, during his Shunrō period, and 1823, after he adopted the name Iitsu. His explicit design of a female diver or fisherwoman, prostrate in ecstasy, as two octopuses fondle her naked body with their tentacles, has repulsed and fascinated viewers for over two centuries (ill. p. 24). Popularly known as *The Dream of the Fisherman's Wife*, the image appeared in the third volume of the book *Pine Seedlings on the First Rat Day* (*Kinoe no komatsu, c.* 1814). The woman's apparent helplessness and the blank,

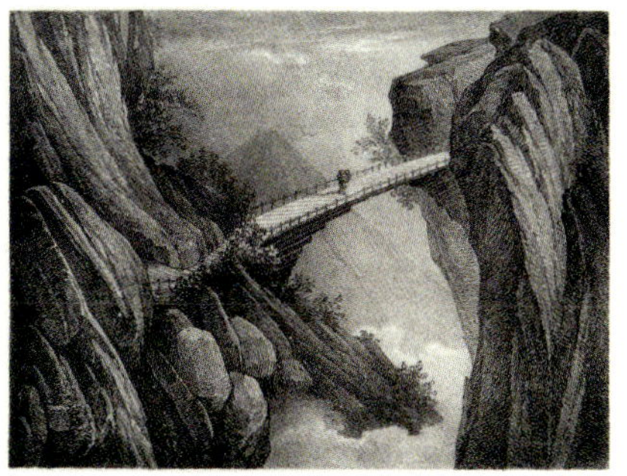

The Stone Bridge at Kume in Shinano, 1852
Lithograph from Philipp Franz von Siebold:
Nippon: A Descriptive Archive of Japan
Leiden, Museum Volkenkunde

PAGE 44
Stone Bridge at Kume in Shinano, 1817
From volume seven of *Hokusai manga*
Published by Eirakuya Tōshirō and others
Woodblock-printed books, 15 volumes
London, British Museum

PAGE 46
Cranes, 1823
From *Illustrated Album of
One-Brushstroke Drawings*
Woodblock-printed book
London, British Museum

BELOW
Combs with Wave Motifs, 1823
From volume one of *Modern Designs
for Combs and Tobacco Pipes*
Published by Nishimuraya Yohachi and others
Woodblock-printed books, three volumes
London, British Museum

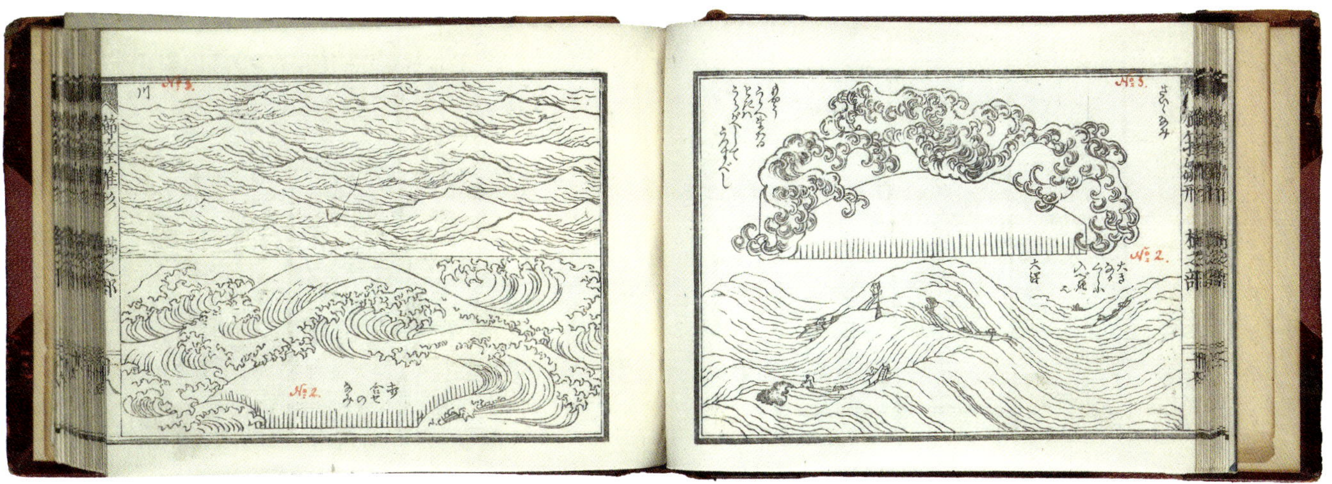

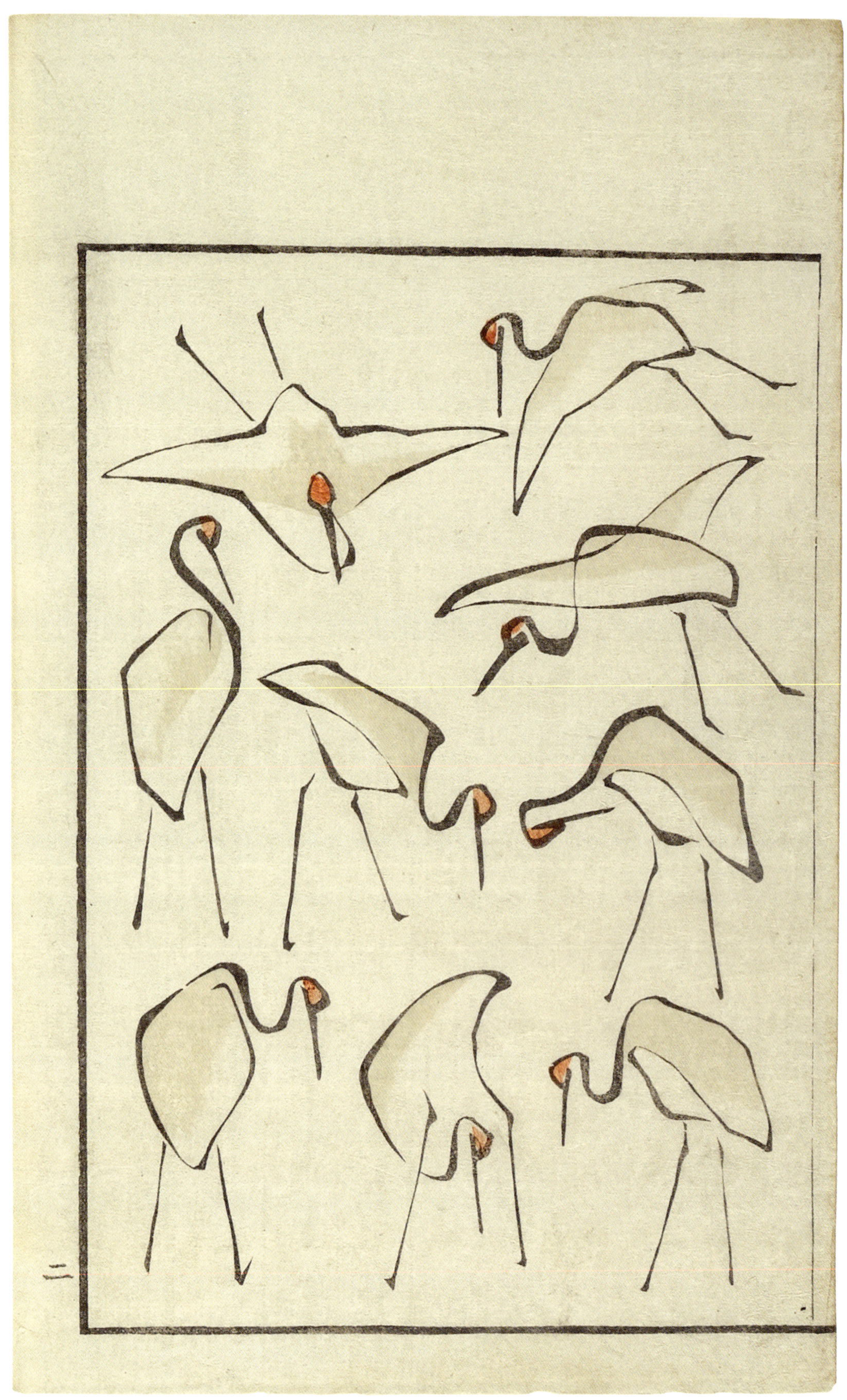

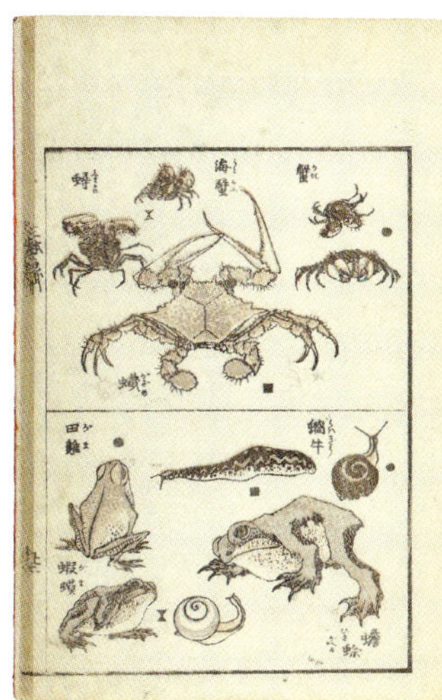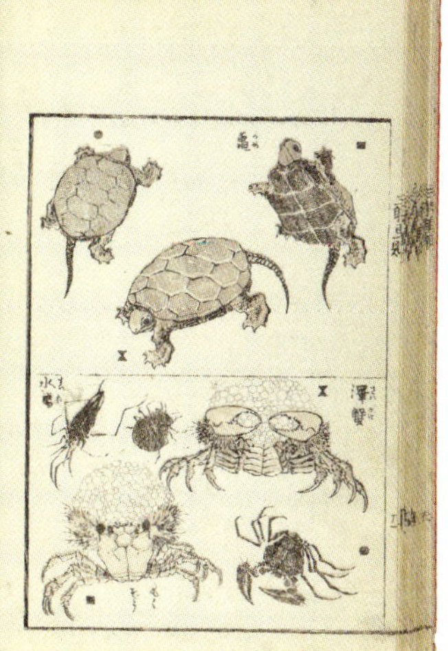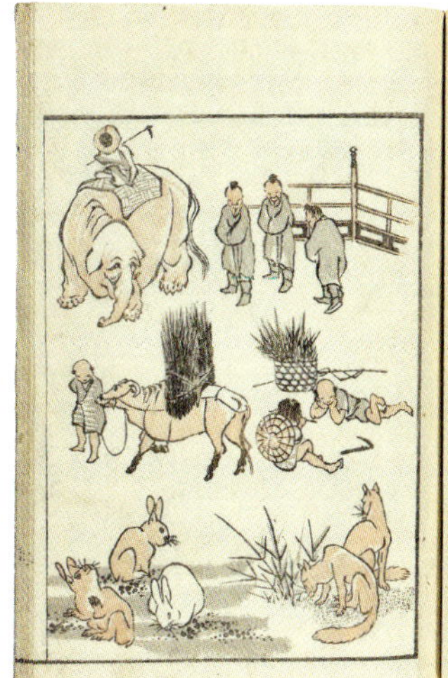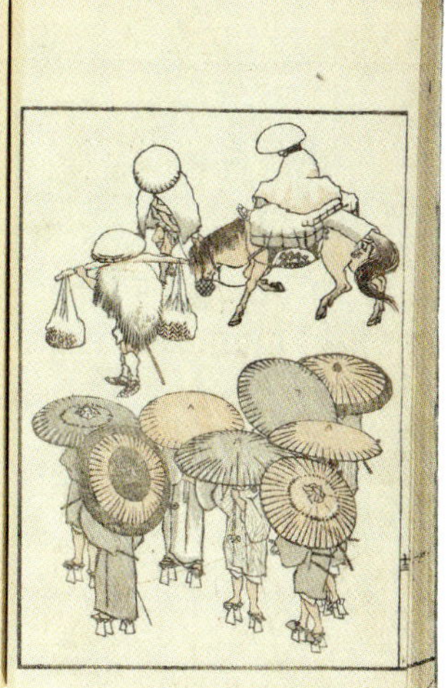

alien eyes of the cephalopods make for an unsettling image, but the text surrounding the image, composed substantially of her instructions to the larger octopus and gasps of pleasure, removes all ambiguity.

The eroticization of *ama* or "women of the sea" was an established trope in Japanese woodblock-printed imagery by Hokusai's time, and he was by no means the first artist to imagine a sexual encounter between a fisherwoman and an octopus. The image was probably inspired by an illustration in Kitao Shigemasa's *Programme of Erotic Noh Plays* (*Yokyoku iro bangumi*) of 1781 or from Katsukawa Shunchō's (active *c.* 1781–1801) *Erotic Book: Lusts of Many Women on One Thousand Nights* (*Ehon chiyo dameshi*) of 1786. Such images may relate to the legend of Princess Tamatori, who had successfully recovered a stolen pearl from the Dragon King. Swimming into the dragon's undersea lair, she lulled him to sleep with music and took the pearl. When the Dragon King awoke and discovered his treasure missing he was enraged and pursued Princess Tamatori with his army of sea creatures. To keep the pearl safe she cut a hole in her breast and placed the pearl inside, but died from her wound.

ABOVE LEFT
Crabs, Shrimp, Turtles, Frogs, Snails and a Slug, 1816
From *Illustrated Album of Three Styles of Painting*, woodblock-printed book
London, British Museum

ABOVE RIGHT
A Crowd in the Rain and Other Scenes, 1814
From volume one of *Hokusai manga*
Published by Eirakuya Tōshirō and others
Woodblock-printed books, 15 volumes
London, British Museum

Friedrich (Fritz) Capelari
Umbrellas, 1915
Published by Watanabe Shōzaburō
Colour woodblock print,
26.7 x 19.8 cm (10⅝ x 7⅞ in.)
Minneapolis Institute of Art, The John and
Shirley Nilson Endowment for Art Acquisition

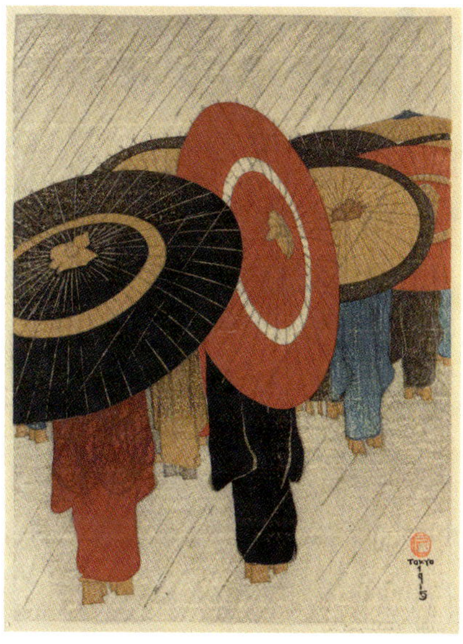

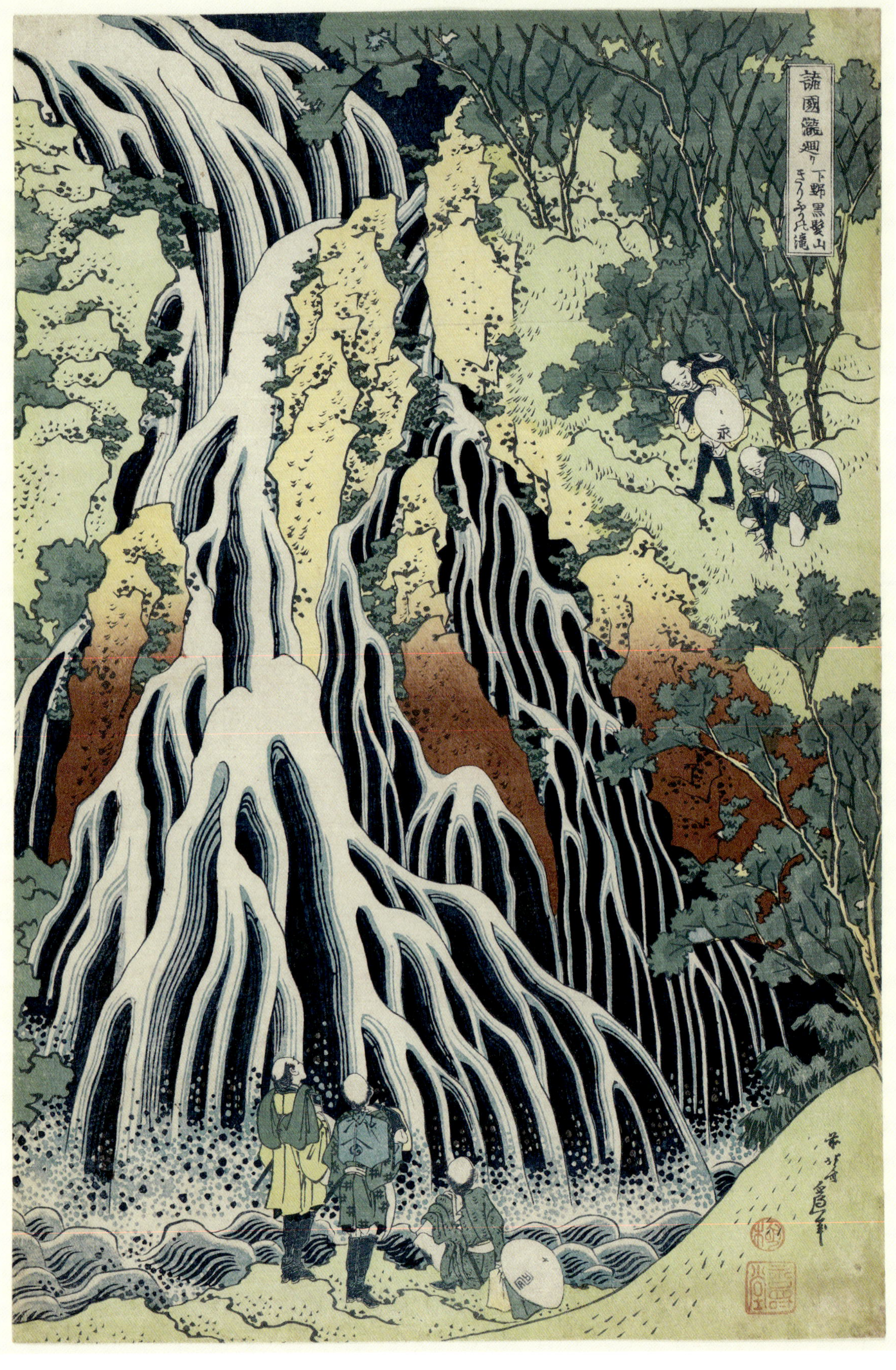

諸國瀧廻り
下野黒髪山きりふりの滝

Born Again

In 1820, the 60-year-old Hokusai adopted the name "Iitsu", meaning "one year old again". According to the East Asian system, a child was considered to be already one year of age at birth. As a full zodiac cycle, that means all possible combinations of the 12 Chinese zodiac sings with the five elements, takes 60 years to complete, turning 61 was akin to being born again.

What should have been a time for celebration for Hokusai, however, was marred by personal tragedy and financial trouble. One of his daughters died in 1821, he was widowed for the second time in 1828, and by 1829 his grandson's gambling debts had put the household into arrears. Around the same time he suffered a stroke which affected his ability to paint. His third daughter, known as Eijo or Ōi (*c.* 1800–*c.* 1866), divorced and returned to her father's household, where she produced works under her own name and possibly also that of her father. In *Operating on Guanyu's Arm*, she depicted an episode from the 16th-century Chinese novel *The Romance of the Three Kingdoms,* which was extremely popular in Japan during the 18th and 19th centuries. After being wounded by a poisoned arrow, the general Guanyu has blood drained from his arm. While his attendants cringe from the gruesome sight, Guanyu is absorbed in a game of Go (ill. p. 49). Although Hokusai had begun his Iitsu period designing *surimono*, the 1820s marked a decisive shift to publishing commercial series of prints that must have provided urgently needed income. Out of necessity came a new creative purpose and it was during this later period that Hokusai created works that have defined his restless genius, including *Under the Wave off Kanagawa.*

Hokusai's major non-commercial projects during the Iitsu period were two large series of *surimono* for the Yomogawa poetry club. The first of these is *Thirty-six Genroku Poets Matched with Shells* (*Genroku kasen kai awase*), a set of 36 designs. Both the number 36 and the term *kasen*, usually translated as "immortal poets", invoke an anthology of 36 classical poems compiled in the Heian period (794–1185) and the literary luminaries that penned them. The theme of this series is based on a Genroku-period (1688–1704) anthology that dealt with the topic of seashells. This choice of subject was to do with the publication year 1821: the Year of the Snake. In the East Asian zodiac calendar this year is associated with shells for the reason that the snake acted as messenger of Benten, one of the Seven Gods of Good Fortune. A shrine to the goddess

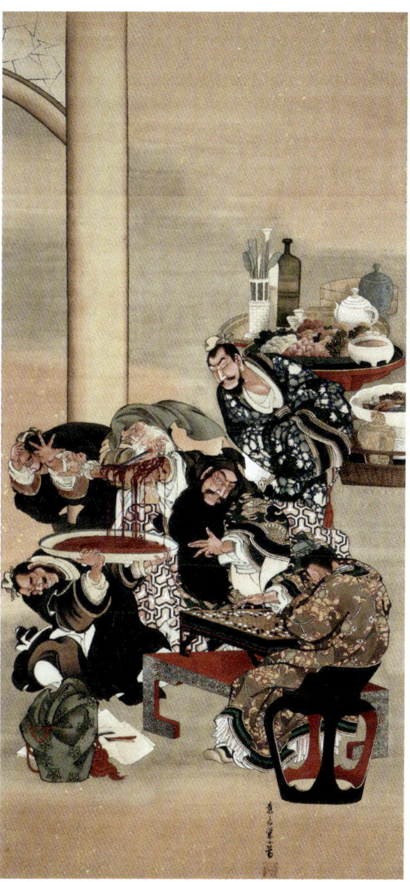

Katsushika Ōi
Operating on Guanyu's Arm, 1850
Hanging scroll, ink, colour and gold leaf on silk, 140.2 x 68.2 cm (55¼ x 26⅞ in.) including mounting
Cleveland Museum of Art, Kelvin Smith Fund

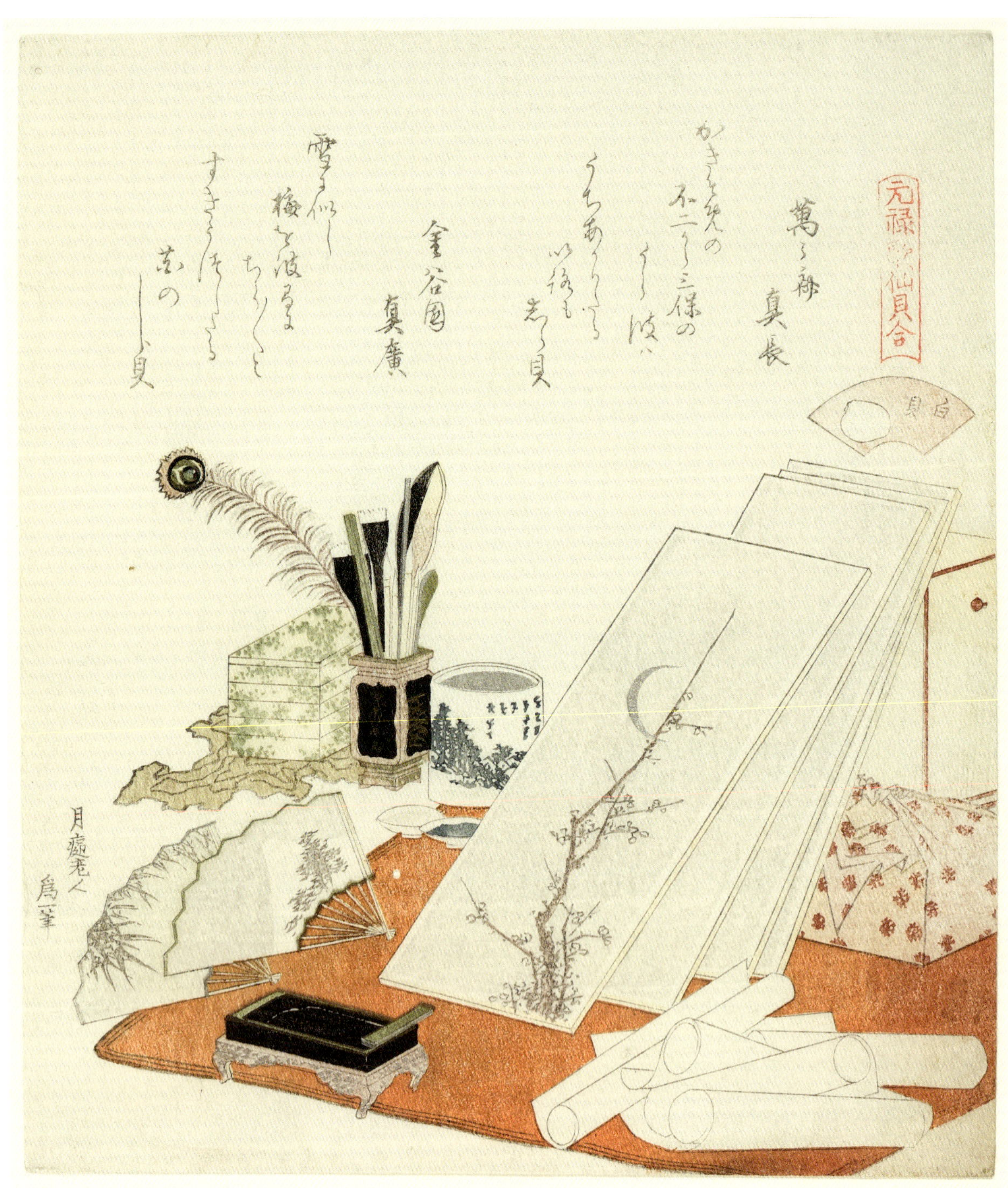

**Kirifuri Waterfall of Mount Kurokami
in Shimotsuke Province**, *c.* 1832
From the series *A Tour of Waterfalls
in Various Provinces*
Published by Nishimuraya Yohachi
Colour woodblock print, *ōban*,
35.7 x 26 cm (14 x 10¼ in.)
Boston, Museum of Fine Arts,
William S. and John T. Spaulding Collection

50

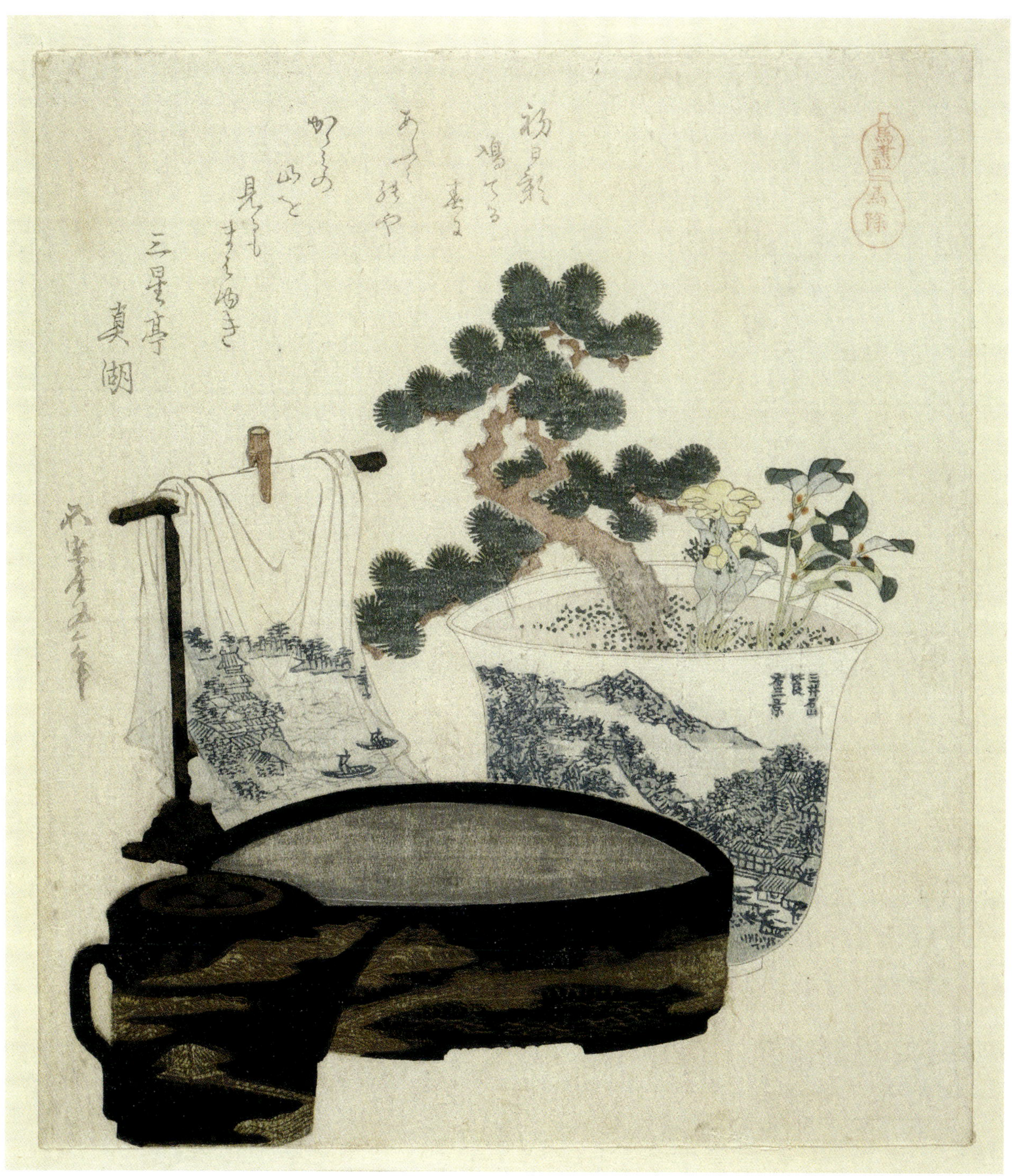

The White Shell, 1821
From the series *Thirty-six Genroku
Poets Matched with Shells*
Colour woodblock print, *shikishiban*,
20.2 x 17.7 cm (8 x 7 in.)
Art Institute of Chicago,
Clarence Buckingham Collection

The Talisman, 1822
From the series *A Set of Horses*
Colour woodblock print, *shikishiban*,
20.1 x 17.6 cm (8 x 7 in.)
London, British Museum

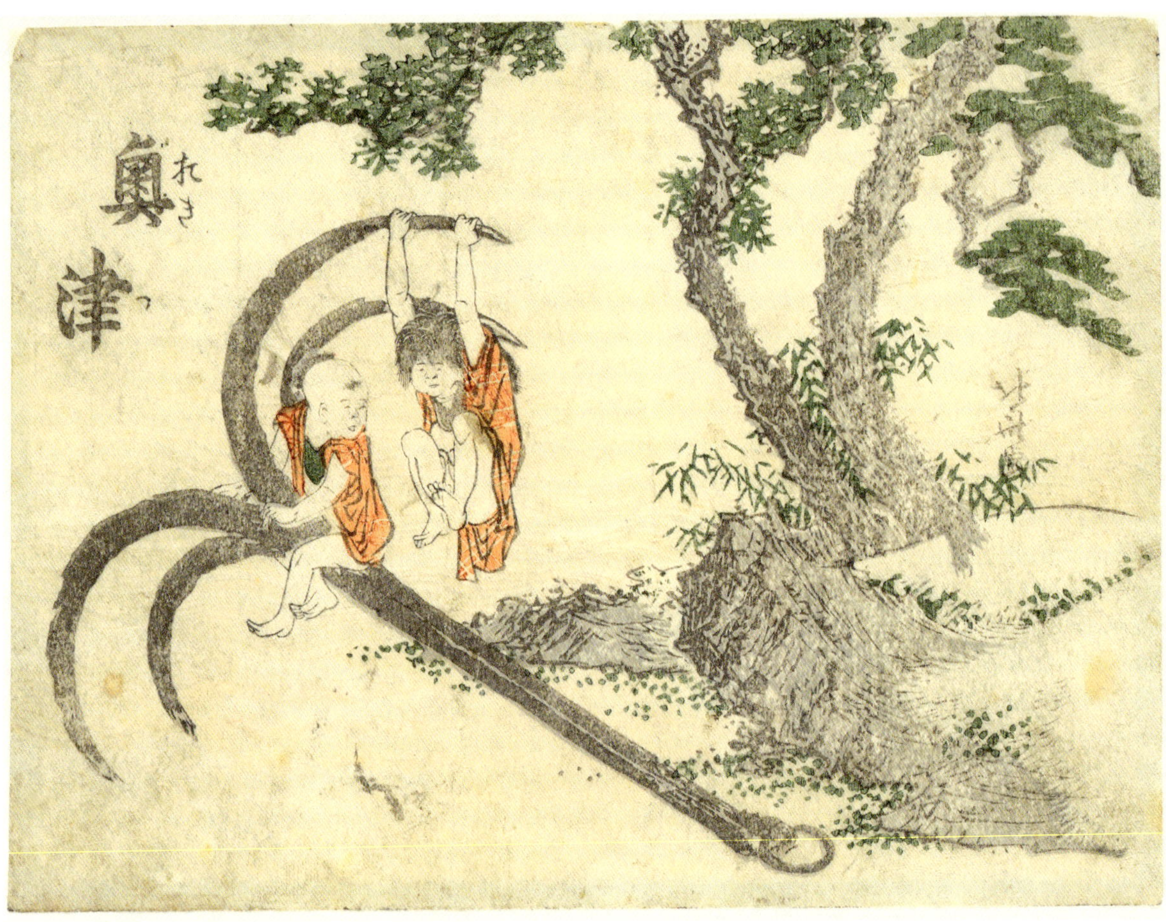

Okitsu, 1802–1810
From an untitled series of prints
on the Tōkaidō
Colour woodblock print, *yotsugiriban*,
12 x 16.3 cm (4¾ x 6½ in.)
Leiden, Museum Volkenkunde

situated on the island of Enoshima, near Kamakura, was a popular spot for gathering seashells. At the time of publication this was the largest set of square-format *surimono* ever produced.

The White Shell is a still life of painters' utensils (ill. p. 50). As well as an ink stone, sticks of ink and brushes, there are several white objects which might suggest the form of seashells: from rolls of crisp paper and paper fans to a porcelain brush pot and ink saucers. The fans, brush pot and completed painting at the centre depict bamboo, pines and plum blossoms – the "three friends of winter" that remain faithfully green or bloom during the most desolate months of the year. The first of two *kyōka* or "mad poems" inscribed above alludes to the first calligraphy or painting executed in the new year. In a red cartouche at the upper right we find the series title while below a fan-shaped cartouche presents the name of the print. Hokusai's signature, "Moonstruck Old Man Iitsu" (*Getchi rōjin Iitsu hitsu*), is in the lower left of the design.

The following year, the Year of the Horse, Hokusai created images for a series of around 30 *surimono* called *A Set of Horses* (*Umazukushi*), with the title of each print containing a pun or reference to the celebrated animal. For example, in the title of *The Talisman* (*Mayoke*), the character for "magic" with which the word is usually written is substituted for one meaning "horse". Both characters have the same reading, "ma". In this image, he depicted an arrangement of objects that evoked the *Eight Views of Ōmi* or *Lake Biwa*, a subject adapted from

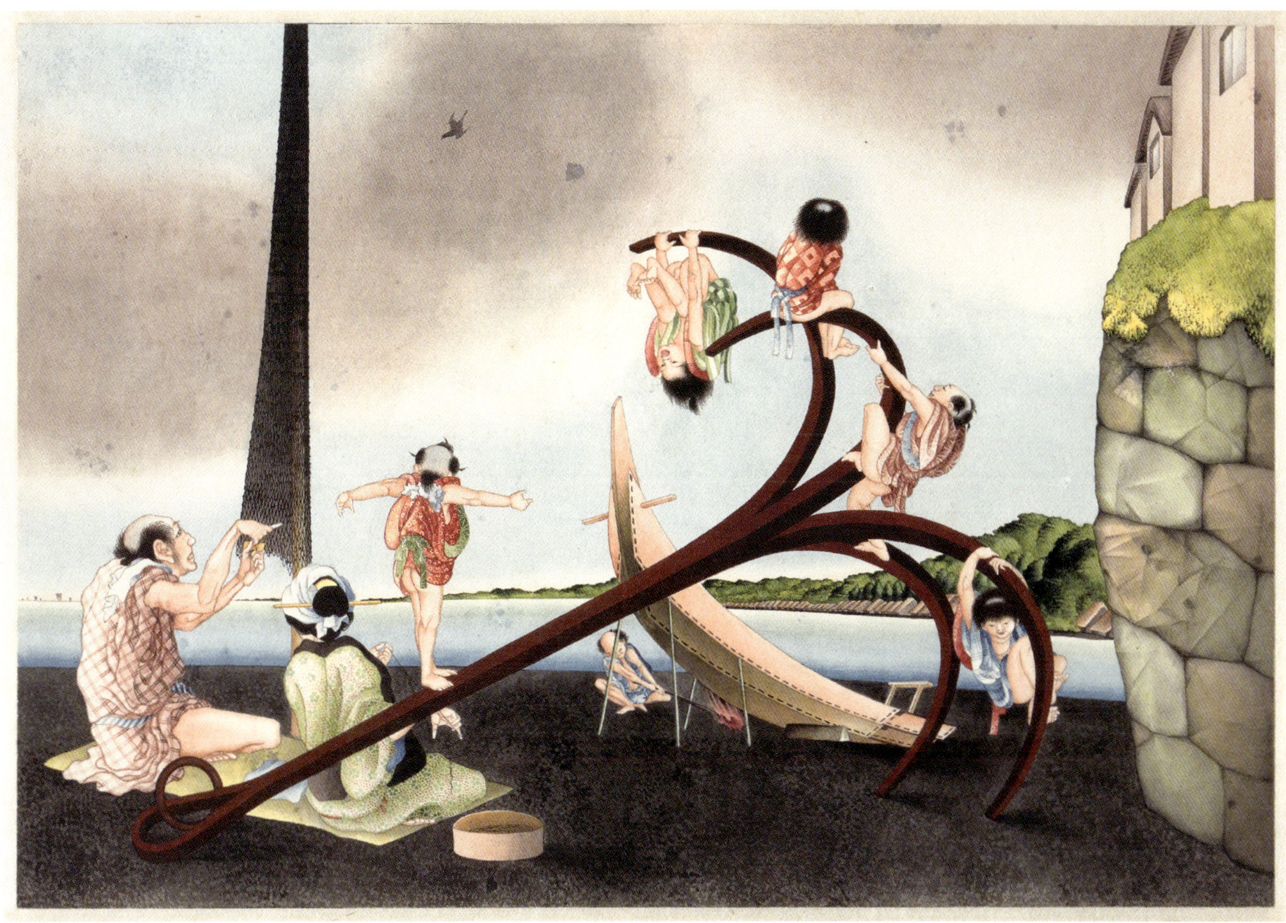

the classical Chinese painting theme *Eight Views of West Lake*. The pot is glazed
with a landscape design identifying Mii Temple, Ishiyama Temple and Mount
Hira. The lacquer basin and pitcher are decorated with the "floating hall" of
Ukimidō at Mangetsu Temple at Katada, and the long bridge of Seta. The image
on the towel, itself suggesting a sail, depicts Zeze Castle in Awazu and boats
returning to shore at Yabase. The dwarf pine represents the solitary pine tree at
Karasaki, and together with the other plants sharing its pot, there is an auspicious
symbol of the New Year. In the upper right the gourd-shaped title cartouche
alludes to the mythical gourd of the Chinese sage Chōkarō, in which he kept
a magical horse (ill. p. 51).

The inscription reads:

In the rays of the spring sun on Lake Biwa, Mirror Mountain also glitters.[1]

Commissions for the Dutch

The 1822 Year of the Horse also brought Hokusai a tantalizing opportunity,
a large commission of paintings from Jan Cock Blomhoff (1779–1853), director
of the Dutch trading port on the man-made island of Dejima. It was initially
constructed in 1634 to quarantine Portuguese traders from the Japanese popu-
lace. In a crackdown on Christianity, which was perceived as a threat to shogunal
authority, the third shogun Tokugawa Iemitsu (1604–1651) expelled the Spanish
and Portuguese traders from Japan altogether by 1638. The Dutch who, compared

to their fervent European counterparts, held little interest in proselytising the Japanese, were allowed to stay, albeit confined to Dejima.

As representative of the Dutch East India Company, Director Blomhoff was required to pay tribute to the shogunal court in Edo every four years. During the 1822 trip, he and his colleague Johannes van Overmeer Fischer (1800–1848) collected objects that represented the daily life, industry and culture of Japan for the recently founded Royal Cabinet of Curiosities in The Hague. In 1837, the Cabinet holdings that included the Japanese pieces assembled by Blomhoff were relocated to Leiden, where they were displayed to the public at the Museum Japonicum, the first ever ethnological museum in Europe.

Among the items Blomhoff and Fischer amassed were *ukiyo-e* prints and printed books, including Hokusai's *Picture Book of Amusements of the Eastern Capital, Picture Book: Both Banks of the Sumida River at a Glance*, the original ten volumes of *Hokusai manga* as well as works by other artists. They evidently admired Hokusai's work, since the Dutchmen arranged a meeting at their inn and commissioned the artist for a number of pictures to be completed by 1826, in time for their return to Edo. Blomhoff supplied Hokusai with 12 sheets of Dutch paper for this project.

With assistance from Ōi and his students, Hokusai completed 11 Western-style landscapes and genre scenes on Dutch paper, along with at least 24 paintings on Japanese paper. Some of the images were adapted from earlier compositions; *A Fisherman's Family*, from the group executed on Dutch paper, is based on two small-format prints published around 15 years earlier (ills. pp. 52, 53). In this re-working, Hokusai achieved greater naturalism by lowering the horizon line, employing spatial recession and linear perspective, and depicting the cloud as a hazy mass. Elements like the form and volume of the figures' flesh or the sea-wall's stones are conveyed through tonal gradations. Cast shadows appear around the composition – from the underside of the boat and the drapery to under the anchor.

In 1826, the Dutch returned to Edo as promised. The party comprised Blomhoff's successor Johan Willem de Sturler (1773–1855), Philipp Franz von Siebold, a German surgeon employed by the Dutch East India Company at Dejima, and the Nagasaki painter Kawahara Keiga (*c.* 1786–1860), who produced hundreds of pictures for the trading colony. At the meeting, Hokusai was accompanied by his student Ōtsuka Hachirō (a.k.a. Ōtsuka Dōan), a scholar of Western learning who may have been able to speak Dutch. After some haggling over the price by Siebold, the Europeans purchased Hokusai's 11 pieces on Dutch paper for the Cabinet. Sturler personally acquired the 24 or so works on Japanese paper and a view of the Sumida River by Ōtsuka on the 12th sheet of Dutch paper. Siebold commissioned an additional 18 paintings, which were produced by Hokusai's students, Hokkei and Ōtsuka.

Several of these paintings, along with images selected from *Hokusai manga*, were adapted into Siebold's *Nippon: A Descriptive Archive of Japan*. An illustration of six mounted couriers galloping around a road-bend appears in the German book, depicted from a more distant, higher vantage point and with a caption that identifies the scene as a horse race (ills. pp. 56, 57). The immediate, graphic quality of the original is diminished in favour of pictorial realism. Hokusai revisited the theme in his *Thirty-six Views of Mount Fuji* with the design *Sekiya Village on the Sumida River* (ill. p. 55).

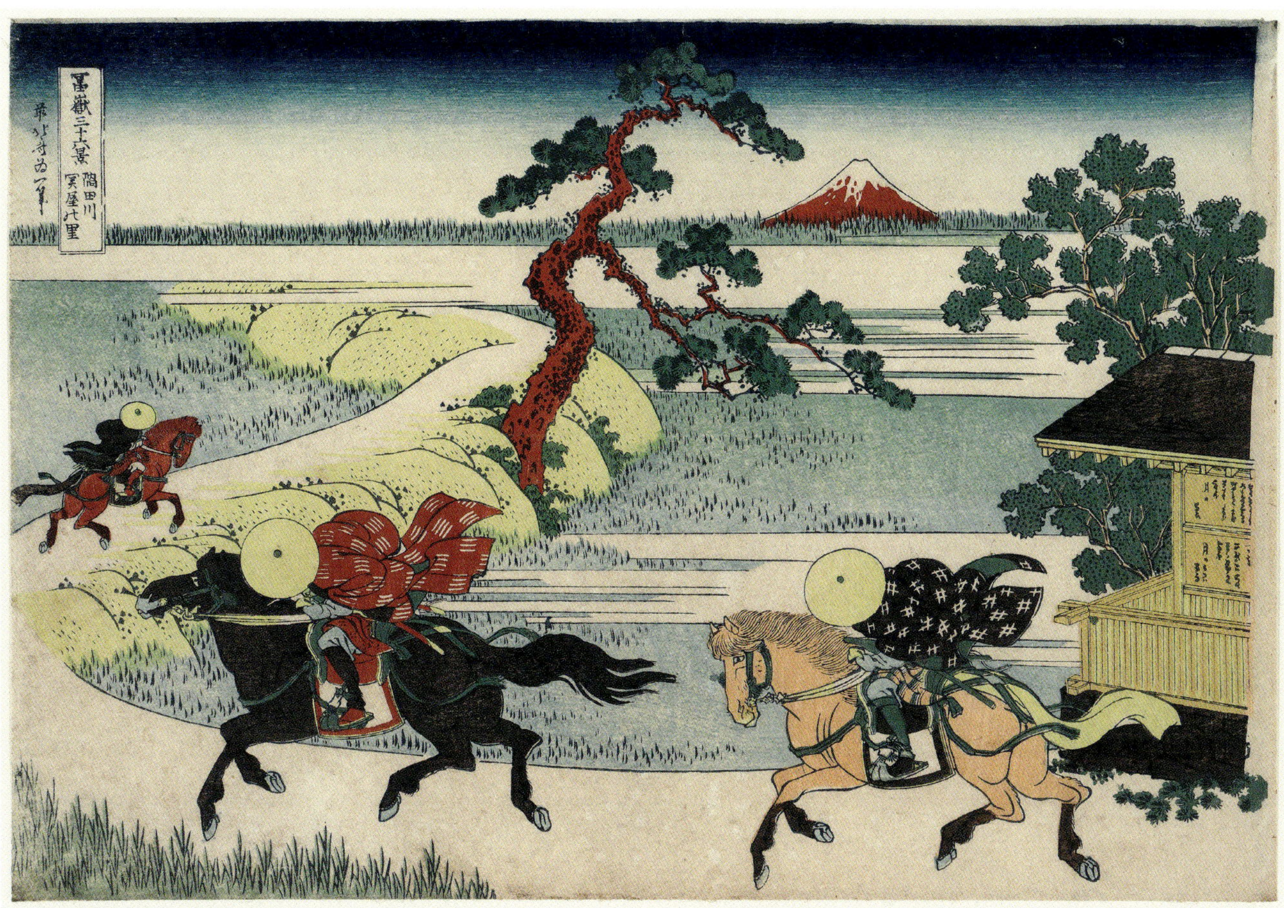

In 2016, art historian Matthi Forrer reattributed a group of six unsigned paintings representing views of Edo in Siebold's collection to Hokusai. The paintings, now at the Museum Volkenkunde in Leiden, lack ink outlines, representing a step further into Western pictorial conventions beyond what had been achieved in the earlier commission. Forrer proposes that Hokusai created the works to demonstrate that he was capable of painting persuasively in the Western style.

Sekiya Village on the Sumida River,
c. 1830/31
From the series *Thirty-six Views of Mount Fuji*
Published by Nishimuraya Yohachi
Colour woodblock print, *ōban*,
25.6 x 37.7 cm (10 x 14⅞ in.)
Boston, Museum of Fine Arts,
William S. and John T. Spaulding Collection

Thirty-six Views of Mount Fuji

The series *Thirty-six Views of Mount Fuji* (*c.* 1830–1834) contains three of Hokusai's best-known designs: *Under the Wave off Kanagawa*; *Fine Wind, Clear Weather*; and *Rainstorm beneath the Summit*. The set features scenic views of Japan's active volcano and holy mountain (also the country's highest peak, at 3,776 metres [12,389 ft]), seen from the city of Edo and various other locales in eastern Japan. The individual designs emphasize the permanence of Fuji amid a world in flux, and contrast the dangerous majesty of nature with the brief and fragile lives of humans.

Fuji has from ancient times held a singular status within Japanese visual and literary expression; a sacred site within Buddhist, Daoist and Shinto belief systems, it was even worshipped as a *kami* (or "god") itself. With the revival of nativist learning during the second half of the Edo period, Fuji emerged as a proto-nationalist symbol hugely celebrated in art and literature. The series also capitalized on increasing popular interest in travel among commoners. Such was its commercial success that the publisher Nishimuraya Yohachi released an additional ten designs, bringing the total number of prints in the series to 46.

The dating of *Thirty-six Views of Mount Fuji* is based on a publisher's advertisement in the first month of 1831, announcing that the project was already underway. The article described the designs as scenes executed "in blues", here referring both to a dye derived from the indigo plant or the day flower customarily used in printing, and a synthetic mineral pigment known as "Prussian blue" or "Berlin blue". Developed in Berlin around 1704–1706, this new pigment was imported to Japan by the mid-18th century. Prohibitively expensive at first, it was initially used only in painting, but in the 19th century, cheaper Chinese-made pigment arrived in Japan, which became hugely popular for prints. With more possible tones, vivid colours and greater resistance to fading, Prussian blue had an exotic appeal and was ideal for depicting depth and distance. It was thus an ideal choice for Hokusai and his publisher for the *Thirty-six Views of Mount Fuji*.

Scholars have divided the 46 prints into four groups. The first ten designs are thought to have been issued before the appearance of the advertisement, probably in 1830. All except one of these are signed "Hokusai aratame Iitsu hitsu" (painted by Hokusai, now Iitsu). Once the first advertisement had been published in 1831, ten more designs, printed mostly in tones of blue and some of them entirely made of the new European pigment, were released with the signature "Saki no Hokusai Iitsu" (Iitsu, formerly Hokusai), a stroke in the final character flicking up at the end to form a hook. Twenty-six prints in various colours followed between 1832 and 1834. The first 16 of these had their outlines printed in blue, as had been the case in the earlier 20 designs. The final ten designs were printed with black outlines as was the custom at the time.

It is in this series that we encounter Hokusai's era-defining image: *Under the Wave off Kanagawa* (ill. p. 64). An enormous white-capped wave is poised to break over three courier boats conveying fish to Edo. The oarsmen flatten themselves against their vessels in anticipation of the oncoming crash. The entire composition seems to rotate clockwise around Mount Fuji, sitting low on the horizon. Spray appears to fall like snow over its peak. In early, unsoiled editions, the breaking wave's form is repeated in the white cloud silhouetted against a buff-coloured sky.

Like other designs in the earlier stages of this series, precursors to *The Great Wave* can be identified in Hokusai's previous works. It is very likely that Hokusai's first explorations of the subject over 30 years before drew inspiration from the work of Shiba Kōkan, such as *Shichirigahama Beach at Kamakura in the Sagami Province*, which was on public display at a shrine in Edo (ill. p. 58 bottom). Hokusai's contribution to the illustrated anthology of *kyōka* poems, *Willow Silk*, depicts a group of figures on the beach of Enoshima, a wave rushing towards them with Mount Fuji in the distance (ill. p. 16). *View of Enoshima*, a *surimono* of 1799 during his Sōri period, features a similar composition, this time omitting the holy peak.

His series of Western-style landscapes contained three more scenes rocked by large foam-crested waves. For *Panoramic View of Enoshima* (*c.* 1804–1810), he reduced the figures to mere silhouettes as to focus attention on the wave (ill. p. 30). In *Express Delivery Boats Rowing through Waves* (*c.* 1800–1805; ill. p. 31),

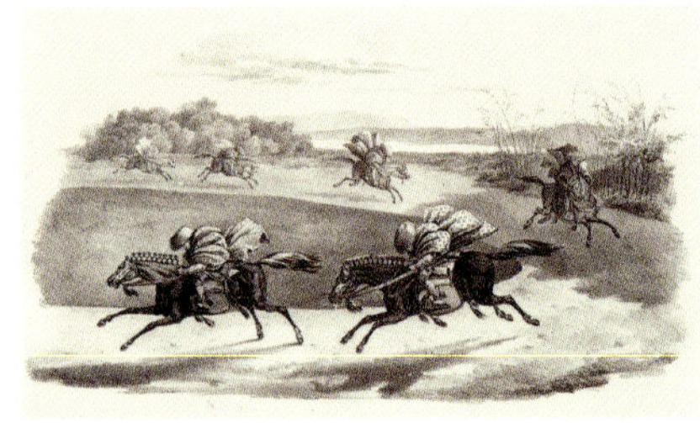

Racers, 1852
Lithograph from Philipp Franz von Siebold:
Nippon: A Descriptive Archive of Japan
Leiden, Museum Volkenkunde

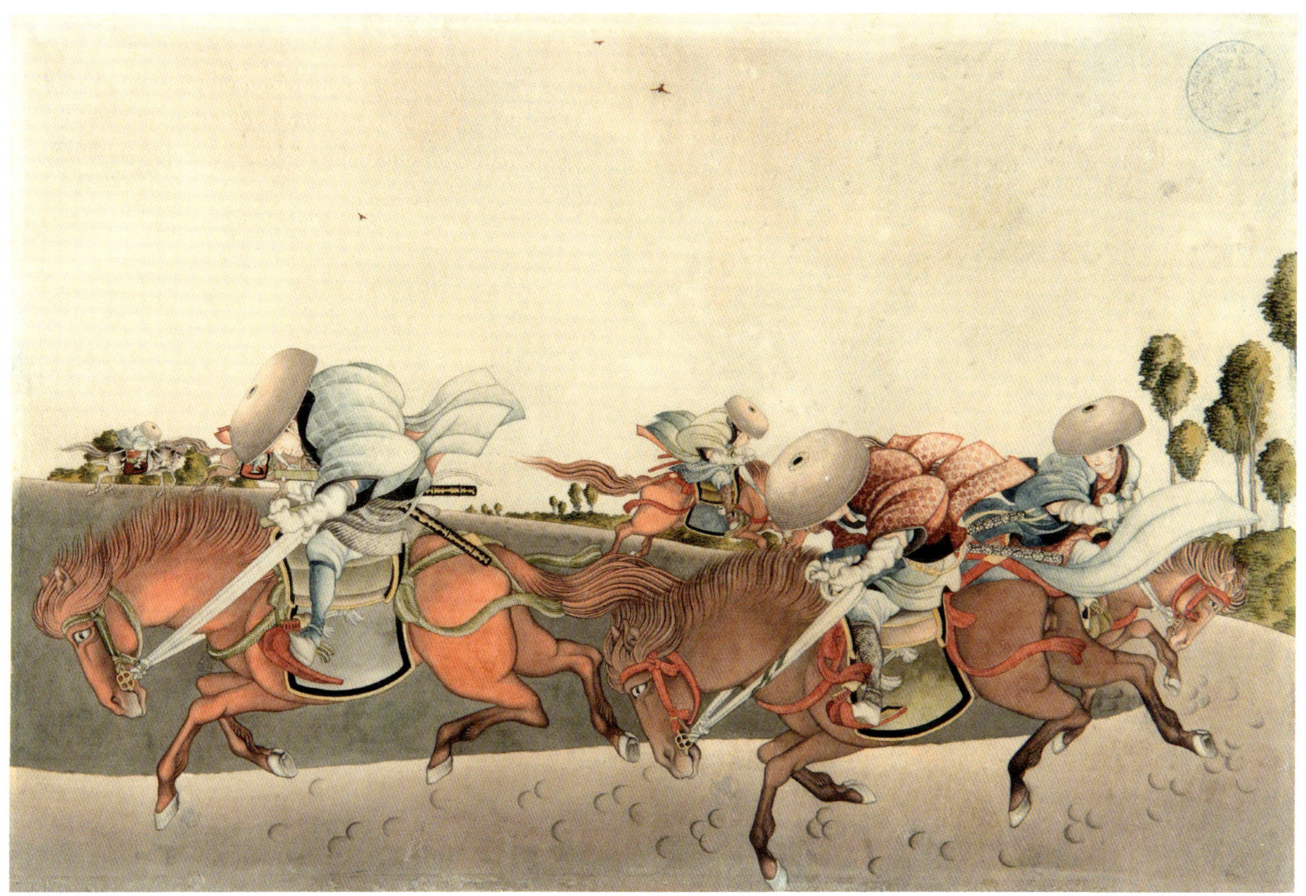

Couriers, 1824–1826
Painting on Dutch paper, *ōban*,
26.7 x 40.1 cm (10⅝ x 15⅞ in.)
Leiden, Museum Volkenkunde

he simplified the landscape elements and made the wall of water even greater in size, then reversed its direction in *View of Honmoku off Kanagawa* (c. 1806/07). For *The Great Wave*, Hokusai brought the viewer closer to water level and gave the wave an arabesque curl, with clawlike projections of sea foam at its crest. The palette of clear, bright blues heightens the visual impact of this monument to nature.

The Great Wave and its reach across all facets of world culture are unparalleled. It is this piece which sparked Gustave Courbet's (1819–1877) exploration of wave forms through some 60 paintings. The composer Claude Debussy (1862–1918) kept an impression in his office and reproduced the design on the cover of his score *La Mer* (ill. p. 66 bottom). To this day, *The Great Wave* is the subject of endless homage and parody. So pervasive is Hokusai's composition that it has even been appropriated for war propaganda. In the days leading up to the United States' invasion of Iraq in 1991, the U.S. military disseminated a leaflet showing a great wave of American forces breaking against the coast of Kuwait, thus fooling the Iraqi forces into reorienting their defences in preparation for an amphibious invasion. Instead, the attack came from the Iraq-Saudi Arabia border.

Yet, this is not the series' only resounding image; *Fine Wind, Clear Weather*, also known as the "Red Fuji", and *Rainstorm beneath the Summit* are two more favourites that depict the volcano from the same vantage point, but under different climactic conditions (ills. pp. 59, 60). The power and elegance of these two images, particularly the unified harmony encountered in the former, derives from the sheer simplicity of forms and colour. Hokusai exaggerated the steepness of Fuji's peak such that the slopes curve exponentially towards the summit, emphasizing its height. Offsetting the cone to the right adds tension and drama to each image. Unlike *The Great Wave*, both landscapes are devoid of human presence, leaving the narrative focused entirely on the majestic, indomitable mountain buffeted by wind and rain.

A similar view of Mount Fuji appeared in volume five of *Hokusai manga* in 1816, but in this earlier monochrome version, the peak is skewed to the left (ill. p. 40 bottom left). Hokusai simplified the composition by reducing or even removing extraneous elements such as the pine forest at the mountain's base, the foothills, water and clouds.

Even his competitors were moved by Hokusai's series. In 1836, his young rival Utagawa Hiroshige (1797–1858) created a homage to *Fujimigahara in Owari Province*, where Fuji appears in the distance through the circular frame of a wooden barrel, as if blessing the honest labour of the cooper (ills. p. 61). Hiroshige made several adjustments to the original composition, such as shifting the setting to a riverbank, adding a village in the background, and increasing the size of the mountain, which now appears as a triangle of vacant, unprinted space.

A Tour of Waterfalls in Various Provinces

A Tour of Waterfalls in Various Provinces (*Shokoku taki meguri*), published *c.* 1832, is a series of eight vertical landscape designs depicting real places in the eastern, western and central locales of Honshū, Japan's main island. Waterfalls were both admired for their beauty and believed to be the dwelling places of gods in local spiritual beliefs. Consequently, they were popular sites of pilgrimage.

A distinct palette makes the eight designs a cohesive suite but the individual images are each strikingly different in terms of composition and their treatment of cascading water, spanning columns of barcode-like stripes, forked rivulets and stippled clouds of spray. As with *Thirty-six Views of Mount Fuji*, the outlines are printed in Prussian blue. The series is remarkable for Hokusai's successful synthesis of the real, the fantastical and the decorative. In *The Amida Falls in the*

Shiba Kōkan
***Shichirigahama Beach at Kamakura
in the Sagami Province***, 1796
Two-panel folding screen, oil on paper,
95.7 x 178.4 cm (37¾ x 70¼ in.)
Kobe City Museum

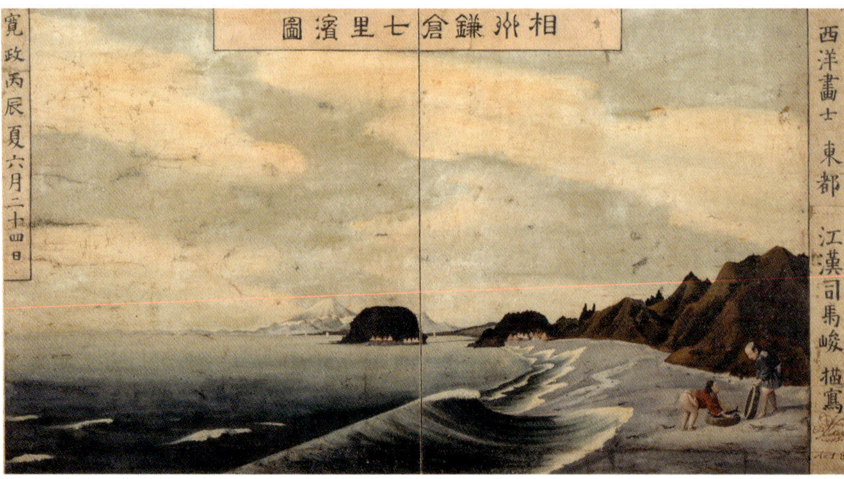

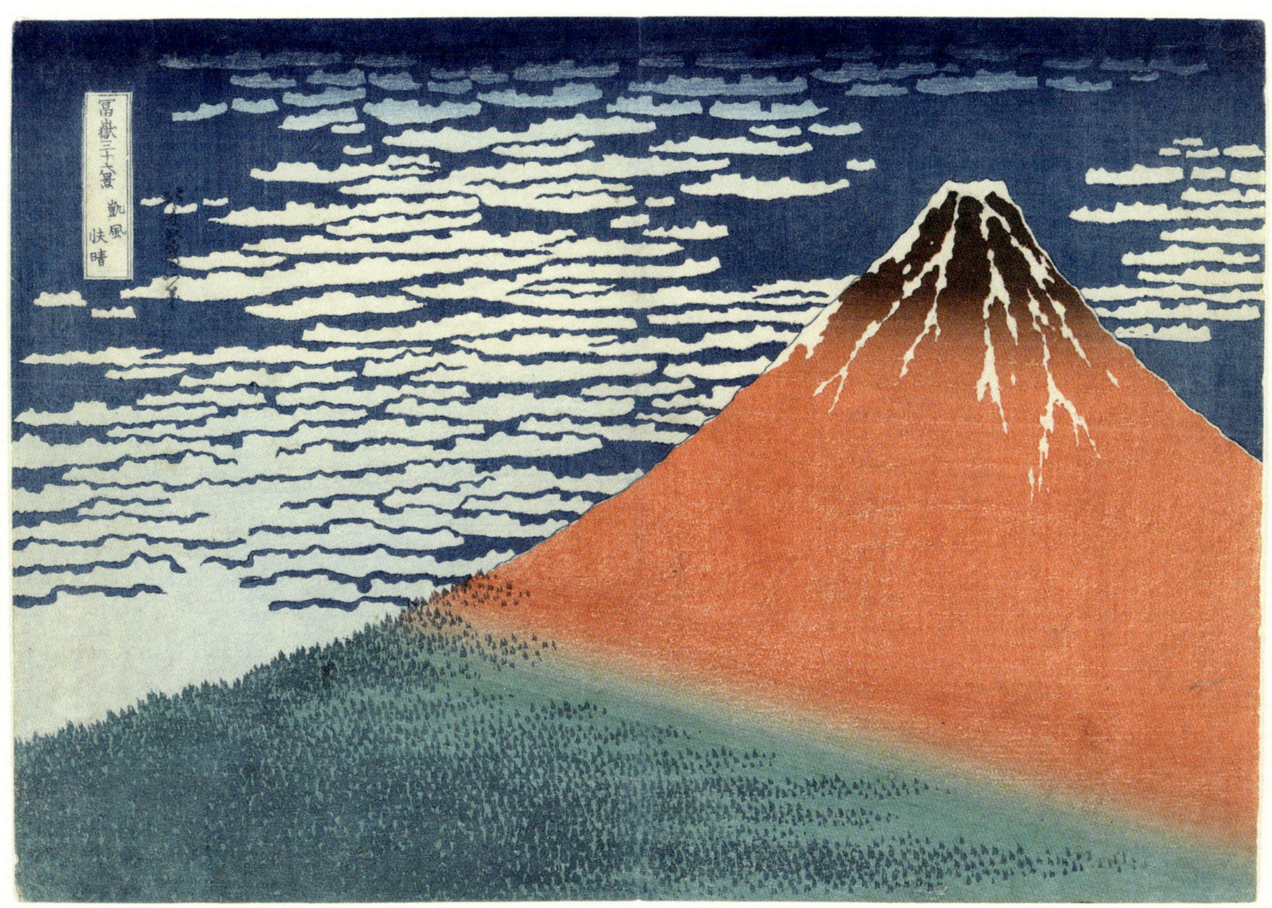

Far Reaches of the Kisokaidō, water cascades from a circular opening in the cliff, spreading as it descends in the form of the Amida Buddha (ill. p. 4). Hokusai gave the surface of the river, above a marble-like pattern that disrupts the composition's illusion of three-dimensional space and gives an otherworldly quality to the scene. Three travellers prepare to have tea on a grassy outcrop overlooking the falls.

Perhaps the most dramatic of the octet is *Kirifuri Waterfall of Mount Kurokami in Shimotsuke Province* (ill. p. 48). The waterfall is located near the historic site and is a favourite tourist destination of Nikkō. Hokusai's print depicts a group of travellers gazing up in wonder at the water fanning out in broad, forking streams over grotesquely shaped rocks.

Eight Views of the Ryūkyū Islands

Eight Views of the Ryūkyū Islands (*Ryūkyū hakkei, c.* 1832) is a series of eight horizontal landscapes, published by Moriya Jihei and commemorating the 1832 diplomatic mission from the court of King Shō Iku (1813–1847) of the Ryūkyū Kingdom to the 11th shogun Tokugawa Ienari in Edo. The Kingdom, which became Okinawa in 1879, comprised a cluster of islands to the south-west of the Japanese archipelago, and had paid tribute to China since the 14th century. After an invasion by the Satsuma domain in south-west Japan in 1609, the Kingdom sent 18 diplomatic missions to Edo. An important regional trade hub

Fine Wind, Clear Weather, *c.* 1830/31
From the series *Thirty-six Views of Mount Fuji*
Published by Nishimuraya Yohachi
Colour woodblock print, *ōban*,
25.7 x 37.7 cm (10⅛ x 14⅞ in.)
Minneapolis Institute of Art,
Gift of Louis W. Hill, Jr.

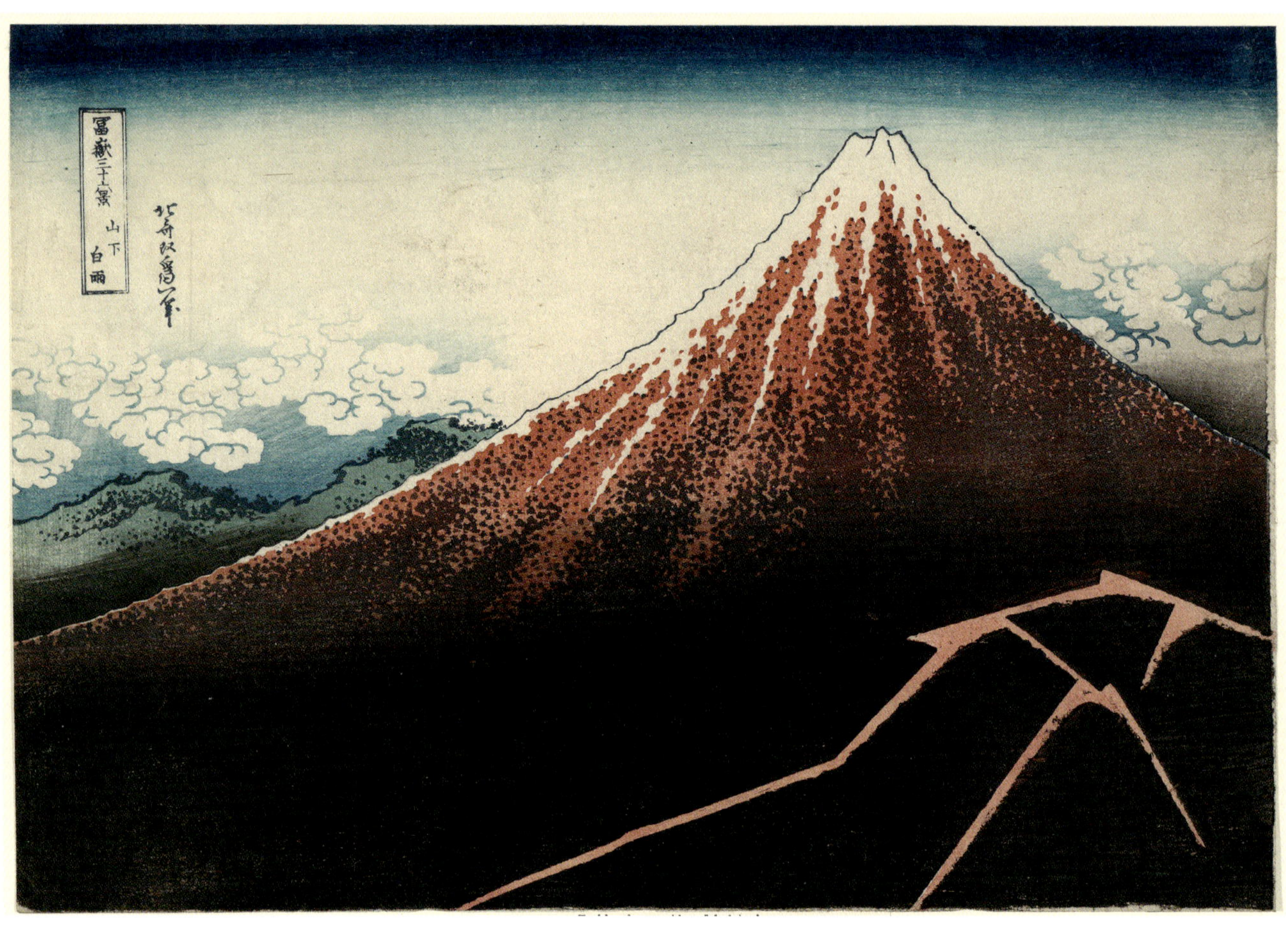

Rainstorm beneath the Summit, *c*. 1830/31
From the series *Thirty-six Views of Mount Fuji*
Published by Nishimuraya Yohachi
Colour woodblock print, *ōban*,
26.2 x 38.2 cm (10⅜ x 15 in.)
Boston, Museum of Fine Arts,
William Sturgis Bigelow Collection

and one of few foreign entities permitted to trade during the Tokugawa period, the Kingdom thus served an intermediary role between Japan and other parts of Asia.

The mission of 1832 was a major event for people in Japan far and wide; as one observer wrote:

> At the arrival of the Ryukyuan tribute mission [of 1832] […] great numbers of spectators, both male and female, flocked to see, lining both sides of the river, and even floating boats out into the middle of the river, clogging the channel […] when they went upriver by boat […] to Fushimi […] it's said the spectators lined the route all the way. What's more […] Imperial Princes, members of the Regent's House, and senior courtiers were pleased to [watch], and it's even rumoured that the retired Emperor secretly made an Imperial Progress to watch.[2]

Rather than represent the spectacle itself, however, Hokusai's series comprises scenic views around the port of Naha, the seat of the Shō court from whence Edo's visitors had come.

Although at first glance the eight designs seem typical of Hokusai's oeuvre, they are in fact each adapted closely from monochrome illustrations in the first volume of a Chinese woodblock-printed, illustrated text *A Brief History of the Ryūkyū Kingdom*. Written by Zhou Huang (d. 1785), deputy ambassador on a mission to the Kingdom from the Qing court in 1757, the text was reissued by

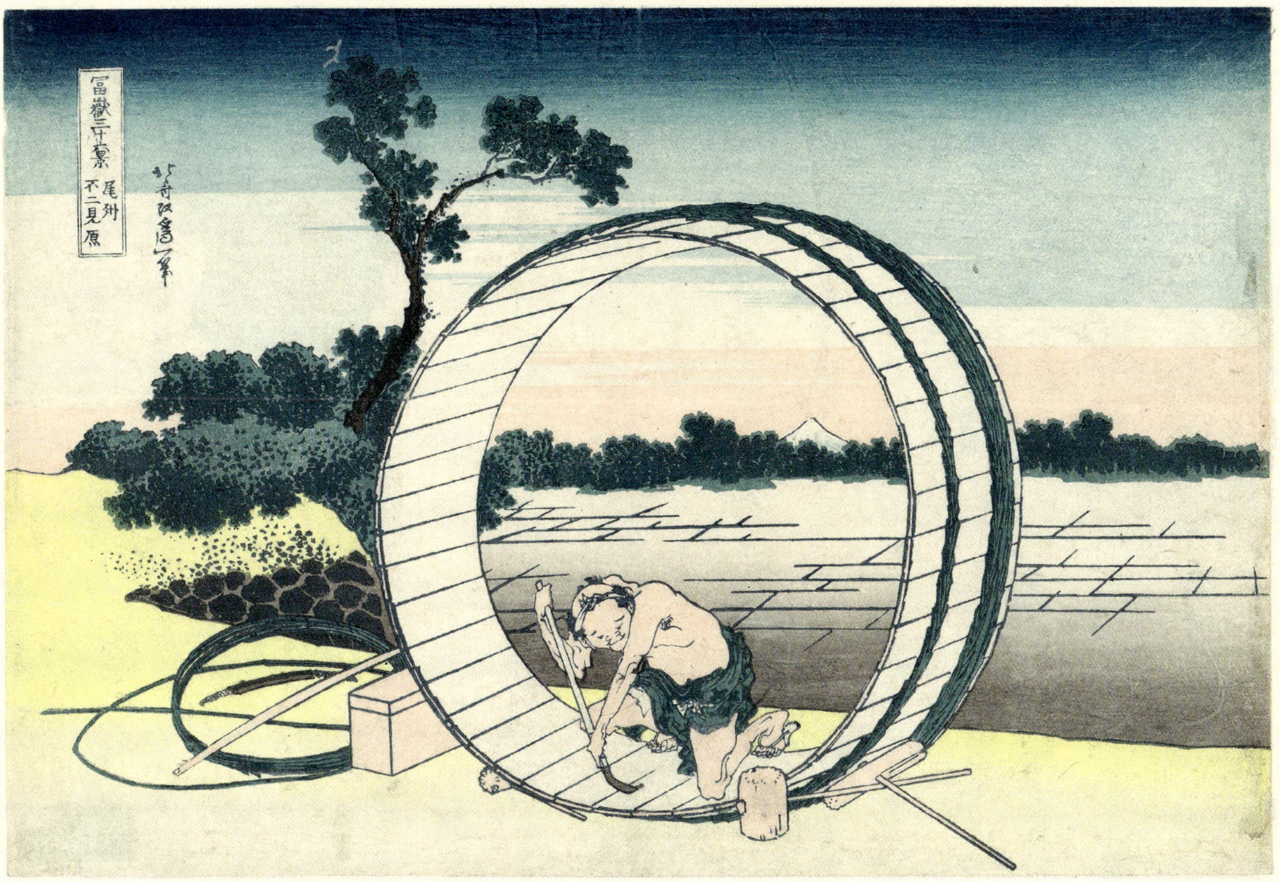

the Tokugawa administration in anticipation of the 1832 visit. Hokusai himself
never travelled to the islands. This practice of copying was by no means unusual;
Hokusai's younger contemporary Hiroshige also relied on woodblock-printed
guidebooks to create compositions of places he had not seen with his own eyes.

While retaining the overall compositions of the illustrations in Zhou Huang's
text, Hokusai assimilated them into his own style by reducing line, thereby sim-
plifying landscape elements, and adding colour. An appealing palette of dark
and light green, buff and shades of Prussian blue clarify the spatial organization
of the scenes as well as enhance the illusion of depth and form. In *Clear Autumn
Weather at Chōkō*, Hokusai emphasized the curve of the kilometre-long Chōkō
bridge and levee structure, enlarged the trees and strengthened the forms of
the islands and promontory (ill. p. 66 top). Lines representing ripples and clouds
are removed in favour of areas of *bokashi* shading (colour gradation). A pair
of boats is added in the bottom left; the lonely oarsman and two figures making
their way across the bridge introduce a sense of melancholy to the scene. The
thatched roofs of the original's buildings are replaced with vivid, bright blue
tiles, and the buff-coloured cone of a Fuji-like mountain rises in the distance,
adding to the curious blend of the exotic and the familiar. Meanwhile, in *Pines
and Waves at Ryūdō*, Hokusai gave the landscape a heavy frosting of snow
(ill. p. 67). While such a scene was impossible in the subtropical Ryūkyūs, scholar
Sakai Nobuo has pointed out that as the embassy marched in Edo, the city

Fujimigahara in Owari Province, c. 1830/31
From the series *Thirty-six Views of Mount Fuji*
Published by Nishimuraya Yohachi, colour
woodblock print, *ōban*, 25.2 x 37.7 cm (10 x 14⅞ in.)
Boston, Museum of Fine Arts,
William Sturgis Bigelow Collection

Utagawa Hiroshige
*Barrel-maker, Copied from a Picture
by Old Master Katsushika*, 1836
Colour woodblock print, *uchiwa-e* on horizontal
aiban sheet, 21.1 x 28.2 cm (8⅜ x 11⅛ in.)
Boston, Museum of Fine Arts,
William S. and John T. Spaulding Collection

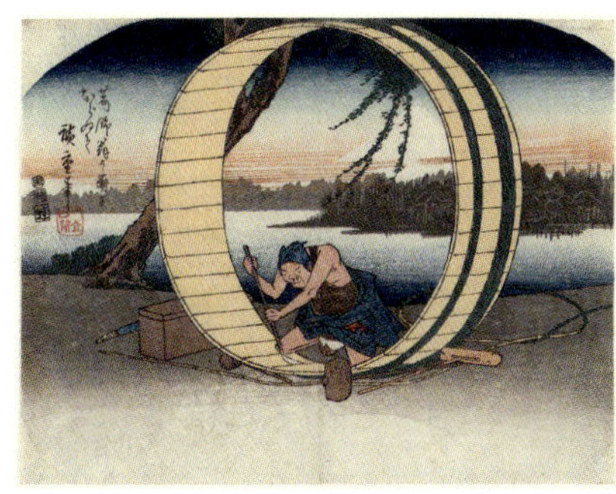

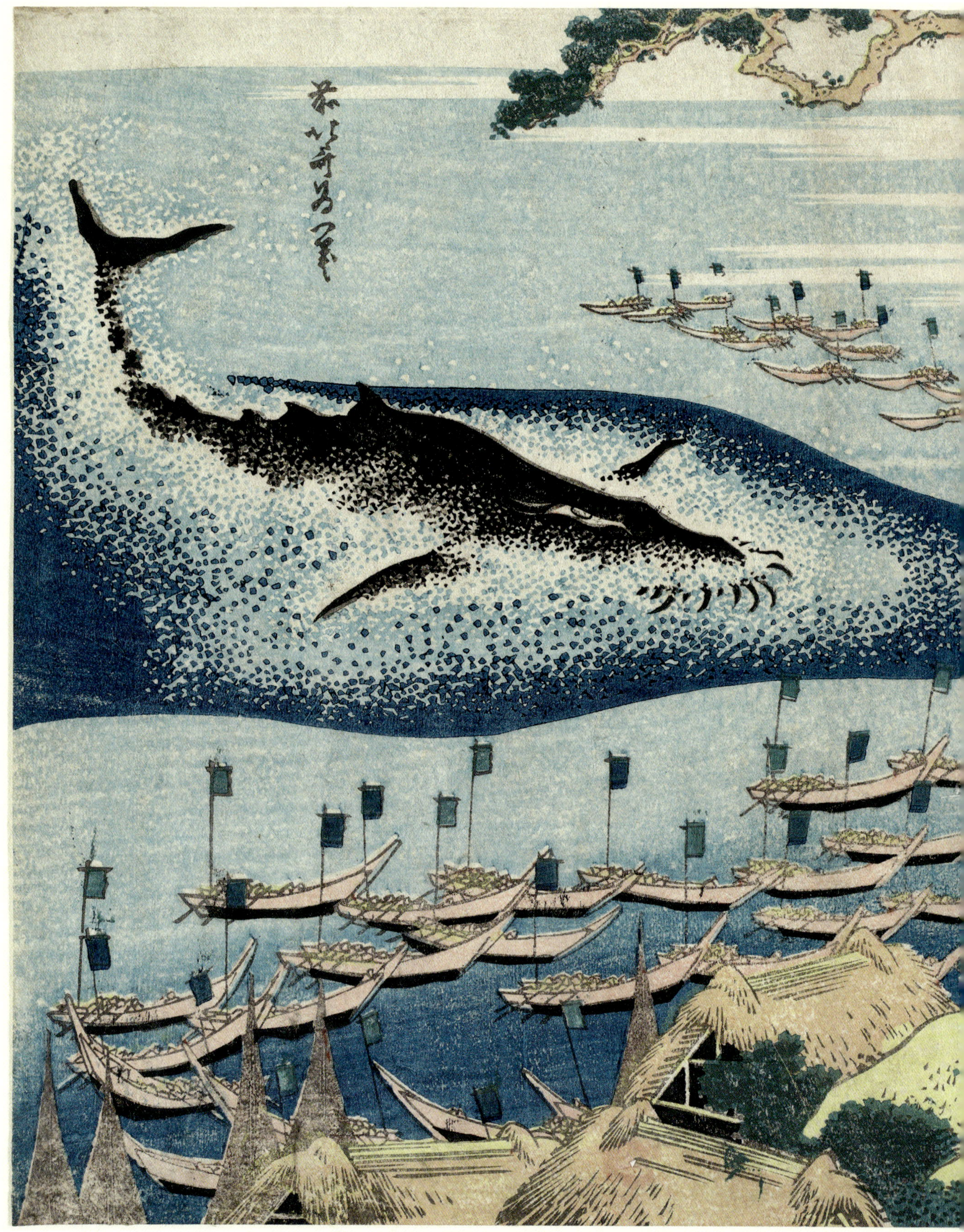
前北斎為一筆

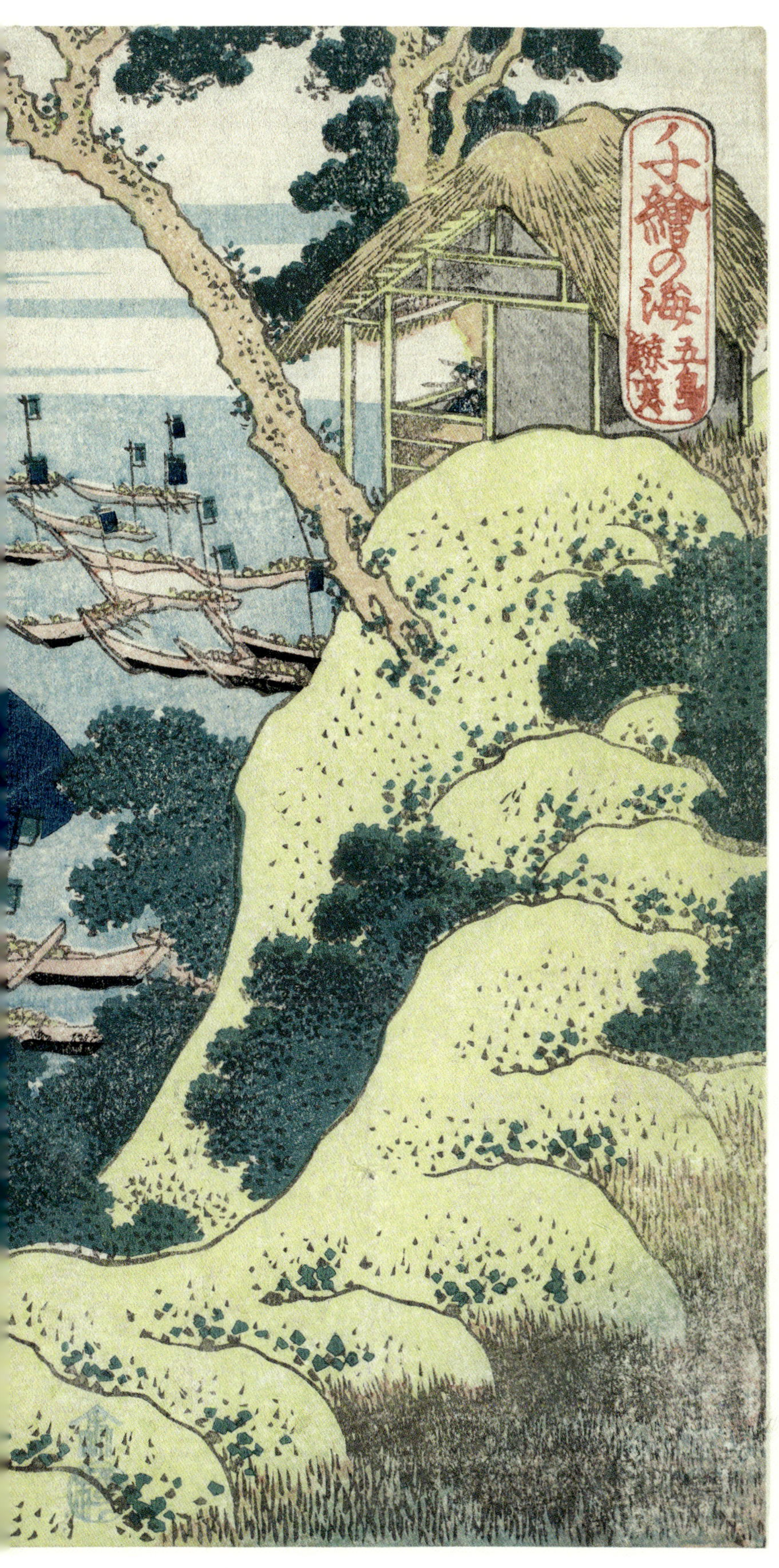

Whaling off the Gotō Islands, *c.* 1833
From the series *One Thousand Pictures
of the Ocean*
Published by Moriya Jihei
Colour woodblock print, *chūban*,
18.7 x 25.7 cm (7⅜ x 10⅛ in.)
Boston, Museum of Fine Arts,
William S. and John T. Spaulding Collection

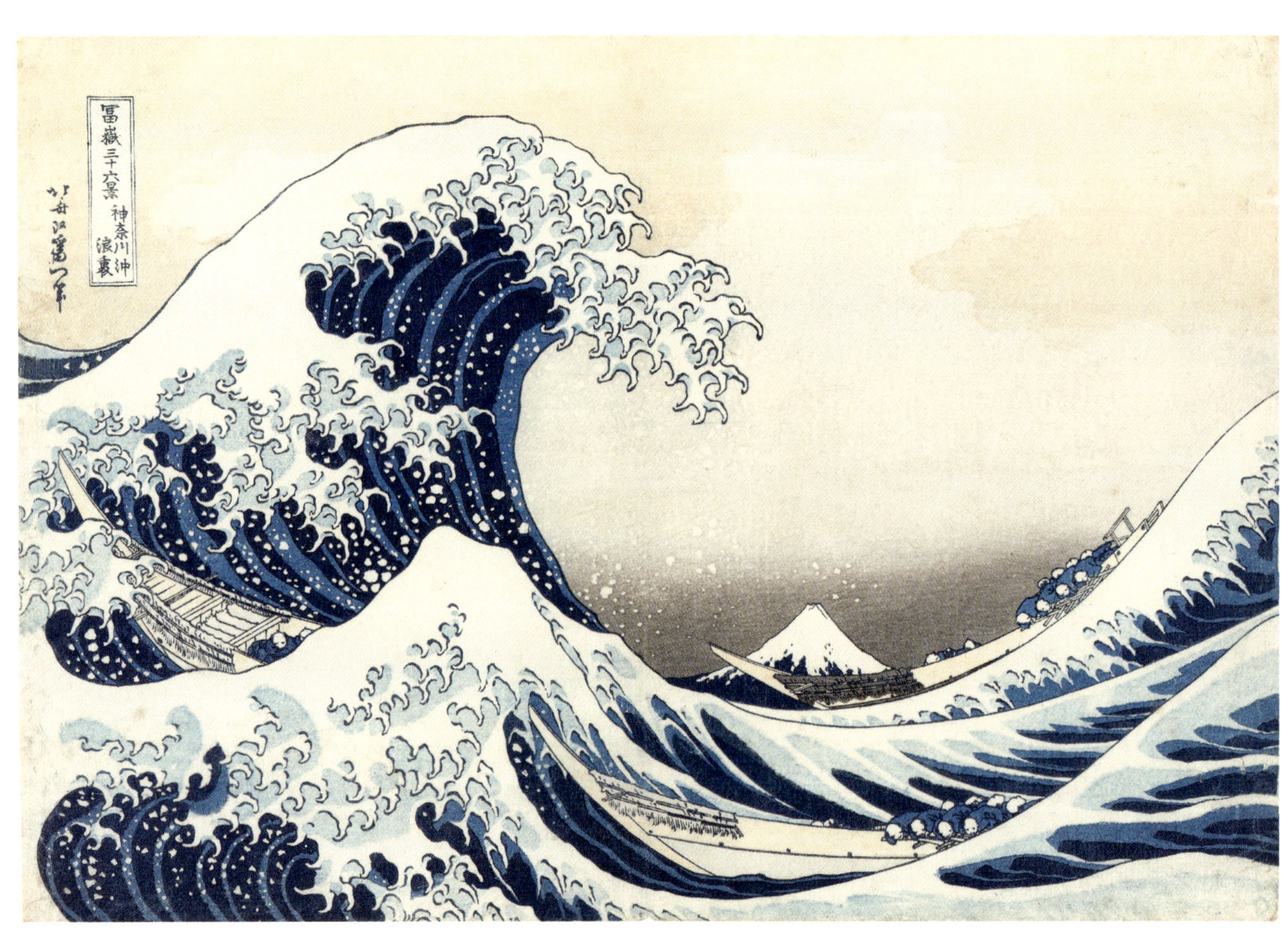

Under the Wave off Kanagawa, *c.* 1830/31
From the series *Thirty-six Views of Mount Fuji*
Published by Nishimuraya Yohachi
Colour woodblock print, *ōban*,
25.7 x 37.7 cm (10⅛ x 14⅞ in.)
Minneapolis Institute of Art,
Bequest of Richard P. Gale

64

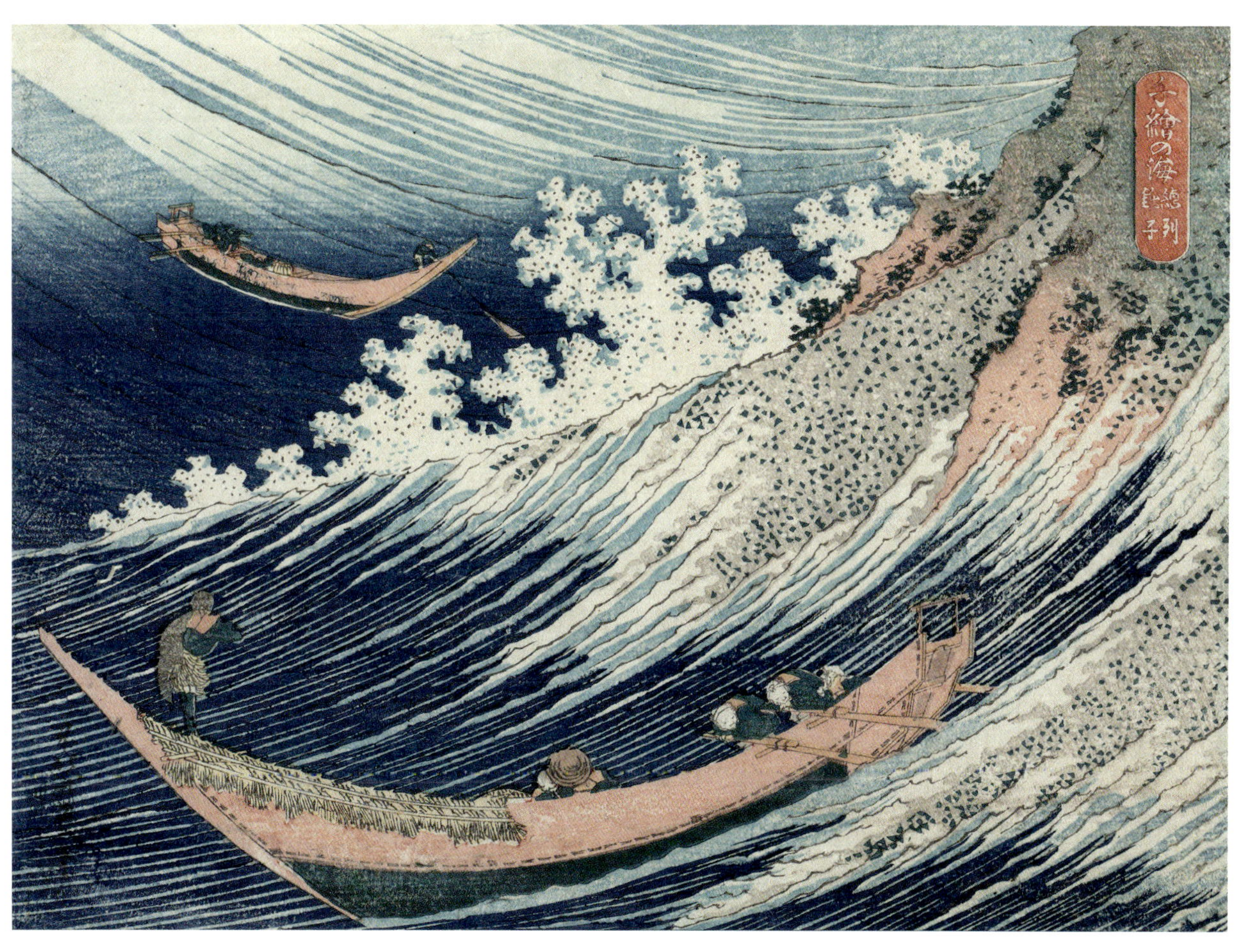

Chōshi in Shimōsa Province, *c.* 1833
From the series *One Thousand Pictures
of the Ocean*
Published by Moriya Jihei
Colour woodblock print, *chūban*,
19.2 x 27.8 cm (7⅝ x 11 in.)
Boston, Museum of Fine Arts,
William S. and John T. Spaulding Collection

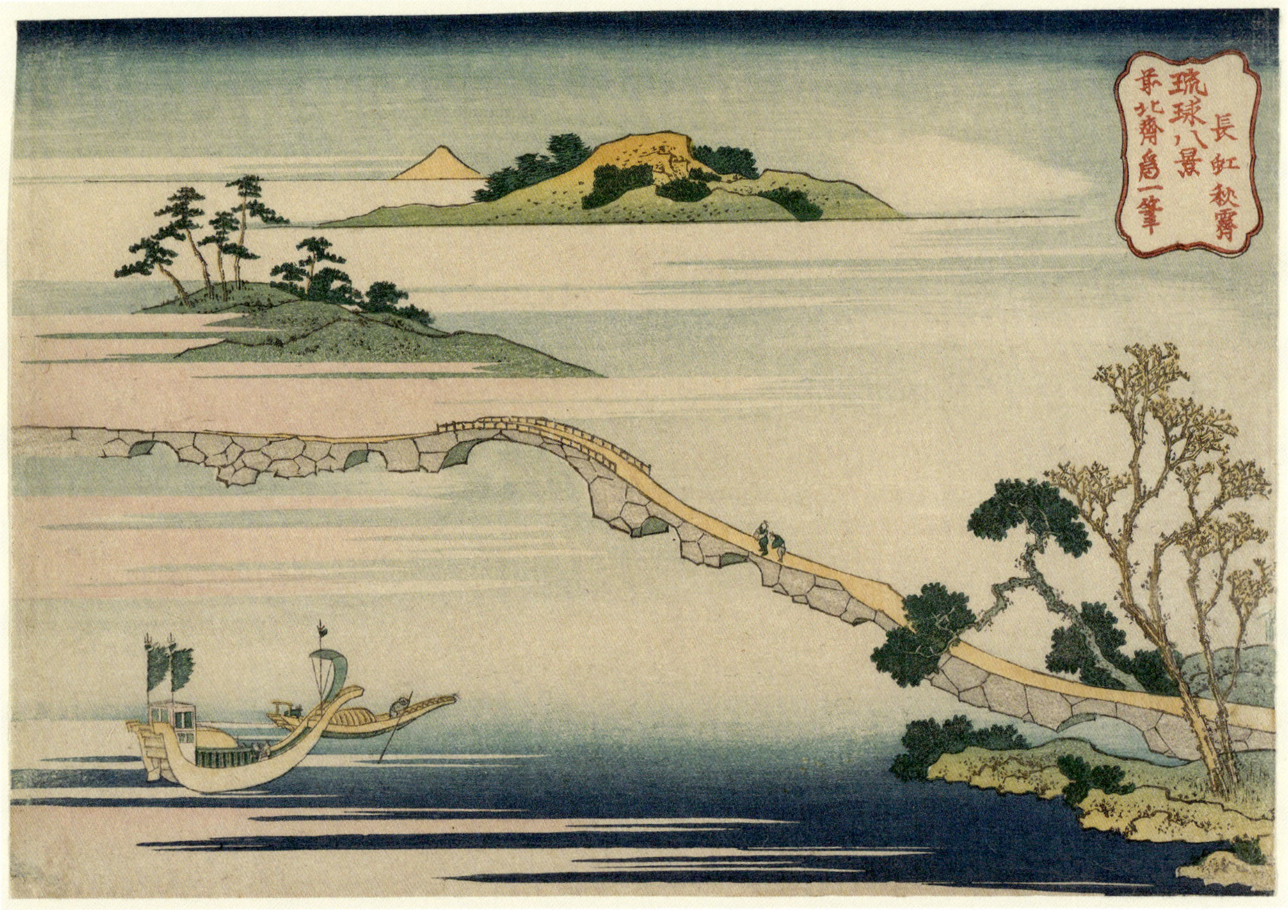

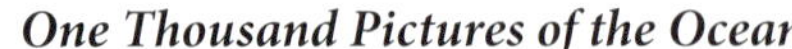

experienced its first snowfall of the year. It may be that Hokusai designed this print to commemorate the diplomatic event, welcomed even by the natural world.

One Thousand Pictures of the Ocean

Each of the ten designs in the series *One Thousand Pictures of the Ocean* (*Chie no umi*, c. 1833) depicts peasants practicing different fishing customs in scenic coastal or river settings, reflecting water's fundamental impact on the Japanese archipelago. Surviving key block impressions for two unpublished designs suggest that the publisher, Moriya, intended a larger series that was never carried out for reasons unknown.

In *Whaling off the Gotō Islands*, an armada of fishing boats surrounds a bewhiskered cetacean (ill. p. 62/63). Group hunting of this kind was developed in around 1677 although whaling itself has a much longer history. Watchmen positioned with telescopes in lookouts, shown in the upper right, would spot the whales and raise the alert. Boats working in concert would drive it into nets set in the shallows. As the whales became entangled, harpooners would descend. Hokusai's whale is poised to slap the surface of the water with its tail; the battle is not yet over.

Chōshi in Shimōsa Province is another variation on the theme of waves, using diagonally sweeping lines and graded colour to convey the ocean's

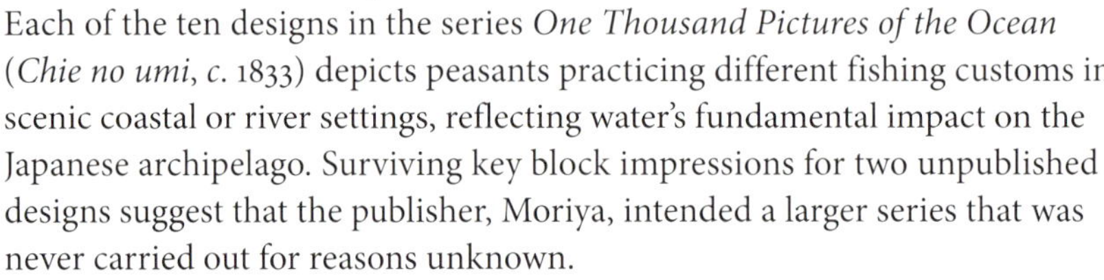

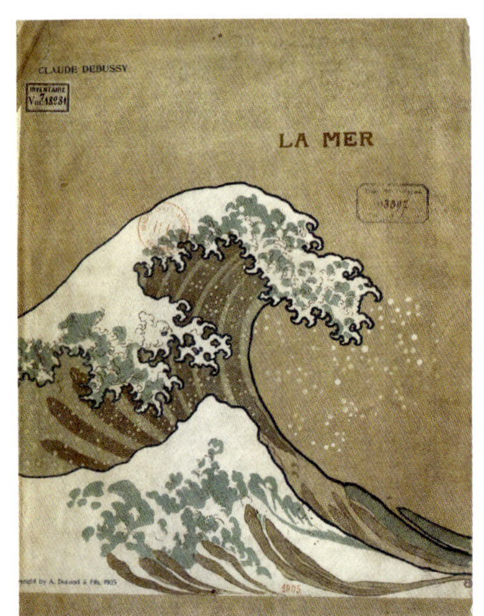

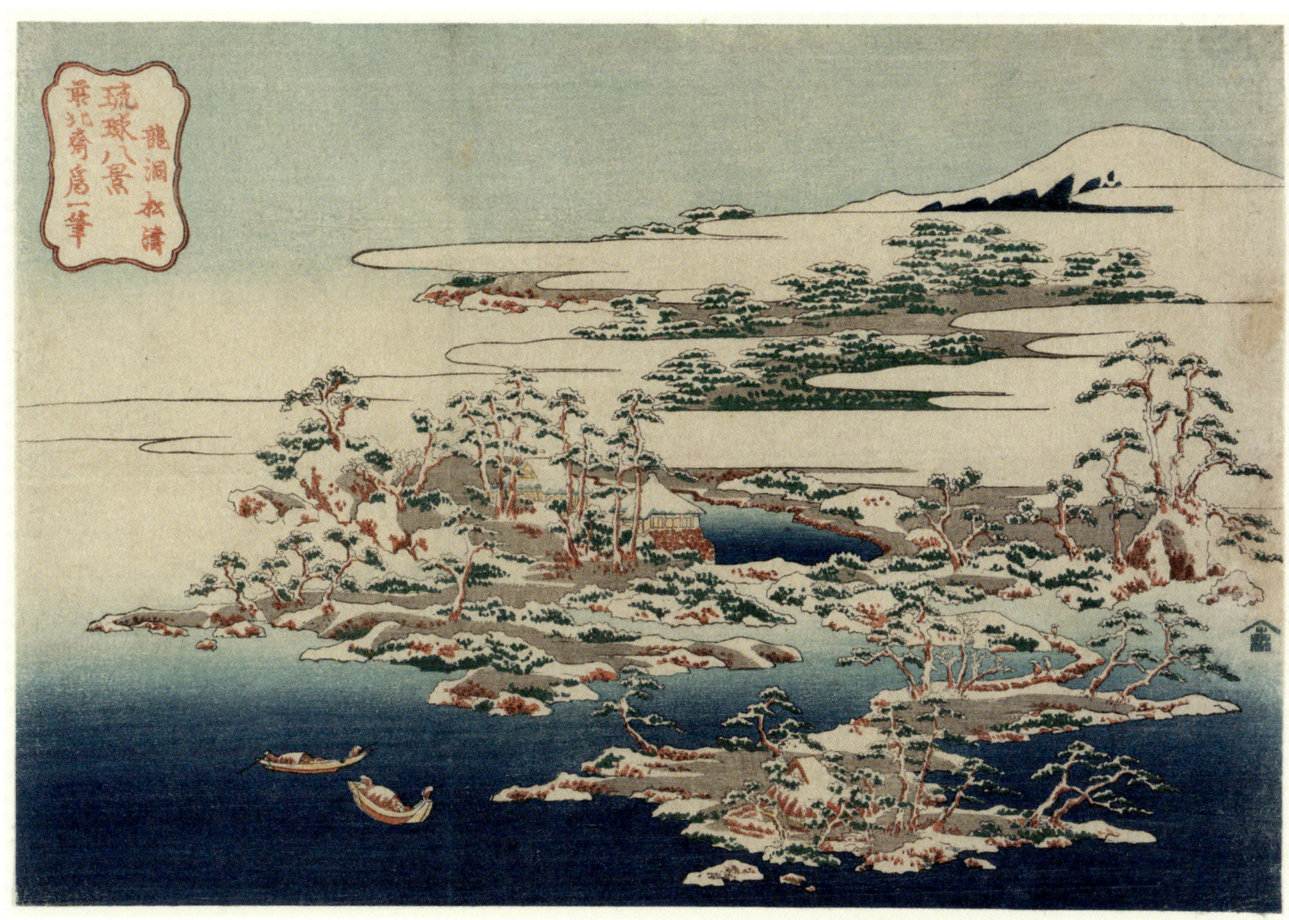

rapid movement (ill. p. 65). In the foreground, a fishing boat launches into turbid seas. The helmsman stands sure-footedly at the bow, guiding the vessel through the surging waters. In the background another boat surfs back on an incoming wave.

Unusual Views of Famous Bridges in Various Provinces

With *Unusual Views of Famous Bridges in Various Provinces* (*Shokoku meikyō kiran*), a series of 11 prints published around 1834, Hokusai carried on his approach of creating series of designs that each offer a different view of a single theme or subject. Hokusai selected bridges outside Edo for his designs but contrary to the title, only some of these sites qualify as "famous bridges". Others are obscure or literary in origin. Hokusai had previously explored the theme of bridges in his print *One Hundred Bridges in a Single View*, *c.* 1823, and bridges feature regularly in his landscape compositions. It is likely that the series was intended as a group of ten prints, but one more was added to commemorate the completion of Tenpōzan, an artificial hill constructed using earth dredged from the mouth of the Ajigawa River at Osaka Bay.

The plank bridges featured in *Old View of the Eight-part Bridge in Mikawa Province* (ill. p. 69) had acquired poetic connotations from the tenth century on, when the site provided the setting for an episode of the classic text *The Tales of Ise* (*Ise monogatari*, *c.* 980). The story's protagonist, a courtier, exiled from

Pines and Waves at Ryūdō, *c.* 1832
From the series *Eight Views of the Ryūkyū Islands*
Published by Moriya Jihei
Colour woodblock print, *ōban*,
25.6 x 37.6 cm (10 x 14⅞ in.)
Boston, Museum of Fine Arts,
William S. and John T. Spaulding Collection

PAGE 66 TOP
Clear Autumn Weather at Chōkō, *c.* 1832
From the series *Eight Views of the Ryūkyū Islands*
Published by Moriya Jihei
Colour woodblock print, *ōban*,
25.8 x 38.1 cm (10¼ x 15 in.)
Boston, Museum of Fine Arts,
William S. and John T. Spaulding Collection

PAGE 66 BOTTOM
Score for *La Mer. Trois esquisses symphoniques de Debussy*, Paris, Durand, 1905
Paris, Bibliothèque Nationale de France

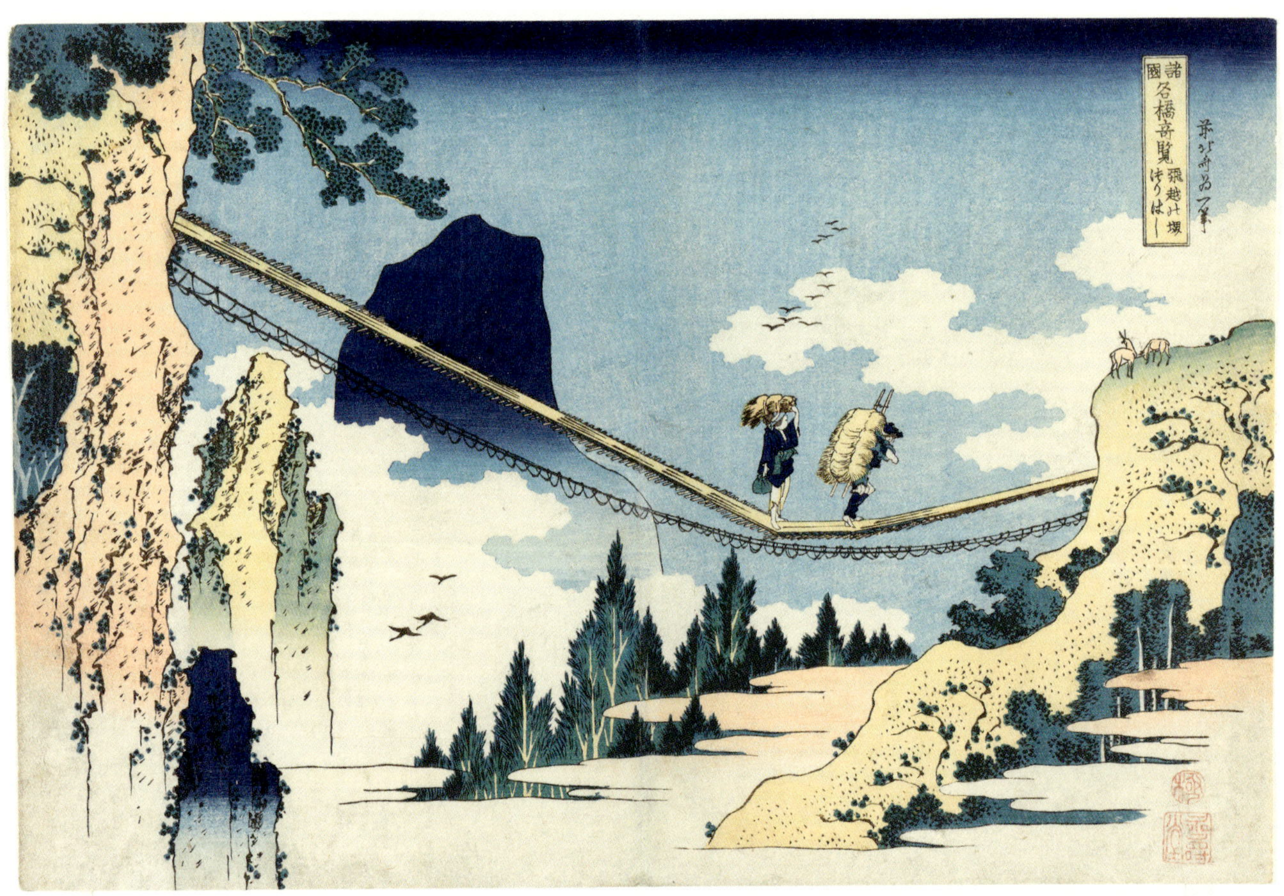

***The Suspension Bridge on the Border
of Hida and Etchū Provinces***, *c.* 1834
From the series *Unusual Views of Famous
Bridges in Various Provinces*
Published by Nishimuraya Yohachi
Colour woodblock print, *ōban*,
25.3 x 37.6 cm (10 x 14⅞ in.)
Minneapolis Institute of Art,
Bequest of Richard P. Gale

the ancient capital of Kyoto after a romantic indiscretion, and his companions break their journey where the Azuma River branches into eight streams, each crossed by a plank bridge. The sight of the irises growing in the shallows move the protagonist to compose an acrostic poem. The "old view" in the title suggests that the depicted scene is intended to take place before the bridges were destroyed in the middle of the Heian period, although the figures crossing the bridge wear contemporary clothing. As with most of Hokusai's depictions of famous places, matters of geography or history did not limit the play of his vivid imagination.

The Suspension Bridge on the Border of Hida and Etchū Provinces is the series' only featured site that has not been identified (ill. p. 68). The Hida-Etchū region, in present-day Gifu and Toyama prefectures, is the most mountainous territory in mainland Japan. The forbidding terrain and long, harsh winters ensured it remained relatively isolated well into the modern period. The image shows a rickety suspension bridge strung loosely across a precipitous ravine. Two farmers carrying loads of straw make the perilous crossing nonchalantly; the second figure, a woman, glances up to contemplate the view.

True Mirrors of Chinese and Japanese Poems
The series *True Mirrors of Chinese and Japanese Poems* (*Shiika shashin kyō,
c.* 1833/34) consists of ten prints featuring famous poets of Japan and China in landscape settings in the tall, narrow *nagaban* format. In better impressions of

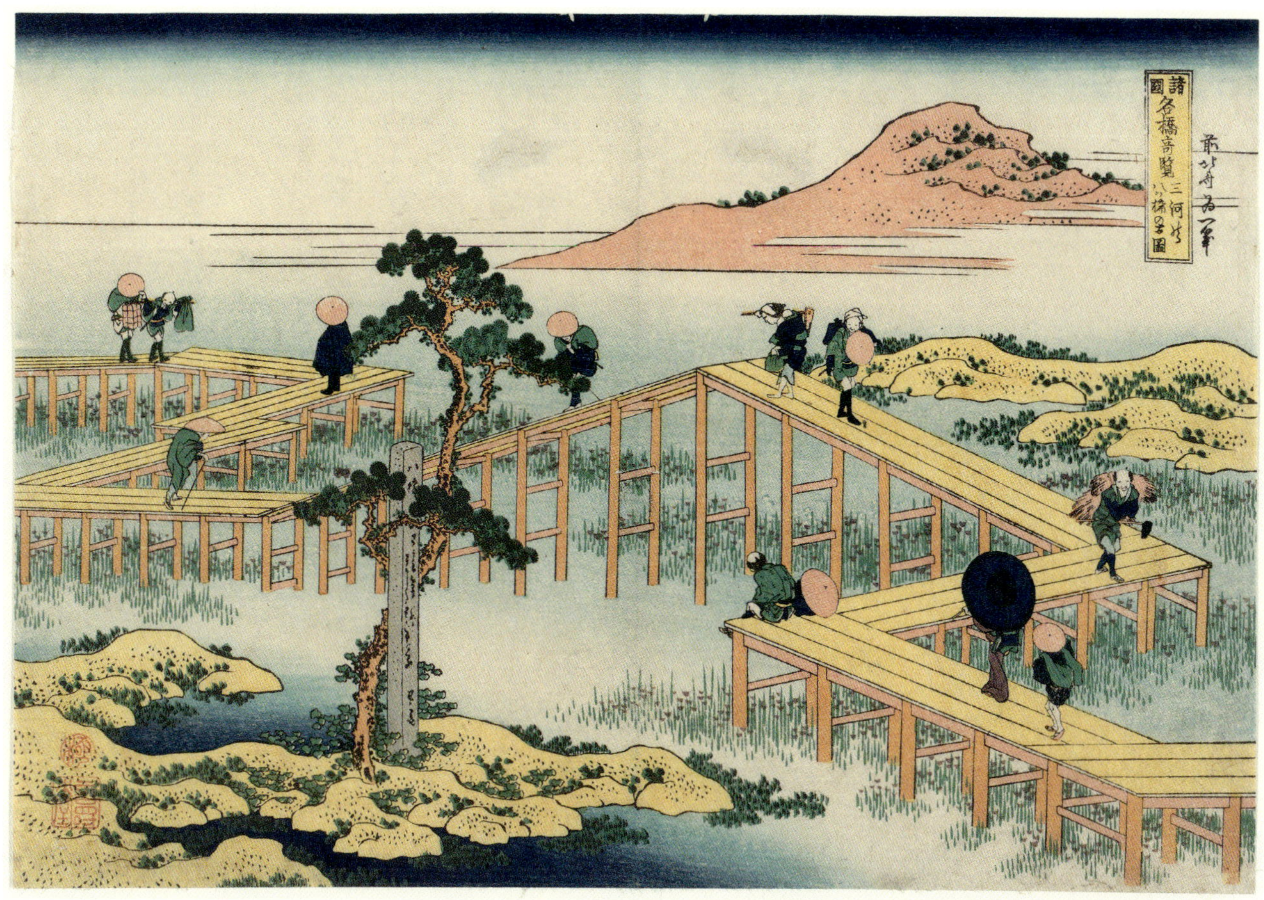

some of the designs, including *Tōru Daijin*, the delicate grain of the cherrywood printing blocks is visible in the background (ill. p. 75). The subject of this design is the courtier Minamoto no Tōru (822–895), son of an emperor so admired for his artistic accomplishments and refined tastes that he purportedly inspired the eponymous hero of Murasaki Shikibu's classic novel *The Tale of Genji* (*Genji monogatari*, *c.* 1008). Hokusai depicted Tōru with attendants in his celebrated garden in Kyoto under a crescent moon.

The subject of *Bai Juyi* is not the Tang dynasty poet per se, but rather a scene from the late 14th-century noh piece *Haku Rakuten* by Zeami Motokiyo (1363–1443; ill. p. 74). In the play, the poet and courtier Bai Juyi (Jp. Haku Rakuten, 772–846) is sent by the Chinese emperor to Japan in order to pacify the country through verse alone. When he arrives he meets Sumiyoshi, Japan's god of poetry, disguised as a fisherman, and a competition between Chinese and Japanese poetry ensues. When Sumiyoshi declares that in Japan, all living creatures sing, the victor is clear and the humbled Bai Juyi returns to China. Hokusai depicts the Chinese poet in courtly attire and flanked by attendants, gazing imperiously down at Sumiyoshi. The mountain peaks wreathed in cloud refer to Bai Juyi's poem:

Green moss, like a cloak, lying on the shoulders of the cliff
White clouds, as though a sash, encircling the waist of the mountain.[3]

Old View of the Eight-part Bridge in Mikawa Province, *c.* 1834
From the series *Unusual Views of Famous Bridges in Various Provinces*
Published by Nishimuraya Yohachi
Colour woodblock print, *ōban*,
24.4 x 36.8 cm (9⅝ x 14½ in.)
Boston, Museum of Fine Arts,
William Sturgis Bigelow Collection

PAGE 70
The Ghost of Oiwa, *c.* 1831/32
From the series *One Hundred Ghost Stories*
Published by Tsuruya Kiemon
Colour woodblock print, *chūban*,
26.3 x 18.9 cm (10⅜ x 7½ in.)
Boston, Museum of Fine Arts,
Gift of Mrs. Edward Jackson Holmes

PAGE 71
The Ghost of Kohada Koheiji, *c.* 1831/32
From the series *One Hundred Ghost Stories*
Published by Tsuruya Kiemon
Colour woodblock print, *chūban*,
26.3 x 18.5 cm (10⅜ x 7⅜ in.)
Minneapolis Institute of Art,
Gift of Louis W. Hill, Jr.

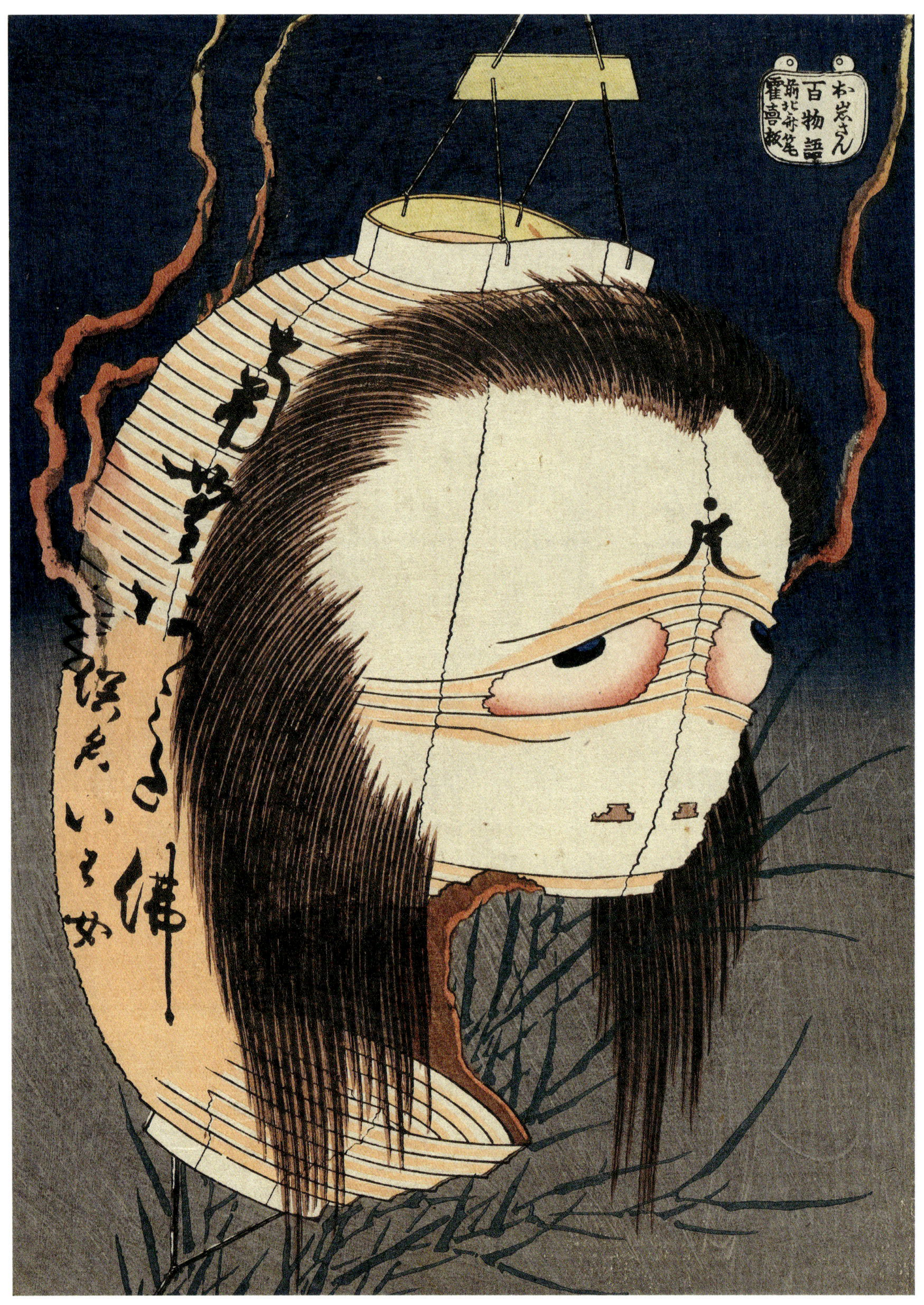

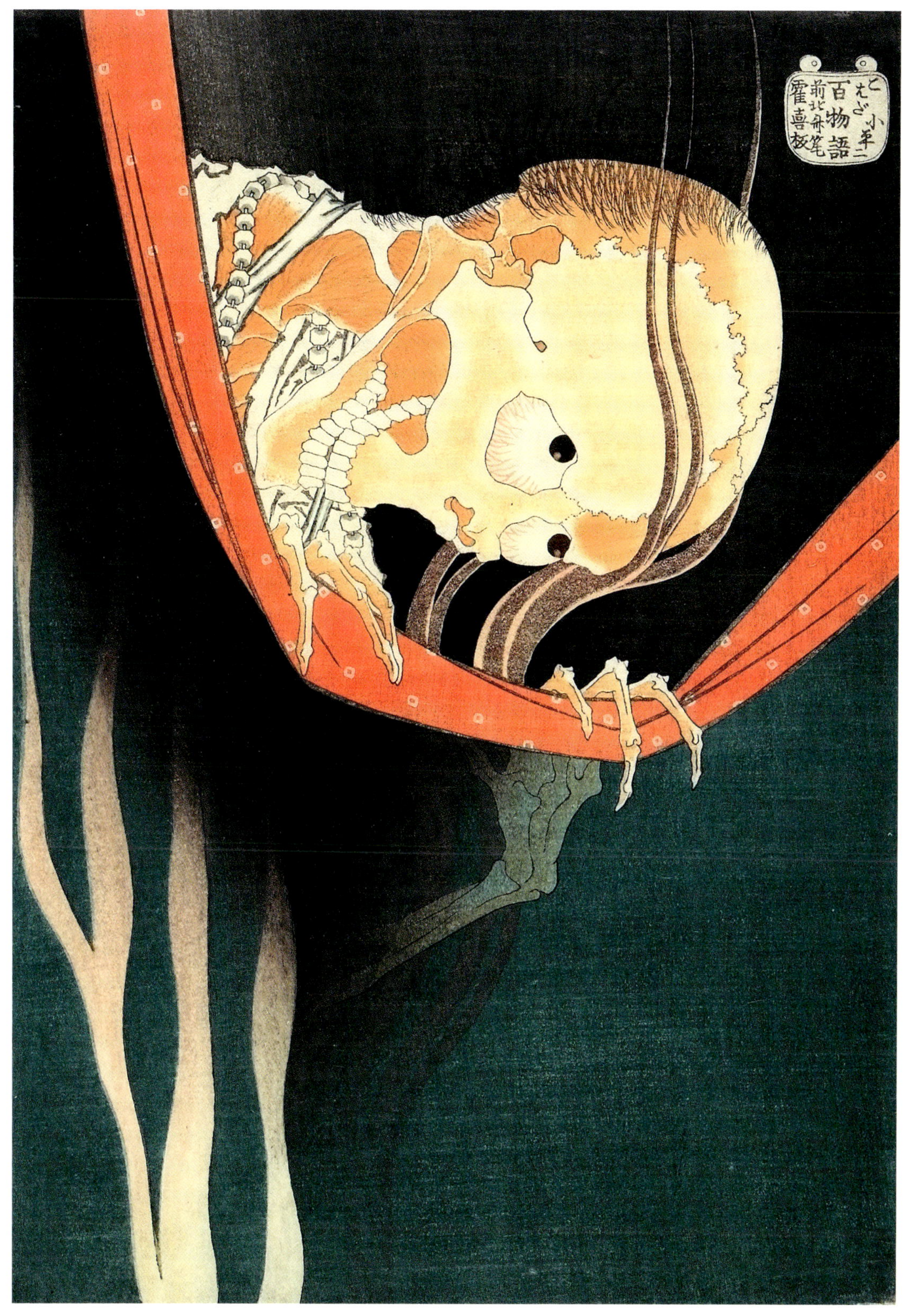
こ
え
ご
小半
二
百
物
語
前北斎筆
蔦喜板

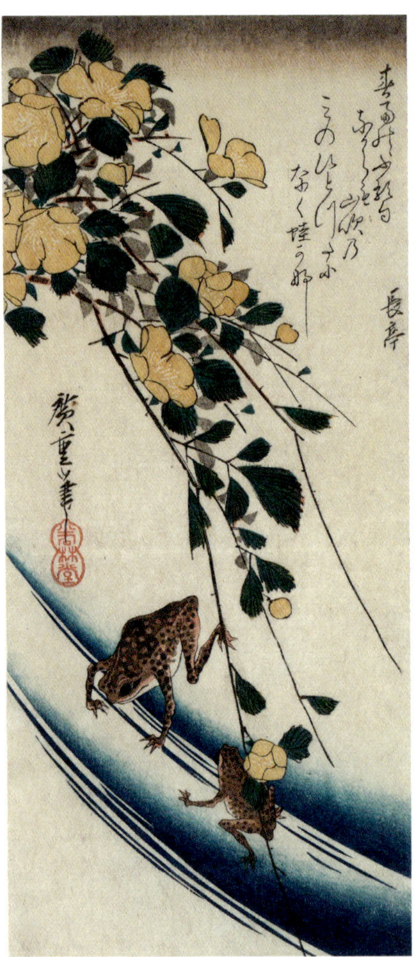

Utagawa Hiroshige
Yellow Rose and Frogs, *c.* 1832
Published by Wakasaya Yoichi
Colour woodblock print, *ōtanzakuban*,
37.5 x 16.5 cm (14⅞ x 6½ in.)
Boston, Museum of Fine Arts,
William S. and John T. Spaulding Collection

One Hundred Ghost Stories

With the series *One Hundred Ghost Stories* (*Hyaku monogatari, c.* 1831/32)
Hokusai returned again to the theme of ghost stories or *kaidan*. This group
comprises five known designs in *chūban* format that ranged from the mildly
creepy to the terrifying. *Kaidan* entered mass print culture with the first of many
anthologies of chilling tales in 1677, and were further popularized by theatre,
illustrated books and woodblock prints. Hokusai himself provided illustrations
for books such as the five-volume *The Stars on a Frosty Night* (ill. p. 35) and
included images of ghosts and demons in *Hokusai manga* (ills. pp. 23, 25).

The narrative associated with *The Ghost of Kohada Koheiji* is based on a
historical event in which an actor was tortured and eventually drowned by his
wife and her lover (ill. p. 71). In a fictionalization from 1803 of the incident by
Santō Kyōden, later adapted for kabuki and performed in 1808, Koheiji returns
to haunt his murderers. Hokusai depicted Koheiji's skull leering through a
mosquito net at the doomed couple as they lie in bed. Bloodshot eyes rolling
in their sockets, clawlike fingers and a grotesque grin make Koheiji's ghost a
dreadful sight. Precise delineation of the musculature and skeleton, particularly
the skull fissures, suggests that Hokusai consulted anatomical texts to make
his image all the more bloodcurdlingly realistic.

The Ghost of Oiwa also stems from kabuki lore. In the play *Ghost Story at
Yotsuya* (*Yotsuya kaidan*), first staged in 1825, Oiwa is horribly disfigured after
being poisoned by the family of her husband's lover (ill. p. 70). Disgusted by
her altered appearance, her husband Iemon persuades a servant to rape Oiwa
to provide grounds for divorce, but she is killed in the ensuing scuffle. Oiwa's
ghost returns to torment Iemon, who ultimately throws himself in a river and
drowns. Hokusai portrayed Oiwa's ghastly face as an apparition in a paper
lantern as it burns. This design was adapted by many contemporaries including
his student Shunbaisai Hokuei (d. 1837) in 1832 and Utagawa Kuniyoshi (1798–
1861) in 1848.

Iris and Grasshopper, *c.* 1831–1834
From an untitled series known as *Large Flowers*
Published by Nishimuraya Yohachi
Colour woodblock print, *ōban*,
24.1 x 36.6 cm (9½ x 14½ in.)
London, British Museum

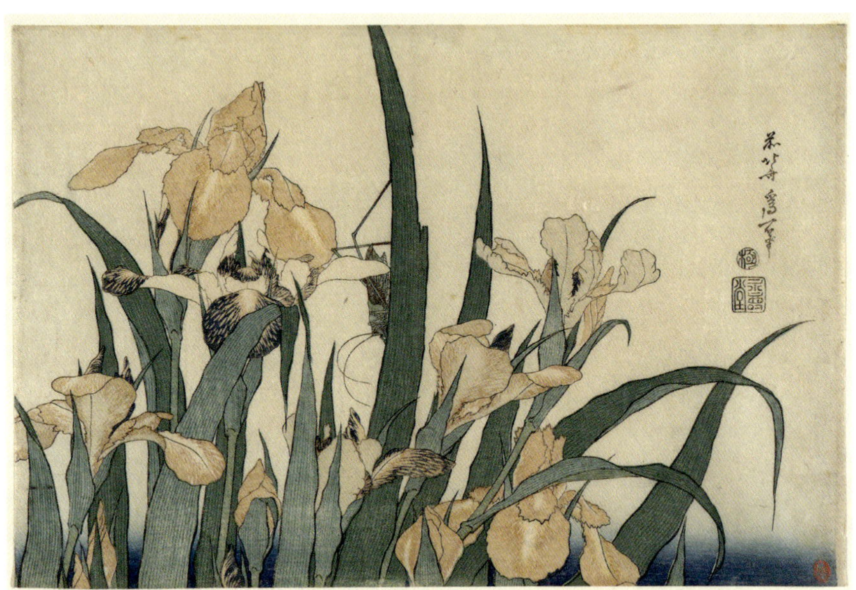

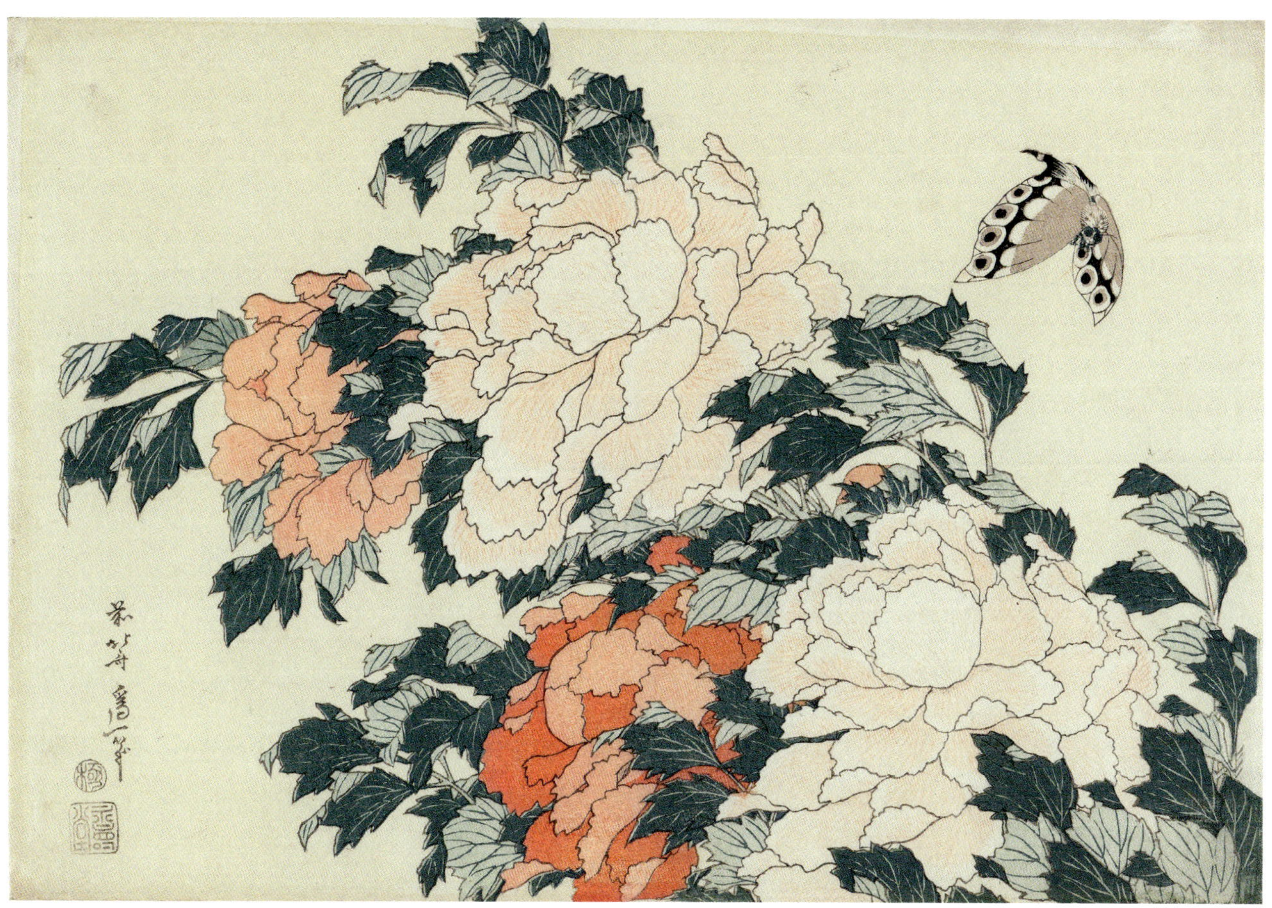

Bird-and-Flower Designs

Hokusai created several bird-and-flower designs during the early 1830s that unite elegant aesthetics with formal realism (ill. p. 72 bottom). Bird-and-flower pictures (*kachō-ga*), a broad term for a painting genre where plants and animals comprised the principal subject, had a long history in Japanese painting. Chinese artists living in Nagasaki during the 18th century introduced a new synthesis of realism with decorative elements that was rapidly adopted by Japanese painters and print designers.

Possibly encouraged by the popularity of bird-and-flower prints produced by the rising star Hiroshige (ill. p. 72 top), publisher Nishimuraya Yohachi commissioned Hokusai to create a series of ten horizontal *ōban* prints known as *Large Flowers*. In contrast to the abbreviated painterly style of Hiroshige, each image is rendered in striking close-up with crisp detail. In *Peonies and Butterfly* (*c.* 1831–1834), for example, Hokusai depicted each wind-buffeted petal, leaf and wing with absolute precision and focus across all facets of the composition (ill. p. 73). No inscription other than Hokusai's signature distracts from the bold design.

Hokusai had created similarly stark, detailed flower compositions in *Hokusai manga* and *Realistic Sketchbook by Hokusai* (*Hokusai shashin gafu*, 1819; ill. p. 78). While the word *shashin* in the title of *Realistic Sketchbook* means "photograph" in modern Japanese, in Hokusai's time it meant to draw or transpose the real, and was associated with scientific illustrations by scholars of

Peonies and Butterfly, *c.* 1831–1834
From an untitled series known as *Large Flowers*
Published by Nishimuraya Yohachi
Colour woodblock print, *ōban*,
26.3 x 39 cm (10⅜ x 15⅜ in.)
Boston, Museum of Fine Arts,
William Sturgis Bigelow Collection

PAGE 74
Bai Juyi (Haku Rakuten), *c.* 1833/34
From the series *True Mirrors of Chinese and Japanese Poems*
Published by Moriya Jihei
Colour woodblock print, *nagaban*,
52.1 x 23.2 cm (20⅝ x 9¼ in.)
Honolulu Museum of Art,
Gift of James A. Michener, 1969

PAGE 75
Tōru Daijin, *c.* 1833/34
From the series *True Mirrors of Chinese and Japanese Poems*
Published by Moriya Jihei
Colour woodblock print, *nagaban*,
49.8 x 23.1 cm (19⅝ x 9 in.)
London, British Museum

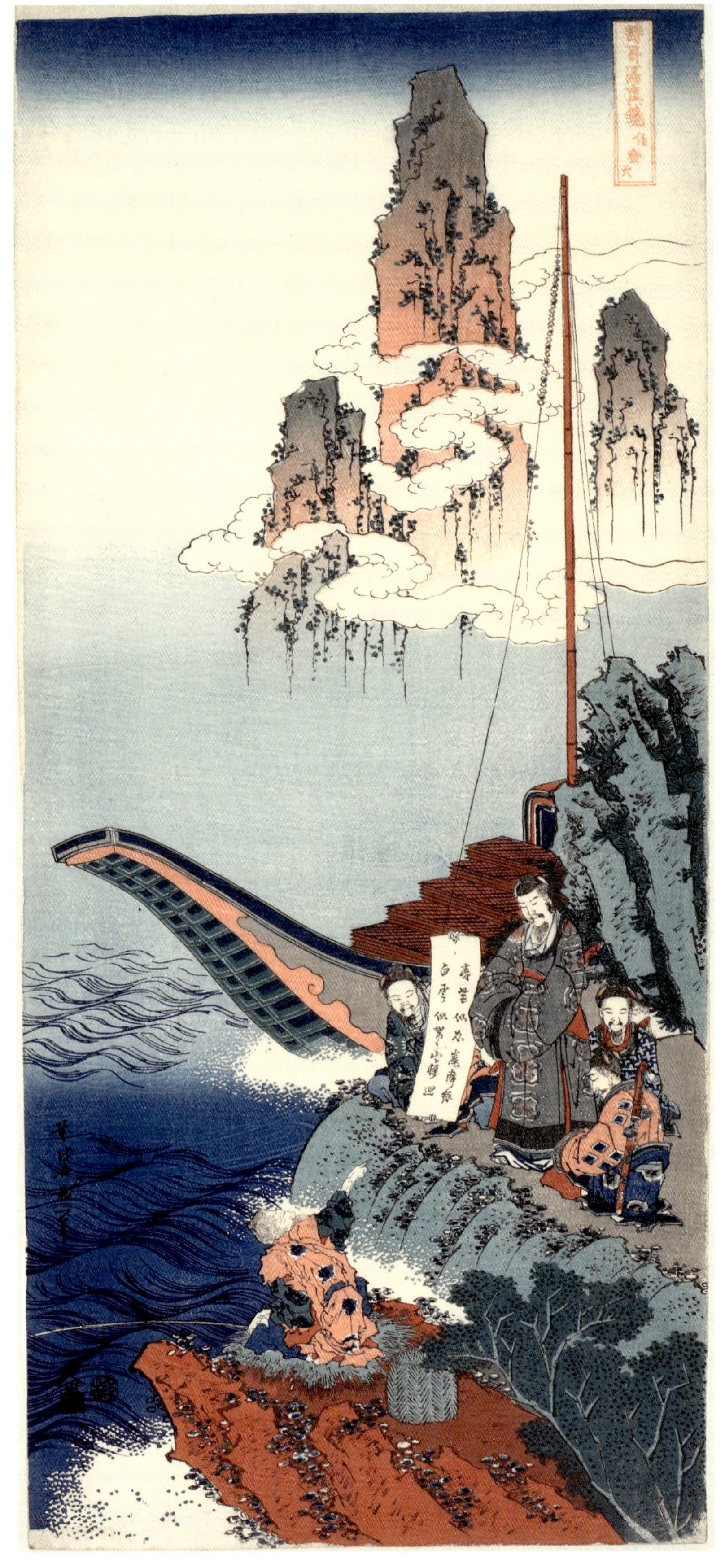

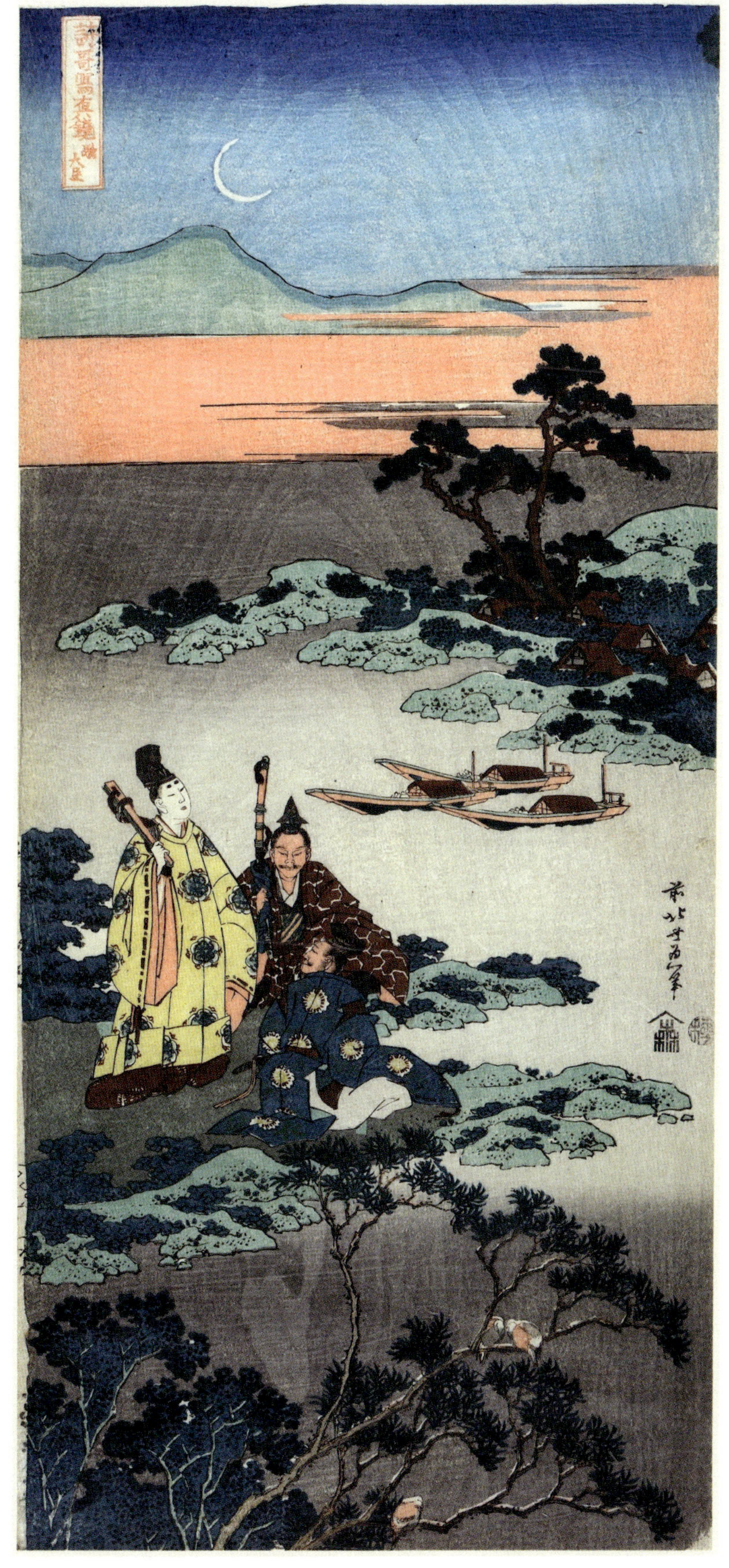

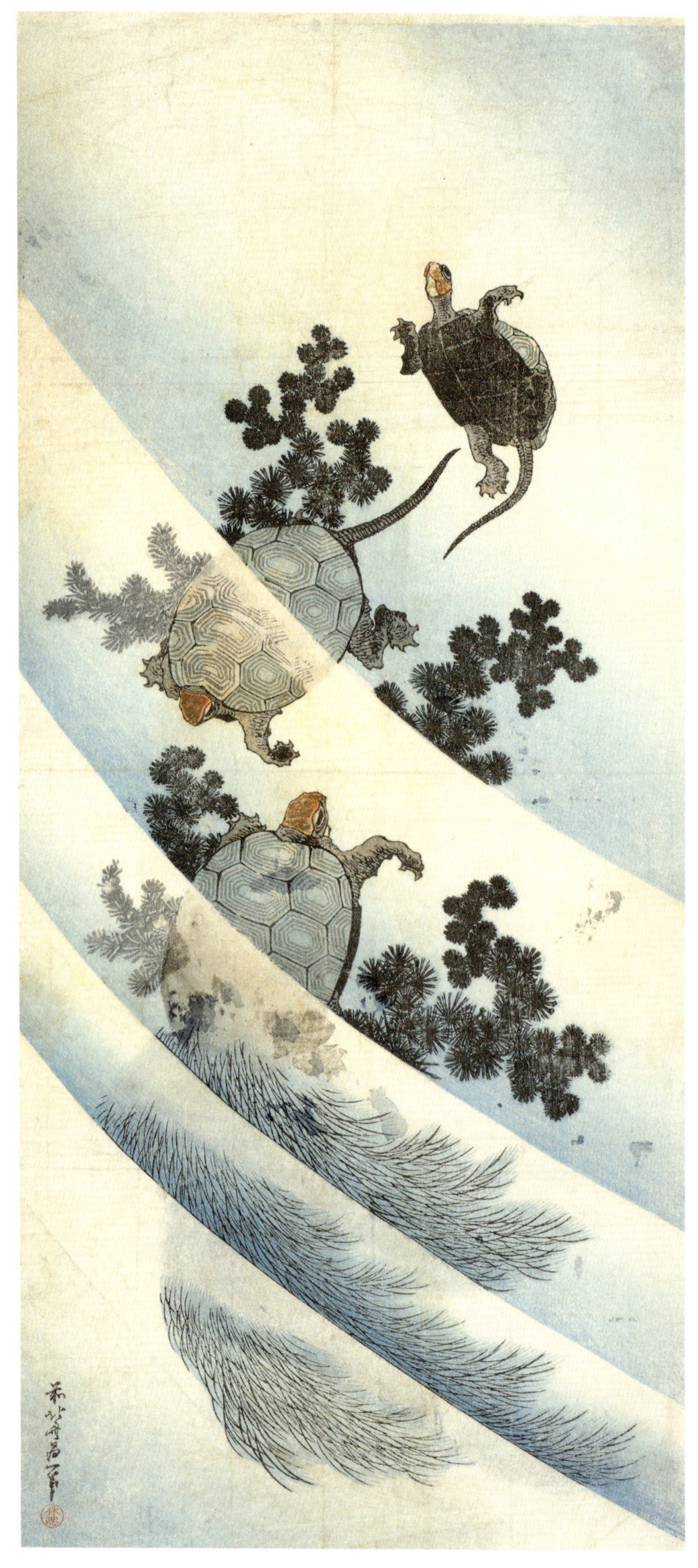

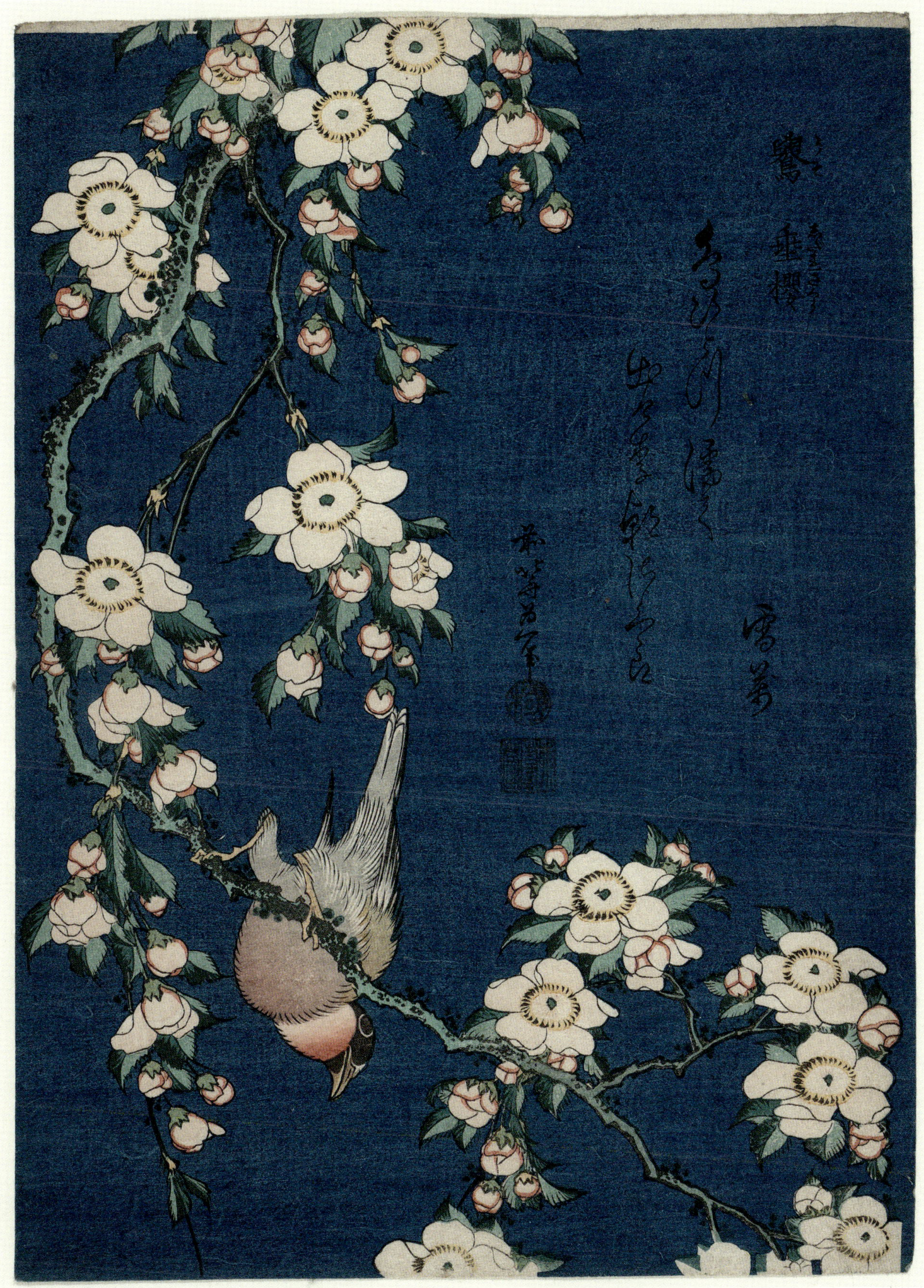
鷽　垂櫻

Western studies. Indeed, Hokusai's approach to composition in both the *Realistic Sketchbook by Hokusai* and *Large Flowers* was probably informed by botanic illustrations. A possible source is *Picture Book of Mountain Grasses* (*Ehon noyamagusa*), a five-volume book set, first published in 1755 and expanded in 1806, which contains a number of similar compositions of subjects found in *Large Flowers*. However, rather than reproducing herbarium specimens, Hokusai's designs of plants and insects pulse with movement and vitality.

Another untitled bird-and-flower series known as *Small Flowers*, this time in vertical *chūban* format and with poetic inscriptions by contemporary literati figures, was released around the same time as *Large Flowers*. In *Bullfinch and Weeping Cherry* (ill. p. 77), Hokusai's intention seems to have been to disorient the viewer: is the bird hanging upside down, or are we looking up at it from below? The inscription, a poem penned by the master shamisen player Sugano Joyu II (1784–1841), reads:

> *One single bird, wet with dew,*
> *Has come out:*
> *The morning cherry.*[4]

Published at approximately the same time were around six tall, narrow *nagaban* prints of subjects with auspicious associations, including a herd of frolicking horses and turtles swimming gracefully amid sprigs of pond weed (ill. p. 76). In the latter design, one of the creatures is of such old age that a plume of algae trails like a tail from its shell. *Minogame*, as such turtles are known, are symbols of long life in East Asian visual culture.

Irises, 1819
From *Realistic Sketchbook by Hokusai*
Published by Tsuruya Kiemon
Woodblock-printed book
Leiden, Museum Volkenkunde

PAGE 76
Turtles, c. 1834
From an untitled series
Colour woodblock print, *nagaban*,
49.9 x 22.7 cm (19¾ x 9 in.)
Honolulu Museum of Art,
Gift of James A. Michener, 1991

PAGE 77
Bullfinch and Weeping Cherry, c. 1834
From an untitled series known as
Small Flowers
Published by Nishimuraya Yohachi
Colour woodblock print, *chūban*,
24.2 x 18.8 cm (9⅝ x 7½ in.)
Boston, Museum of Fine Arts,
William Sturgis Bigelow Collection

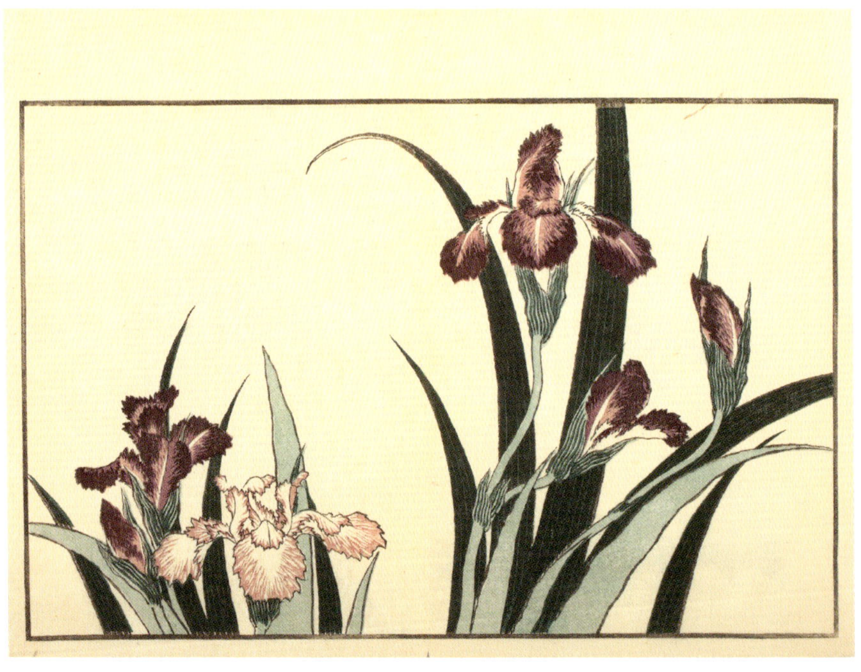

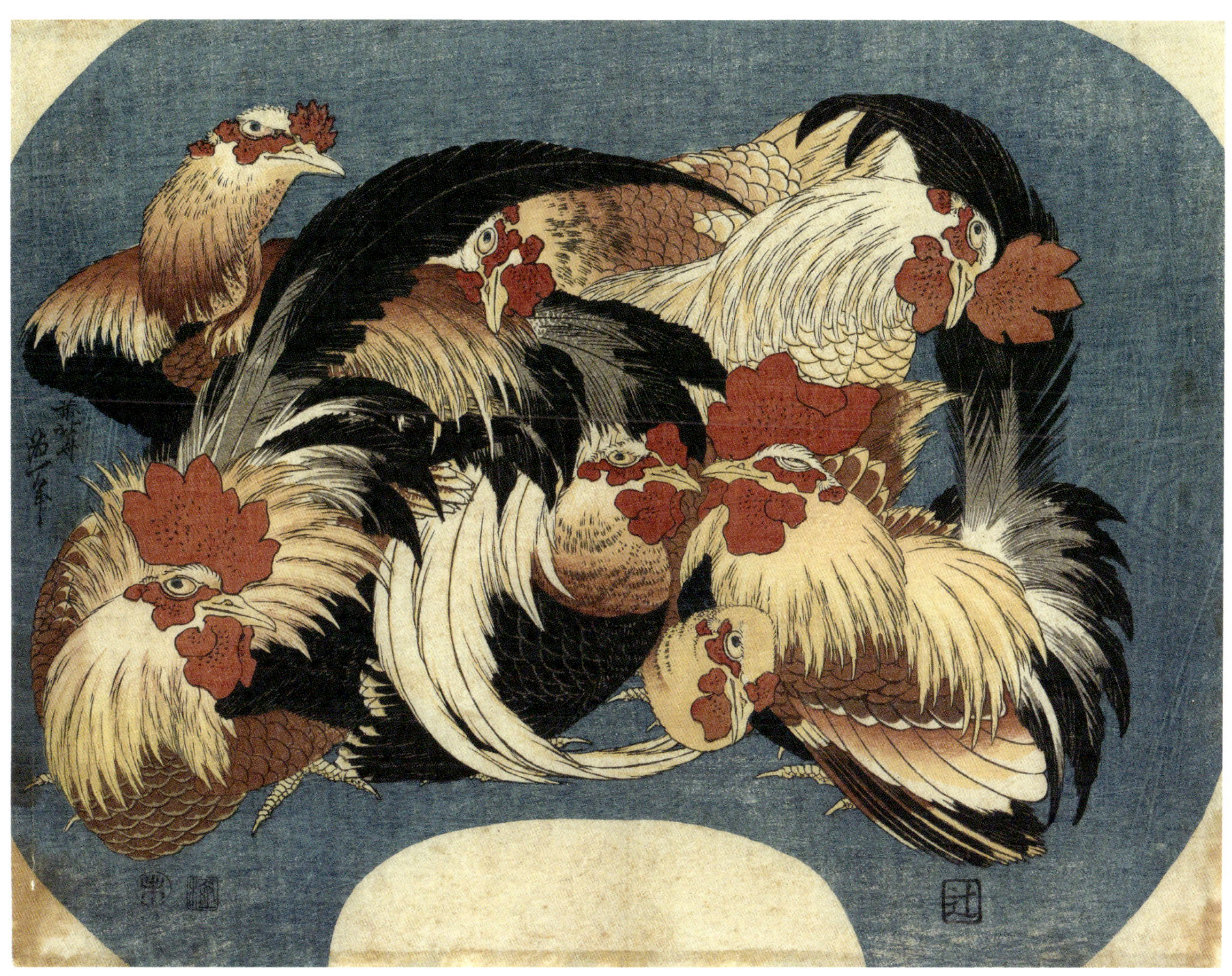

It is around the same time that Hokusai's striking fan print *Group of Hens and Roosters* was probably published, in late 1835 for the 1836 Year of the Rooster (ill. p. 79). Fans were an affordable and practical fashion accessory during Japan's hot and humid summers. Rather than creating a formally realistic composition of his avian subjects, Hokusai drew an eye-catching pattern of splendid plumage and bright red cockscombs against a deep blue ground. The birds' sharp expressions and beady eyes fixed warily on the viewer make them seem ready to dart off the page.

Group of Hens and Roosters, 1835
Published by Tsujiya Yasubei
Colour woodblock print, *uchiwa-e*,
22.5 x 29 cm (8⅞ x 11½ in.)
Tokyo National Museum, Important Art Object

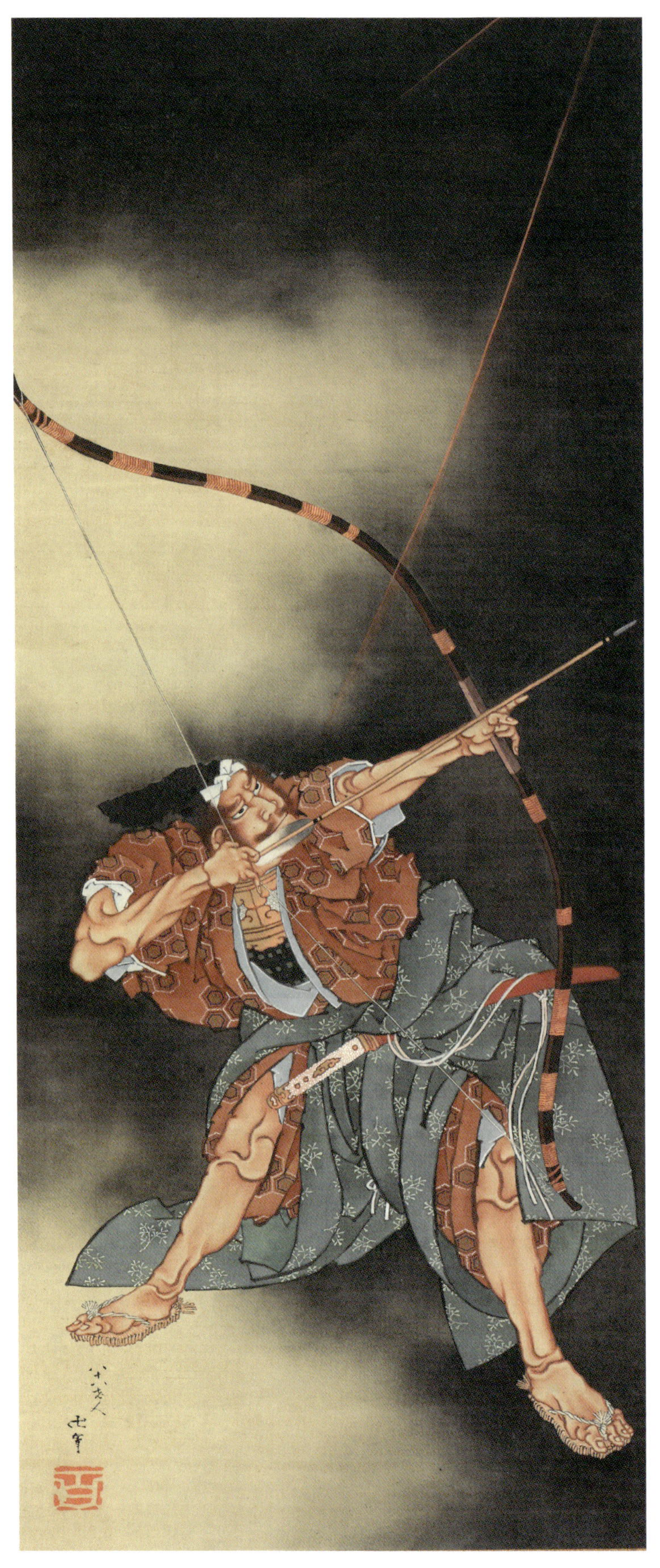

Divine Madness

In the third month of 1834, in the first volume of the illustrated book *One Hundred Views of Mount Fuji* (*Fugaku hyakkei*), Hokusai formally adopted his final name, one that he had periodically used in the past and would continue to use until his death: "Gakyō rōjin manji", meaning "old man mad about painting". The final character *manji* is written using a left-facing swastika, an auspicious Buddhist symbol that can also mean "ten thousand". Parodying a passage from Confucius's *Analects*, Hokusai added a spirited postscript to the volume:

> From the age of six I had a penchant for copying the form of things, and from about 50, large numbers of pictures were published; but until I reached the age of 70, nothing that I drew was worthy of notice. At the age of 73, I was somewhat able to grasp the form of birds, animals, insects and fish, and the growth of plants and trees. Therefore, when I am 80 years I will have made increasing progress, and at 90 I will penetrate the secrets of art. When I am 100 years old, I will have attained a mysterious level, and at 110, every dot and stroke will be alive. To those who outlive me, please observe that I have not spoken falsehoods.

The three elegantly conceived volumes aimed to capitalize on the popularity of *Thirty-six Views of Mount Fuji*. They followed a similar concept, depicting the majestic form of Japan's premier mountain from different angles and in a variety of moods. However, while the first series gathered compositions printed in colour and in the large *ōban* format, each a self-standing, independent work of art, Hokusai designed these images in monochrome to be produced in the relatively small book format to be enjoyed as a sequence.

This reduced scale and absence of colour strained the artistry and skill of the designer and artisans. The first two volumes were produced by a consortium of four publishers including Nishimuraya in 1834 and 1835; the third during the 1840s by Eirakuya Tōshirō, one of the publishers of *Hokusai manga*. The printing blocks of volumes one and two were expertly carved by Egawa Tomekichi and others whose names are recorded on each page in recognition of their masterful work. Delicate gradations of grey and the grain of the wood are visible in early editions. The three books were a remarkable success and went into several reprints.

Although Hokusai travelled widely, no in-situ sketches for any of the designs survive. The images must have been drawn from his own imagination or adapted

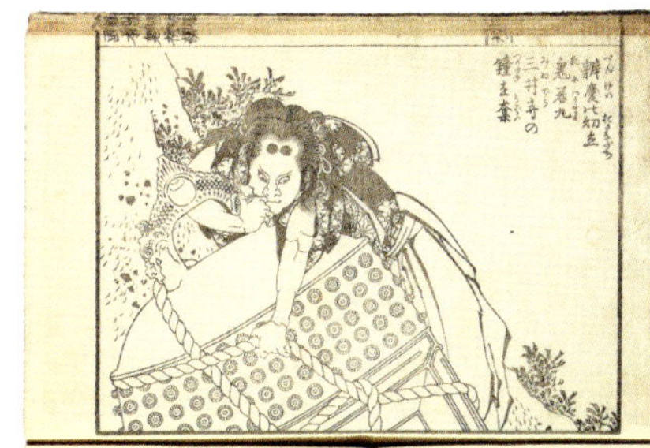

Benkei Stealing the Bell from Mii Temple, 1836
From *Picture Book of Japanese and Chinese Warriors in the Vanguard*
Published by Eirakuya Tōshirō and Wanya Kihei
Woodblock-printed book
London, British Museum

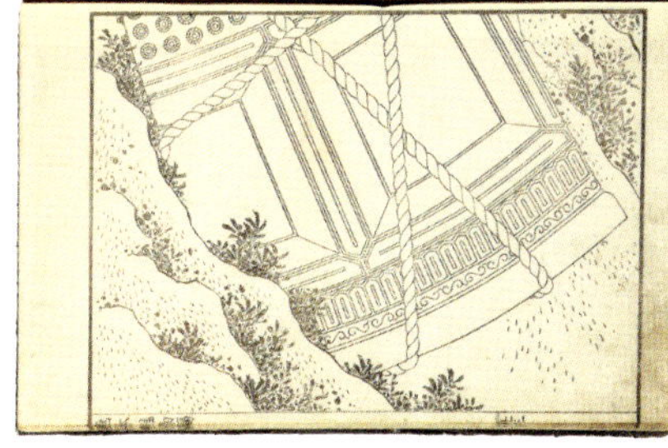

Minamoto no Yorimasa Aiming an Arrow, 1847
Hanging scroll, ink and colour on silk,
99 x 42.2 cm (39 x 16⅝ in.)
Cambridge, Arthur M. Sackler Museum,
Promised gift of Robert S. and
Betsy G. Feinberg

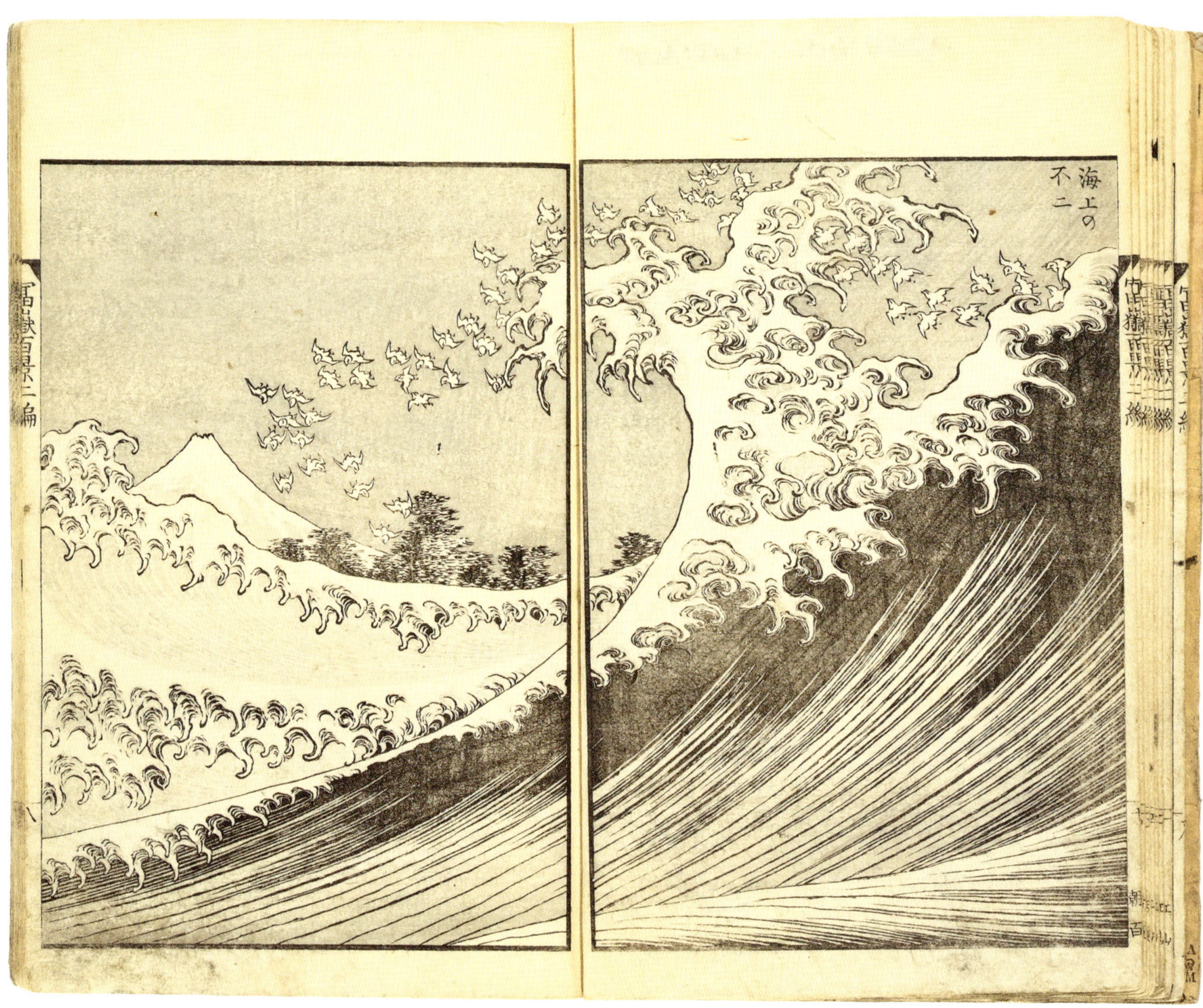

Fuji over the Sea, 1835
From volume two of *One Hundred
Views of Mount Fuji*
Published by Nishimuraya Yohachi
and Nishimura Sukezo
Woodblock-printed books, three volumes
London, British Museum

PAGE 83 TOP
Fuji through a Bamboo Forest, 1835
From volume two of *One Hundred
Views of Mount Fuji*
Published by Nishimuraya Yohachi
and Nishimura Sukezo
Woodblock-printed books, three volumes
London, British Museum

on from other artists' illustrations. While Hokusai's images refer to actual places, and Western pictorial techniques were used to give a sense of realism, he exaggerated and enhanced the natural world to create a familiar yet fantastic landscape.

Fuji over the Sea from the second volume of *One Hundred Views of Mount Fuji* continues Hokusai's exploration of wave forms that begun in the 1790s (ill. p. 82). Instead of moving laterally across the composition the two waves depicted here seem to rush perilously toward the viewer. Hokusai elaborated on the decorative potential of sea foam, one that he had already exploited in *The Great Wave*. He added a flock of swallows that appears to materialize from the crest of the wave. We are able to glimpse Fuji's peak and the tops of pine trees over the turbid water. Like *The Great Wave* this image continues to enjoy a long afterlife. Hiroshige later adapted the design in his series *Thirty-six Views of Mount Fuji* (1858). It was the inspiration for a Royal Copenhagen plate, which was subsequently copied by the Hirado kilns in western Japan.

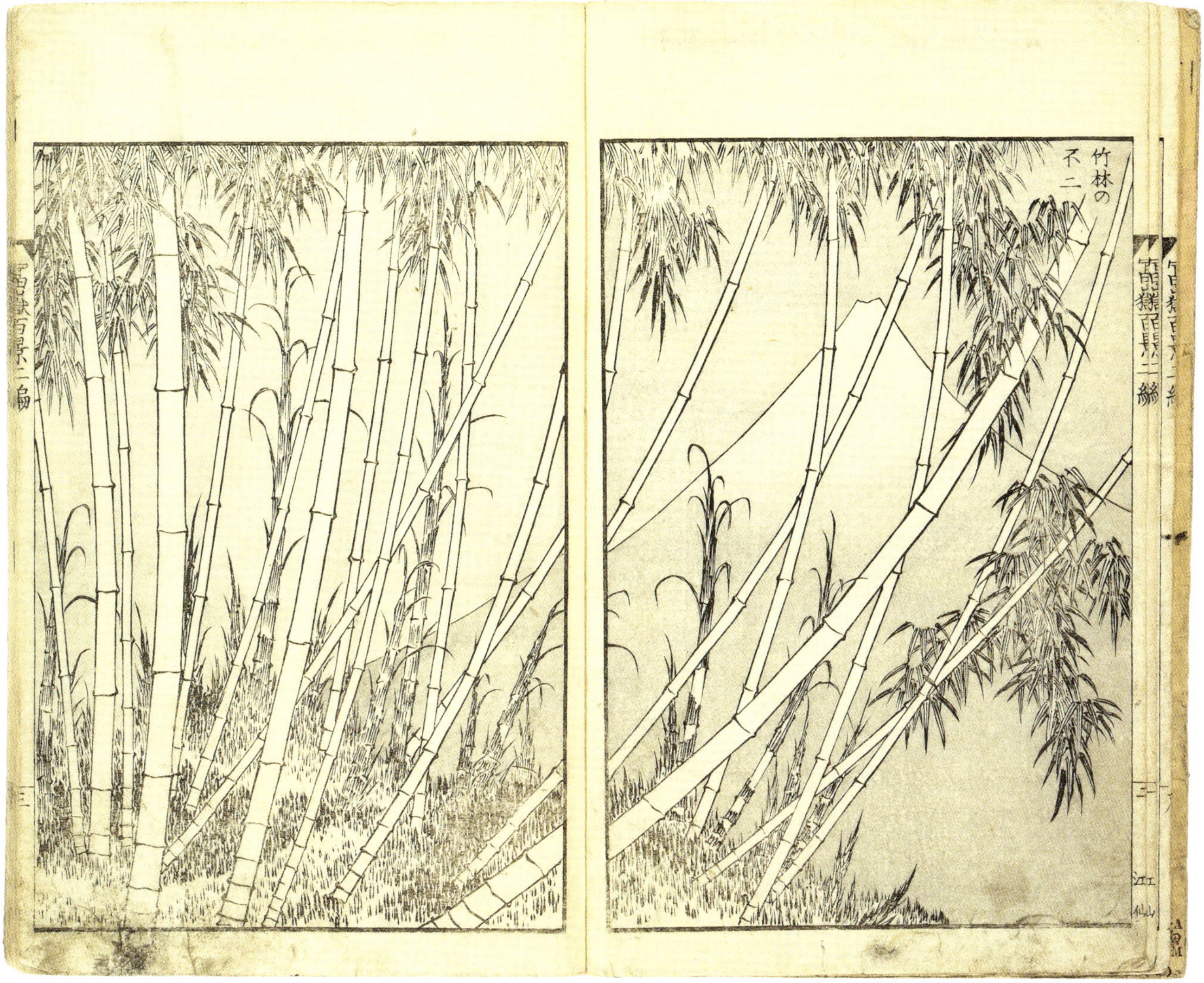

Fuji through a Bamboo Forest depicts the mountain through a thicket of
bamboo (ill. p. 83 top). It is this design that inspired *Mont Fuji Vase* (1878) by
the French crystal manufacturer Baccarat (ill. p. 83 bottom). By layering new
spring shoots with more mature culms Hokusai juxtaposes the effervescence of
the seasonal cycle with Fuji's steady, immortal presence. The graceful bending
of forms echoes the contours of the mountain's cone shape. One can almost hear
the soft rustling of leaves as they sway in the breeze.

Fuji over Torigoe (*c.* 1849), from the final, later volume, shows Japan's holy
mountain as if seen from the observatory on Torigoe Hill, Asakusa. In 1782, the
shogunate had established the site in order to make astronomical and meteoro-
logical measurements for devising the Japanese calendar. As the observatory was
relocated from Torigoe to Kudanzaka in 1842, Hokusai presumably completed
the design before then.

The device at the centre is a model of the terrestrial sphere called a *kantengi*.
Hokusai's enduring curiosity in the Western sciences and the elegant geometry of
the instrument's interlocking rings representing the horizon, meridian, equator

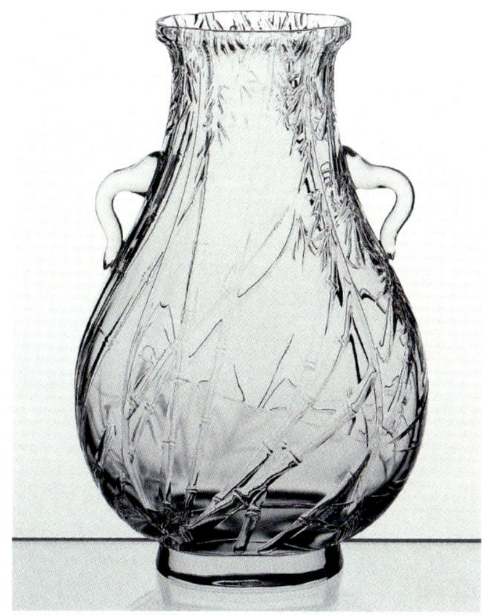

Mont Fuji Vase
Created for the Universal Exhibition, Paris 1878
Inspired by Hokusai engraving
Clear crystal, cut engraved decoration
(intaglio), height 29 cm (11½ in.)
Baccarat, Heritage Collection

and four displacements, would have made the *kantengi* an appealing subject to him. His depiction of the instrument is fairly consistent with diagrams in the *Compendium of the Kansei Calendar* (*Kansei rekisho*, *c.* 1844) by Shibukawa Kagesuke (1787–1856), the principal calendrical astronomer to the shogun at the time. A brilliant scholar of Western astronomy, Kagesuke's research and translations of Dutch treatises were the foundation for important 19th-century calendar reforms. In Hokusai's image, an astronomer – perhaps Kagesuke – gazes out from the observatory, not into the heavens but rather at the celestial peak of Mount Fuji.

Hokusai's last major print series was *One Hundred Poems Explained by the Nurse* (*Hyakunin isshu uba ga etoki*, *c.* 1835/36). The series consists of 27 prints, vividly coloured and in *ōban* format, but an additional 64 designs are known through Hokusai's hand-drawn drafts, printing proofs and 19th-century European reproductions of now lost pieces. Nishimuraya Yohachi released the first five designs earlier than the rest, perhaps due to financial difficulties associated with the Tenpō crisis of 1835/36, and passed the series onto another publisher as he had done following the first two volumes of *One Hundred Views of Mount Fuji*. Iseya Sanjirō subsequently issued 22 more designs before shelving the project. It is difficult to say for certain why the series was abandoned. It may have been that in the difficult economic climate, the bookish theme failed to appeal to the print-buying public. Hokusai's prints may have also suffered from competition with works by rival artists, such as Hiroshige, whose star was rising in the 1830s. It is also possible that Hokusai's personal circumstances may have prevented the series' completion.

The series is based on the premise of courtly poems' interpretations from the classic anthology *One Hundred Poems by One Hundred Poets* (*Hyakunin isshu*), as told by an old woman or wet nurse of limited education. Compiled in 1235 by the courtier Fujiwara no Teika (1162–1241), the poems are *waka*, a form usually comprising 31 syllables arranged in five alternating lines of five and seven syllables each, ending on two lines with seven syllables. By Hokusai's time the poems

Chūnagon Yakamochi, *c.* 1835/36
From the series *One Hundred Poems Explained by the Nurse*
Published by Nishimuraya Yohachi
Colour woodblock print, *ōban*,
25.5 x 37.8 cm (10 x 15 in.)
Honolulu Museum of Art,
Gift of James A. Michener, 1991

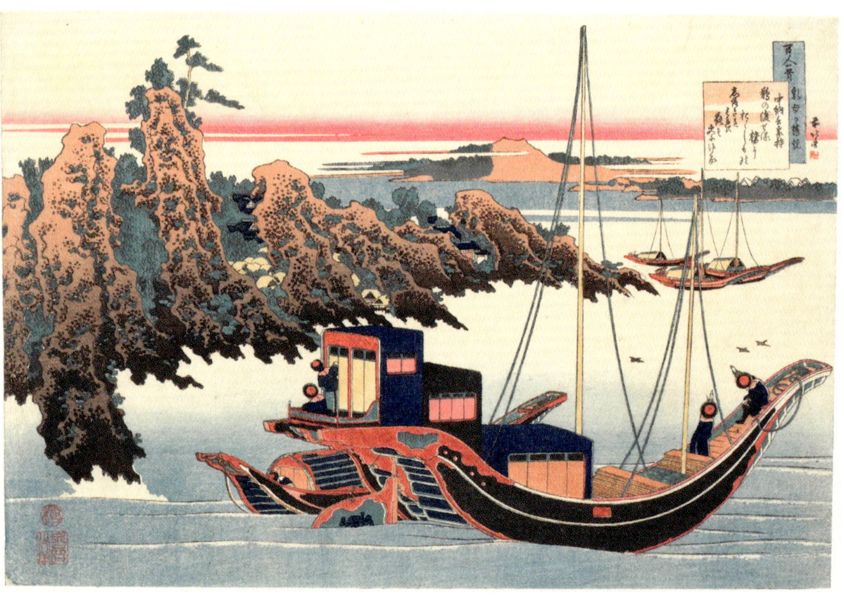

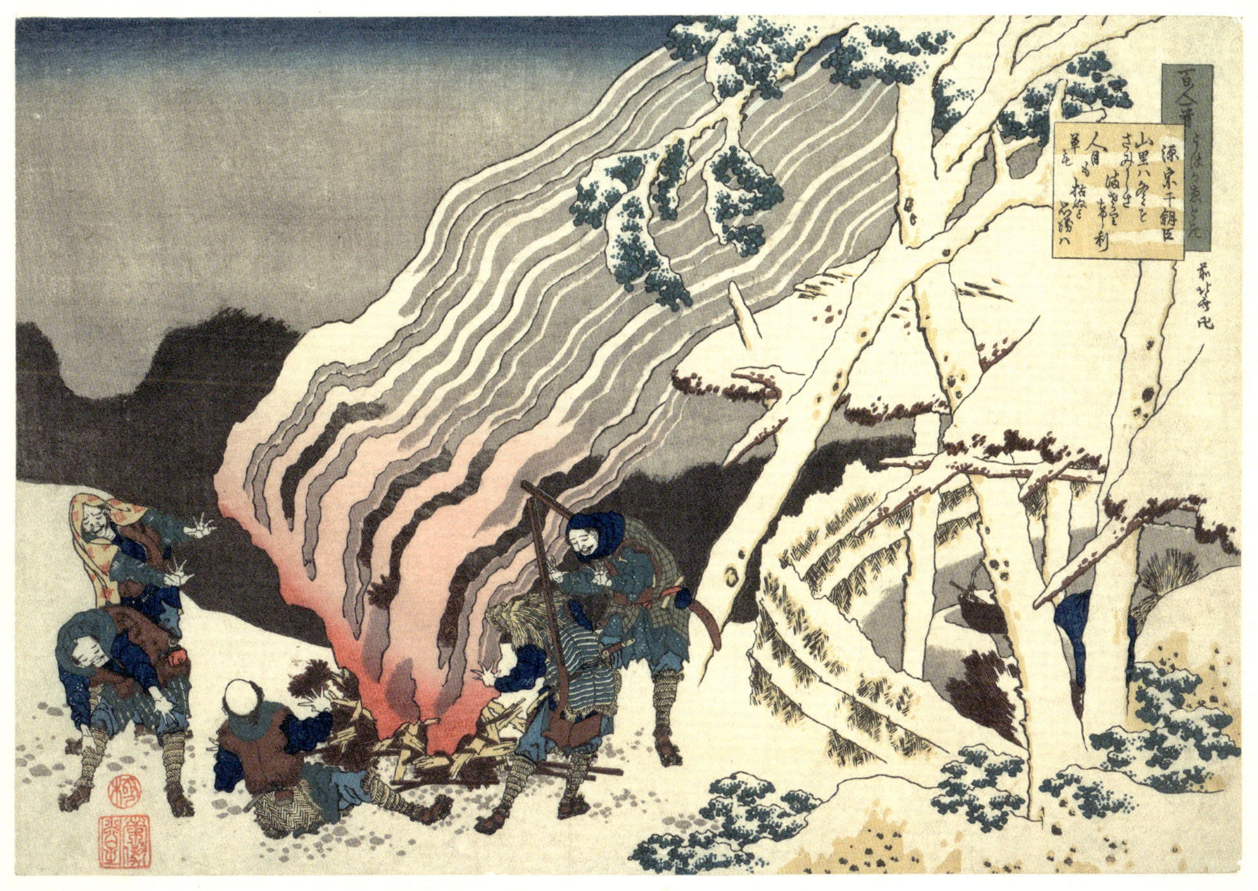

Minamoto no Muneyuki ason, c. 1835/36
From the series *One Hundred Poems
Explained by the Nurse*
Published by Nishimuraya Yohachi
Colour woodblock print, *ōban*,
25.1 x 36.8 cm (10 x 14½ in.)
New York, The Metropolitan Museum of Art,
The Howard Mansfield Collection,
Rogers Fund, 1936

would have been familiar even to commoners, thanks to the card-matching game *utagaruta* customarily played on New Year's Day. However, the various nuances intended by their authors may have been lost on the average person.

The nurse's guileless, at times comical, retellings of the poems were an ideal device for Hokusai to create imaginative designs, whose connections to the poems are elaborate and open to interpretation.

The print *Chūnagon Yakamochi* represents the sixth poem in Fujiwara no Teika's anthology, penned by Middle counsellor (*chūnagon*) Yakamochi (718–785; ill. p. 84). The poem reads:

When I see the whiteness
of the frost that lies on the bridge the magpies spread,
Then do I know, indeed,
that the night has deepened.[5]

Yakamochi likens the magpie bridge to separated lovers of Japanese folklore, the weaver princess and the cow herder (personifications of the stars Altair and Vega respectively), who travel across the Milky Way from their respective places of banishment and meet on the seventh day of the seventh month on a bridge leading into the imperial palace. Meanwhile, Hokusai's fantastical design of an imaginary Chinese setting, complete with ornate pleasure boats and a peninsula of grotesque rock formations, seems to have little connection to the clandestine meeting described by the poem. We thus see how Hokusai's reinterpretations of

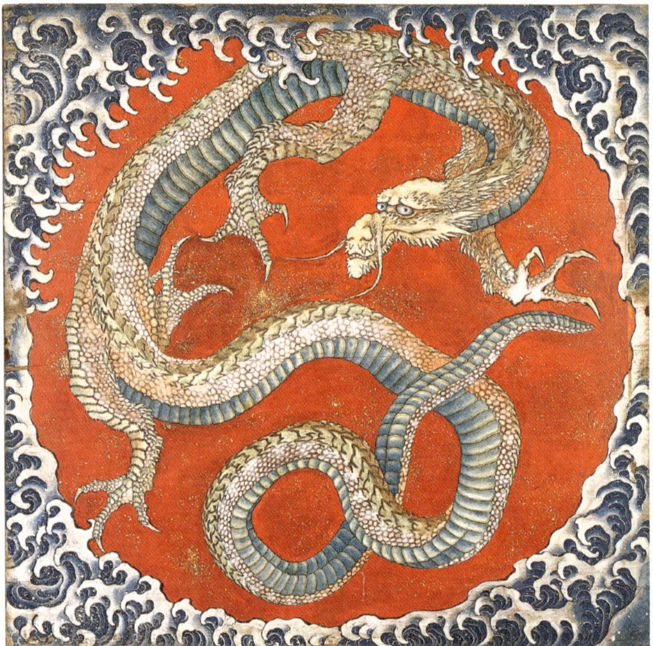
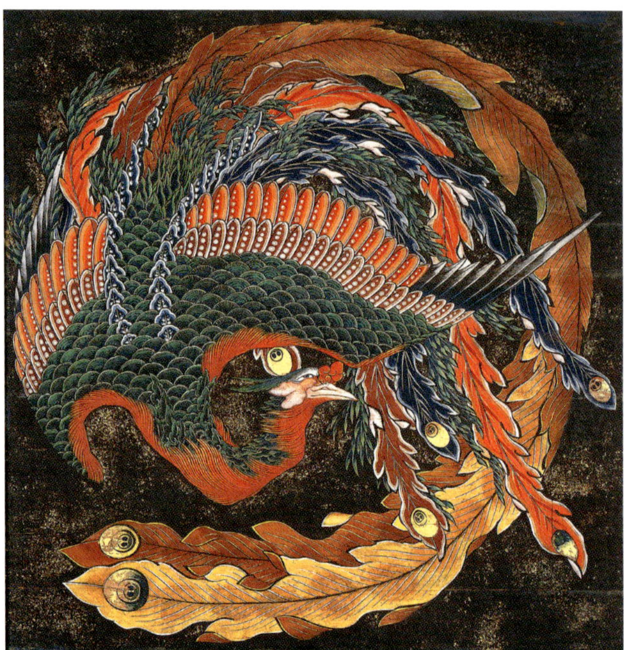

Dragon and Phoenix, *c.* 1844
Ceiling paintings on the Obuse
Higashimachi Ward festival floats
Painting on panel,
each 123.1 x 126.7 cm (48½ x 50 in.)
Obuse, Hokusai-kan Museum

the classics through the untutored lens of an old woman offer an irreverent perspective on Japan's cultural pillars.

The print *Minamoto no Muneyuki ason* features a poem by the Heian period nobleman (*ason*) of that name, the 28th poem of the classic anthology (ill. p. 85):

In the mountain village,
It is in winter that my loneliness
increases most,
when I think how both have dried up,
the grasses and people's visits.[6]

Rather than a scene of winter desolation, however, Hokusai depicted a group of jovial hunters basking in the warmth of a blazing fire by their camp. The two standing figures on the right carry matchlock rifles slung over their shoulders. Ribbons of flame and smoke cut a dramatic diagonal swath across the composition. The silhouetted form of the mountains in the background is printed with no outline and a soft, feathered edge, as if blurred by the frosty night air.

Hokusai's final major illustrated book project was a trilogy of warrior books *Picture Book of the Warrior Vanguard in Japan and China* (*Wakan ehon sakigake*), *Picture Book of the Stirrups of Musashi* (*Ehon Musashi abumi*), and *Picture Book of the Pride of Japan and China* (*Ehon wakan no homare*). The first two volumes were published collaboratively in 1836 by six publishers in Edo, Osaka and Nagoya. The third volume's illustrations were probably completed by 1836, but the project was passed on to a new syndicate of publishers that would not release it until after Hokusai's death in 1850.

The books were a compilation of warrior portraits from Chinese and Japanese lore, with short captions explaining their subjects. Many of the scenes were designed as striking vertical diptychs spanning two open pages, in such a way that the viewer had to turn the book 90 degrees counterclockwise to view them properly. The images' clear linear style makes them more visually legible than the

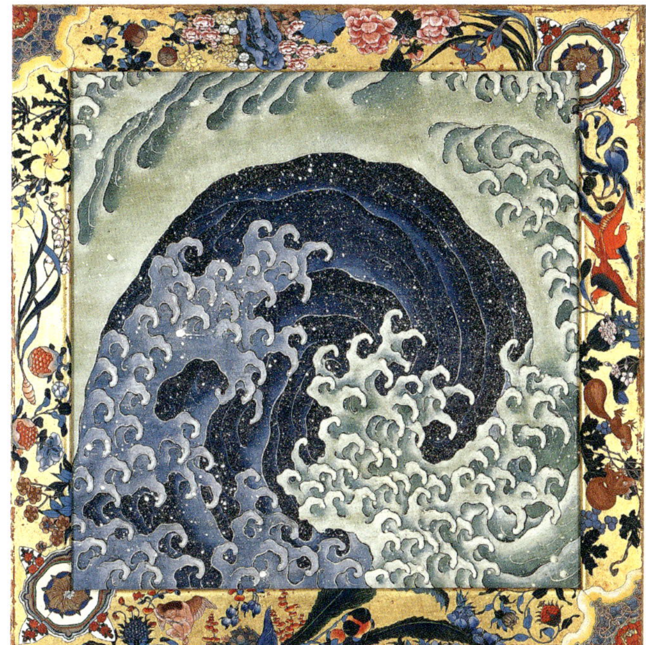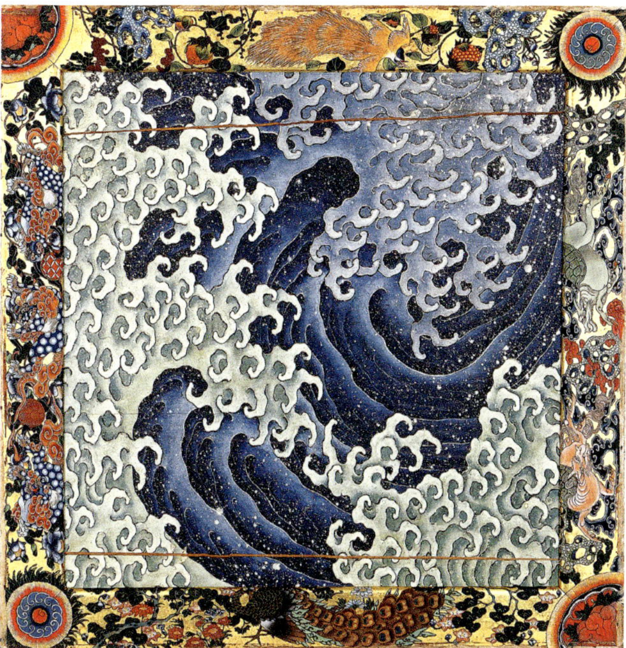

more tonal, sometimes cluttered illustrations Hokusai executed for *yomihon* in the 1810s. One design depicts the legendary warrior monk Musashibō Benkei (1155–1189) in his youth, when he went by the childhood name Oniwakamaru ("demon boy"; ill. p. 81). Benkei, who possessed otherworldly strength, is shown hauling a three-tonne bell he has stolen mischievously from Mii Temple (in present day Shiga prefecture), up the precipitous incline of Mount Hiei. According to legend, when the bell, famed for its exquisite tone, refused to ring for him, Benkei hurled it back down the mountain to its rightful home.

Painting with a Brush Unchanged

The Manji period is also distinguished by Hokusai's prolific output of paintings, many considered to be pinnacle achievements of his career. As he wrote in the postscript to *New Designs for Craftsmen* (*Shin hinagata*, 1836):

> When one is old, one's skill quickly declines. Fortunately, however, I am not bound by these long-established ways of thinking. In making my pictures, I may regret last year or even be ashamed of what I did yesterday, but I continue on my own path, alone. Now I am close to 80, but the strength of my brush is unchanged – it is like that of a young man's. Therefore, I ask for the perseverance to live to 100, to keep trying until I reach what I judge as perfection.

In 1839, Hokusai painted the enigmatic still life *Drying Watermelon Rind*, depicting a cleaver resting on a halved fruit with shaved coils of rind drying from a rope above (ill. p. 88). The sharp realism, the strange forms of the watermelon rinds and the unattended knife give the scene an eerie quality, anticipating the disquieting still life paintings of the oil painter Takahashi Yuichi (1828–1894). However, this work is believed to relate to Kikkōden, the "Festival to Plead for Skills", during which young women would appeal to the gods for prowess in weaving and needlework. A precursor to the Tanabata festival, Kikkōden marked the iconic, brief, celestial meeting of the earlier-mentioned

Attributed to Hokusai
Feminine and Masculine Waves, *c.* 1845
Ceiling paintings on the Obuse
Kanmachi Ward festival floats
Painting on panel,
each 118.0 x 118.5 cm (46½ x 46¾ in.)
Obuse, Hokusai-kan Museum

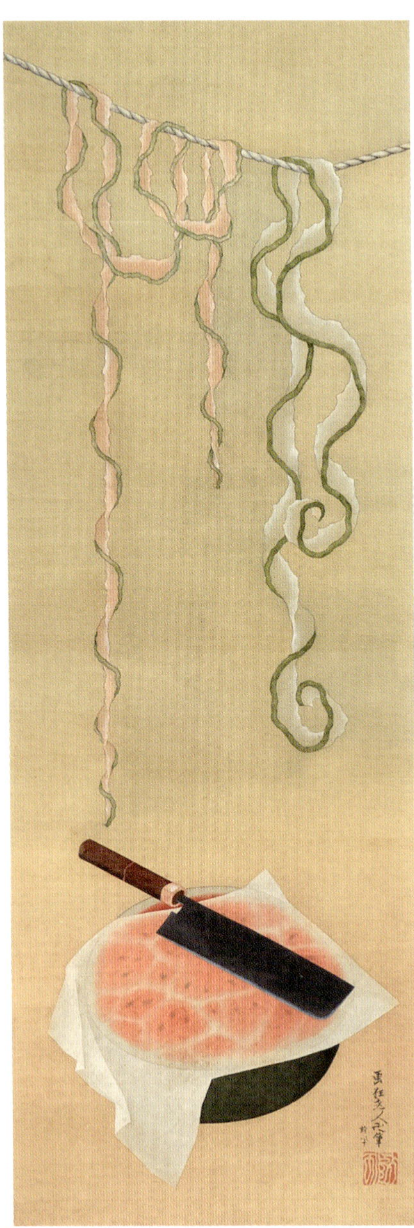

Drying Watermelon Rind, 1839
Hanging scroll, colour on silk,
86.7 x 29.7 cm (34¼ x 11¾ in.)
Tokyo, The Museum of the Imperial
Collections/Sannomaru Shōzōkan

herdsman, representing Altair, and his lover the weaver maiden or the star Vega. In premodern Japan and China, it was customary to assemble offerings including sewing needles, coloured thread and fruit such as watermelon on the night of the festival.

Around 1844, Hokusai began work on a commission in Obuse (present-day Nagano prefecture) requested by Takai Kōzan (1806–1883), a wealthy local merchant and amateur painter who had been briefly a student of Hokusai. Among the works he created in the region are four paintings on the ceilings of floats for the Higashimachi (ills. p. 86) and Kanmachi festivals (ills. p. 87). He also created the design for *Phoenix Staring in Eight Directions*, measuring almost 34 square metres, for the ceiling of Ganshōin Temple, although the finished work was probably executed by local artists following Hokusai's instructions. The painting's name refers to the phoenix's eyes, which appear to follow the viewer around the space below.

Another splendid artwork in an unusual format came in 1844: a gift cover or *fukusa* decorated with a prancing *shishi* or Chinese guardian lion, in ink with a colourful border of peonies (ill. p. 89). Featured in Buddhist literature, the combination of these two motifs was highly auspicious. The *shishi* was a familiar subject to Hokusai. Between 1842 and 1843, he painted the mythological creatures every day as part of a "daily exorcism" performed to attract good fortune and ward off disaster.

In 1847, when he was 88 years old, Hokusai painted the semi-historical subject *Minamoto no Yorimasa Aiming an Arrow* (ill. p. 80). The epic warrior narrative *Tales of the Heike* (*Heike monogatari*, 1371) describes an episode in which the emperor is tormented by a bird-beast with the head of a monkey, the body of a racoon dog (*tanuki*), limbs of a tiger, a viper's tail and the bewitching cry of a thrush hovering night after night in a dark cloud over the imperial palace. Priests were summoned to chant sutras and perform exorcisms but to no avail. At last Minamoto no Yorimasa (1104–1180), a distinguished archer, was called and felled the creature in a single shot. For his deeds, the emperor rewarded Yorimasa with a sword. Many *ukiyo-e* images show Yorimasa victorious, but Hokusai depicted the archer as he narrows his eyes, draws his bow and takes aim into the dark cloud. Needles of red light suggest the beast's malevolent spirit. Using red pigment, Hokusai delineated Yorimasa's tightly clenched muscles and sinews to endow the scene with palpable tension. He impressed a seal reading "ten thousand" in the lower left corner – an expression of his hopes for longevity. The same seal appears in the following two paintings.

With *Ducks in a Stream* (1847), Hokusai presented yet another testament to his ability to imaginatively reinterpret established themes and genres (ill. p. 94). In East Asian art and literature, a mated pair of ducks is a prevalent symbol of marital fidelity; works depicting such a duo might be presented to newlyweds to wish them a happy life together. Here, Hokusai wanders from the well-worn poetic image and opts for a more obscure theme, choosing to paint migratory water birds instead – in effect, such birds evoke the bittersweet change of the seasons. Hokusai's painting depicts two male mallards, one negotiating the swift current on the surface, the other diving beneath. Red maple leaves drift, indicating that it will soon be time for the birds to fly south. The fine detail and jewel-like colours with which Hokusai rendered the birds' plumage is set off by the largely monochromatic background. The graphic rendering of the water surface – seen earlier in such artworks as his print *Turtles* (ill. p. 76) – and the shifting perspective, whereby we seem to look sharply down at one bird and laterally at the other, disrupt the sense of naturalism. Hokusai's restless creativity continued up until shortly before his death. In the first month of 1848, he published what would be his last painting manual, *Picture Book: The Essence of Colouring*, which professes to lay out the principles and techniques of his vocation.

The following year, only months before he passed away, Hokusai painted one of his most beloved works, *Li Bai Admiring a Waterfall* (ill. p. 91). The celebrated poem "Viewing the Waterfall at Mount Lu", of the Tang dynasty poet Li Bai, was a popular theme in both Chinese and Japanese painting, and Hokusai had included a print on the subject in his series *True Mirrors of Chinese and Japanese Poems* some 15 years earlier. Here, his dramatic treatment of the falling water as columns of ink wash and blue extending almost the entire height of the image, the delicate spray of foam at its base, and the child attendant clinging to the poet as he contemplates this force of nature from below, make this a striking and charming painting.

That same year Hokusai painted *Tiger in Snow* (1849). With its green eyes narrowed, whiskers erect and ears flattened, the feline moves purposefully through a wintry landscape. The tiger's undulating body and the lack of ground lines bring to mind a dragon in flight (ill. p. 90). Although Hokusai used tonal modelling and finely brushed detail to give form and texture to the animal's body, he was more concerned with conveying the feisty character of his grinning

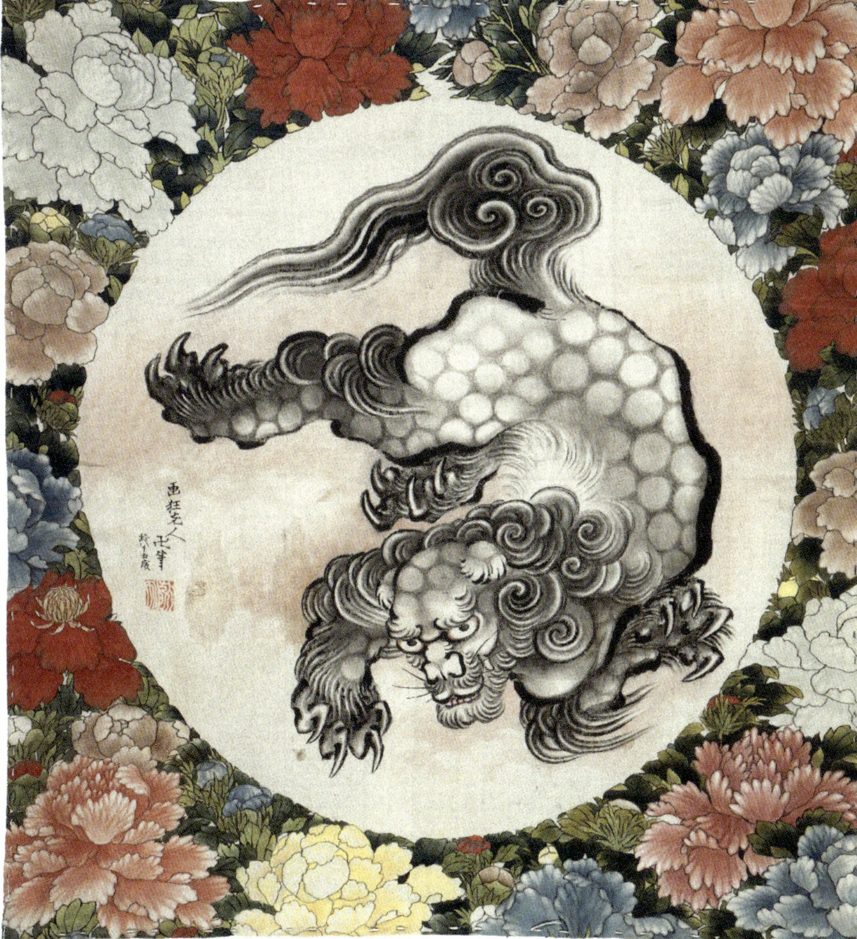

Gift cover with Chinese lion, 1844
Silk plain weave with ink and colour,
71.6 x 66.6 cm (28¼ x 26¼ in.)
Boston, Museum of Fine Arts,
William Sturgis Bigelow Collection

beast than formal realism. It has been suggested that Hokusai, indefatigable in his advanced age, painted the tiger as a self-portrait; while there is no tangible evidence of this, there is no doubt that the animal embodies the fierce will and tenacious spirit that defined the artist, even in the winter of his life.

Hokusai's Death

Hokusai died on the 18th day of the fourth month (10 May) of 1849 at the age of 90. The following day, a cortege of over 100 people escorted his remains to the site of the family grave at Seikyōji Temple, Asakusa. It seems he took his leave from the world with great reluctance, believing his life's work unfinished. As he felt death was near he is said to have lamented, "If only heaven would give me another ten years… If heaven would give me just five more years, I might become a true painter."

Of his immediate students, only Yashima Gakutei outlived his master by more than a few months. His daughter Ōi retreated into obscurity, perhaps taking to the road as a wandering hermit. Hokusai's legacy, however, lived on in other ways. His drawing manuals and prints were circulated on an unprecedented scale both within Japan and beyond its borders.

Tiger in Snow, 1849
Hanging scroll, ink and colour on silk,
39.4 x 50.5 cm (15 ⅝ x 20 in.)
Private collection

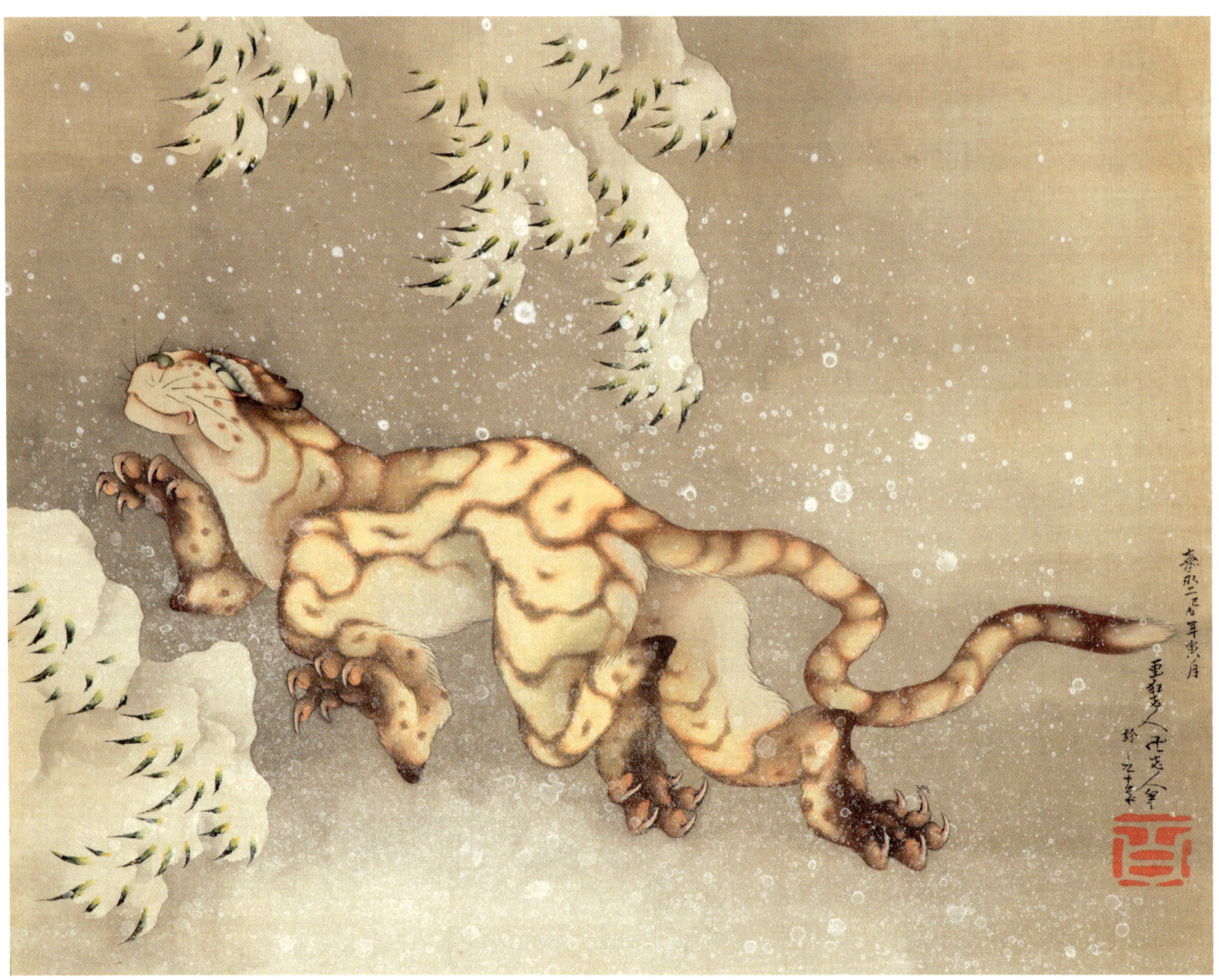

Following his death Hokusai was the focus of several exhibitions in the West. The first exhibition dedicated to him – and the first ever devoted to a single Japanese artist – was held at the Fine Arts Society in London in 1890. This was followed in 1893 by *Hokusai and His School*, organized by Ernest Fenollosa (1853–1908) at the Museum of Fine Arts in Boston. Studies of Hokusai's work were already being proliferated in English, French and German.

It may have taken longer for Hokusai to be accorded a place in the art-historical canon of his own country; however, one must bear in mind that art history and criticism were still emerging disciplines during the *Japonisme* booms in the West. Because of its low-brow, commercial character, *ukiyo-e* itself only gradually gained acceptance as a legitimate field of scholarly study, but even so, Iijima Kyoshin published his biography of Hokusai in 1893, with Yone Noguchi's (1875–1947) monograph on the artist following in 1925. The collection of the Japan Ukiyo-e Museum in Matsumoto, which contains many prints and paintings by Hokusai, was established by the paper wholesaler Yoshitaka Sakai (1810–1869). The collection of the Ōta Memorial Museum of Art began in the 1920s, when the businessman Ōta Seizō (1893–1977) began collecting works by Hokusai and other *ukiyo-e* artists.

Today, Hokusai is Japan's most celebrated and internationally known artist. More than a century and a half since his death, his images continue to arrest viewers and inspire artists across all disciplines and all over the world. Like his *Great Wave*, holding viewers in perpetual awe, Hokusai's brilliant legacy shows no sign of ever diminishing.

Li Bai Admiring a Waterfall, 1849
Hanging scroll, ink and colour on silk,
93.4 x 30 cm (36⅞ x 11⅞ in.)
Boston, Museum of Fine Arts Boston,
William Sturgis Bigelow Collection

いくら歳
[署名] 筆

1760 Born Kawamura Tokitarō in the eastern outskirts of the city of Edo. At around four years of age he is adopted into the Nakajima family, mirror smiths to the shogun, and is given the name Tetsuzō.

1774 First begins work as a printing block carver.

1779 Enters the studio of Katsukawa Shunshō and has his first print designs published under the name Shunrō. As a member of Shunshō's studio, Hokusai designs portraits of actors, sumo wrestlers and beauties in the Katsukawa school style, and produces illustrations for works of popular fiction.

1785/86 Designs illustrations for books and other works under the name Gunbatei, thereby suggesting a temporary rift with the Katsukawa studio.

1792 Katsukawa Shunshō dies in the 12th month.

1793 Hokusai begins designing *surimono*, privately published programmes, calendars and other deluxe printed matter. His first wife dies, leaving Hokusai with their two daughters and a son.

1794 Adopts the name Sōri, after the Rinpa artist Tawaraya Sōri. Hokusai's first designs under this name, marked by their elegant, decorative and whimsical tendencies appear the following year. Designs for *surimono* and poetry albums comprise the bulk of his activity during this stage of his career. Prints bearing the signature "Tōshūsai Sharaku" begin to appear on the market during an apparent lull in his productivity, leading some to believe that they were created by Hokusai; however, there is little evidence to support this.

1797 Hokusai marries his second wife Koto.

1798 Bequeaths the name Sōri to a student and begins signing work as Hokusai Tokimasa,

also read "Hokusai Tatsumasa". Under this new name he mainly produces illustrated poetry albums and *surimono*, along with a few of paintings including the diptych *Chinese Immortal Yuzhi and Her Dragon* (ills. p. 21). Hokusai also designs commercially published prints under the name Kakō.

c. 1800 *Fine Views of the Eastern Capital at a Glance* is published (ill. p. 26 top). Hokusai's third daughter and future artistic collaborator Ōi is born. Over the next few years, Hokusai designs several series of landscapes that mimic Dutch engravings.

1801 This year the first known images, signed "Hokusai, the fellow mad about painting" (Gakyōjin Hokusai), are published.

1802 Hokusai's anthology *Picture Book of Amusements in the Eastern Capital* is published (ill. p. 26 bottom).

1803 Hokusai's first contribution to the genre of full-length, serialized novels called *yomihon* is published by Maruya Jin'emon and others: *Ancient Curious Tales Left by Fishermen*, written by Ryūgasō Hirozumi.

1804 *Kyōka Picture Book: Mountains upon Mountains* is published (ill. p. 27). In the fourth month Hokusai paints a monumental half-length portrait of Bodhidharma (Daruma), covering an area of 120 *tatami* mats (almost 200 square metres) at Edo's Gokokuji Temple.

c. 1805 *Picture Book: Both Banks of the Sumida River at a Glance* is published (ills. pp. 28, 29) and designs bearing the signature "Katsushika Hokusai" first appear. Hokusai shifts his focus to producing illustrations for *yomihon* until around 1812.

1806 Around this time Hokusai paints *Gathering Shellfish at Low Tide* (ill. p. 32).

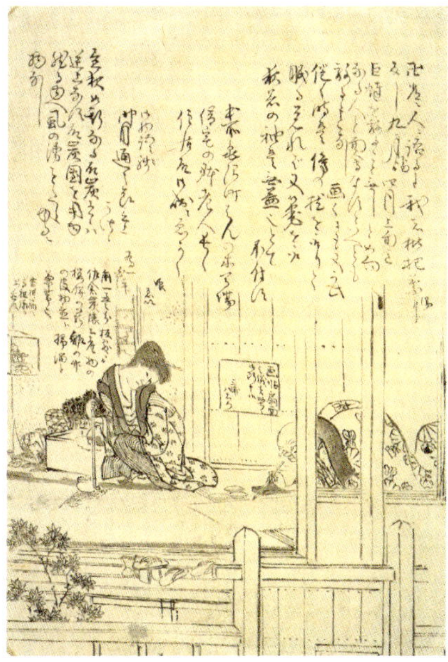

Tsuyuki Kōshō
Hokusai and Eijo (Ōi) in their lodgings,
before 1893
Ink on paper, 25 x 17.5 cm (10 x 7 in.)
Tokyo, National Diet Library

Self-portrait, aged eighty-three, 1842
Drawing in a letter, ink on paper,
26.9 x 16.9 cm (10½ x 6¾ in.)
Leiden, Museum Volkenkunde

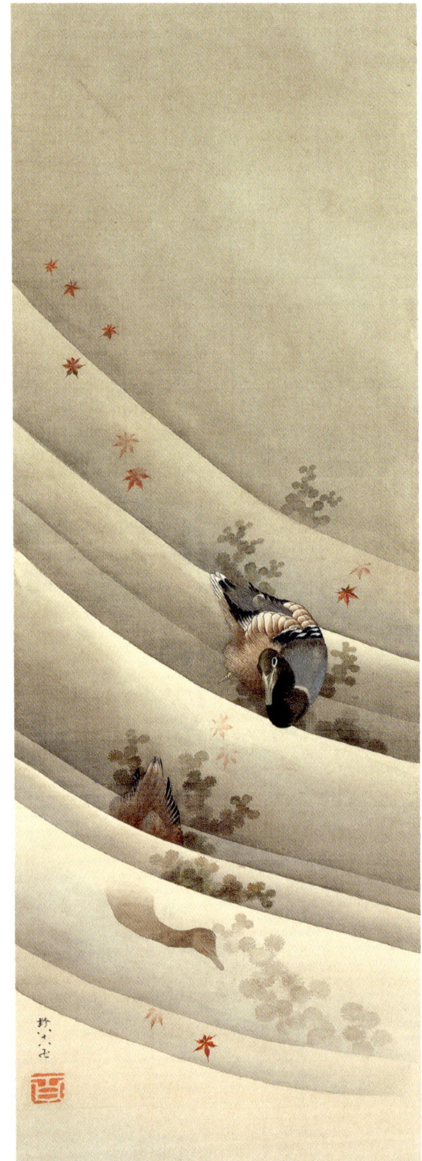

Ducks in a Stream, 1847
Hanging scroll, ink and colour on silk,
111 x 40 cm (43¾ x 15¾ in.)
London, British Museum

Dragon Rising above Mount Fuji, 1849
Hanging scroll, ink and slight colour on silk,
95.5 x 36.2 cm (37½ x 14¼ in.)
Obuse, Hokusai-kan Museum

1807/08 Hokusai allegedly paints *Maple Leaves on the Tatsu River* for the shogun Tokugawa Ienari by dipping a chicken's foot in red paint and allowing it to run across a sheet of paper. The warrior saga *Snow in the Garden* by Takizawa Bakin and Ryūtei Tanehiko's ghost story *The Stars on a Frosty Night*, both featuring illustrations by Hokusai, are published (ills. pp. 34, 35).

1810 Hokusai publishes his first drawing manual (*edehon*) *Foolish Ono's Nonsense Picture Dictionary*. From 1812, he devotes his energies to producing drawing manuals.

1811 Celebrating the completion of the *yomihon Strange Tales of the Crescent Moon*, Hokusai paints *Tametomo and the Inhabitants of Onigashima Island* (ill. pp. 38/39).

1812 From the autumn of 1812, Hokusai spends six months in Nagoya at the home of his student Gekkōtei Bokusen. During this time he makes around 300 sketches which form the basis of the first instalments of *Random Drawings by Hokusai* (*Hokusai manga*; ills. pp. 23, 25, 40, 44, 47 top right).

1813 Hokusai adopts the name Taito.

1814 In the first month of 1814, the first of 15 volumes of *Hokusai manga* is published. The final three volumes are released posthumously and the last is, today, considered spurious. Around the third month, work bearing the name Taito begins to appear. Around the same time Hokusai creates erotic images for the book *Pine Seedlings on the First Rat Day* (ill. p. 24).

1816 The drawing manual *Illustrated Album of Three Styles of Painting*, a collaboration between Hokusai and his students Bokusen, Hokuun, Hokusen und Hokkei is issued in the spring (ill. p. 47 top left).

1817 On the fifth day of the tenth month Hokusai paints a portrait of the Zen Buddhist patriarch Bodhidharma (Daruma), almost 20 metres high, on a 200-square-metre quilt of paper at Honganji Betsuin Temple in Nagoya.

1820 At the age of 60 years Hokusai begins to sign works with the name "Iitsu", meaning "one year old again".

1821 Hokusai's *surimono* series *Thirty-six Genroku Poets Matched with Shells* is published (ill. p. 50).

1822 Another *surimono* series *A Set of Horses* is published (ill. p. 51). Hokusai is commissioned by Director Jan Cock Blomhoff of the Dutch East India Company and merchant Johannes van Overmeer Fischer to complete a set of paintings by their return trip to Edo four years later.

1823 In the first month *Illustrated Album of One-Brushstroke Drawings* is published by Eirakuya Tōshirō (ill. p. 46). In the fifth month a sourcebook for craftsmen *Modern Designs for Combs and Tobacco Pipes* is issued (ill. p. 45 bottom).

1826 When the Dutch return to Edo, the German surgeon Philipp Franz von Siebold commissions Hokusai to execute another group of paintings.

***c.* 1828** Hokusai's second wife dies. Ōi leaves her husband, artist Minamisawa Tōmei, and returns to her father's household.

***c.* 1830** Publication of *Thirty-six Views of Mount Fuji* begins (ills. pp. 42/43, 55, 59, 60, 61 top, 64). New designs are issued until as late as 1834.

***c.* 1831/32** *One Hundred Ghost Stories* is released (ills. pp. 70, 71).

1832/33 The series *Eight Views of the Ryūkyū Islands* (ills. pp. 66, 67) and *A Tour of Waterfalls in Various Provinces* (ills. pp. 4, 48) are published. Several images from *Hokusai manga* are reproduced in Siebold's illustrated *Nippon: A Descriptive Archive of Japan* (1832–1852; ills. pp. 45 top, 56).

1833/34 The series *One Thousand Pictures of the Ocean* (ills. pp. 62/63, 65), *Large Flowers* (ills. pp. 72 bottom, 73), *True Mirrors of Chinese and Japanese Poems* (ills. pp. 74, 75) and *Unusual Views of Famous Bridges in Various Provinces* (ills. pp. 68, 69) are published.

1834 Hokusai changes his name to "Gakyō rōjin Manji", meaning "old man mad about painting", followed by a left-facing swastika, an auspicious Buddhist symbol in East Asian culture. The untitled series today known as *Small Flowers* is published (ill. p. 77) and in the third month the first volume of *One Hundred Views of Mount Fuji* is released.

***c.* 1835/36** The series *One Hundred Poems Explained by the Nurse* is published (ills. pp. 84, 85).

1836 The book *New Designs for Craftsmen* is published.

1839 Hokusai paints *Drying Watermelon Rind* (ill. p. 88).

***c.* 1844/45** He undertakes a group of commissions from the wealthy merchant Takai Kōzan in Obuse (present-day Nagano prefecture), including ceiling paintings for festival floats and the Ganshōin Temple (ills. pp. 86, 87).

1847 Among other major works Hokusai paints *Minamoto no Yorimasa Aiming an Arrow* (ill. p. 80) and *Ducks in a Stream* (ill. p. 94).

1849 Hokusai paints *Tiger in Snow* (ill. p. 90) and *Li Bai Admiring a Waterfall* (ill. p. 91). He passes away in the fourth month at the age of 90 years.

Selected Bibliography

Calza, Gian Carlo, *Hokusai*, London 2010

Carpenter, John T. (ed.), *Hokusai and His Age: Ukiyo-e Painting, Printmaking and Book Illustration in Late Edo Japan*, Amsterdam 2005

Clark, Timothy (ed.), *Hokusai: Beyond the Great Wave*, exhibition catalogue, London, British Museum, London 2017

Forrer, Matthi (ed.), *Hokusai: Prints and Drawings*, exhibition catalogue, London, Royal Academy of Arts, Munich 1991

Forrer, Matthi, *Hokusai*, Munich 2010

Guth, Christine M. E., *Hokusai's Great Wave: Biography of a Global Icon*, Honolulu 2015

Hiller, Jack Ronald, *The Art of Hokusai in Book Illustration*, London and Berkeley, CA, 1980

Iijima Kyoshin and Jūzō Suzuki, *Katsushika Hokusai den*, Tokyo 1999

Kawakita Michiaki, *Modern Currents in Japanese Art*, translated and adapted by Charles S. Terry, New York 1974

Keyes, Roger S., *The Art of Surimono: Privately Published Japanese Woodblock Prints and Books in the Chester Beatty Library, Dublin*, London 1985

Keyes, Roger S. and Wilfred Lockwood, *Surimono from the Chester Beatty Collection*, Alexandria, VA, 1987

Keyes, Roger S., "The Dragon and the Goddess. Using Prints to Date, Identify and Illuminate Hokusai's Early Paintings", in: *Hokusai and His Age*, edited by John T. Carpenter, Amsterdam 2005, pp. 16–31

Kishi Akimasa, "Hokusai no 'Ryūkyū hakkei' ni tsuite", in: *Ukiyo-e geijutsu*, vol. 13, 1966, pp. 36–39

Kobayashi Tadashi, "The Real Hokusai: 'Artist Mad about Painting'", in: *Hokusai*, vol. 2, edited by Ann Yonemura, pp. 9–15

Kubota Kazuhiro, "The 'Surimono Artist' Hokusai in the Society of Edo Kyōka Poets", in: *Hokusai and His Age*, edited by John T. Carpenter, pp. 181–215

Mostow, Joshua S., *Pictures of the Heart: The Hyakunin Isshu in Word and Image*, Honolulu 1996

Nagata Seiji, *Katsushika Hokusai Nenpu*, Tokyo 1997

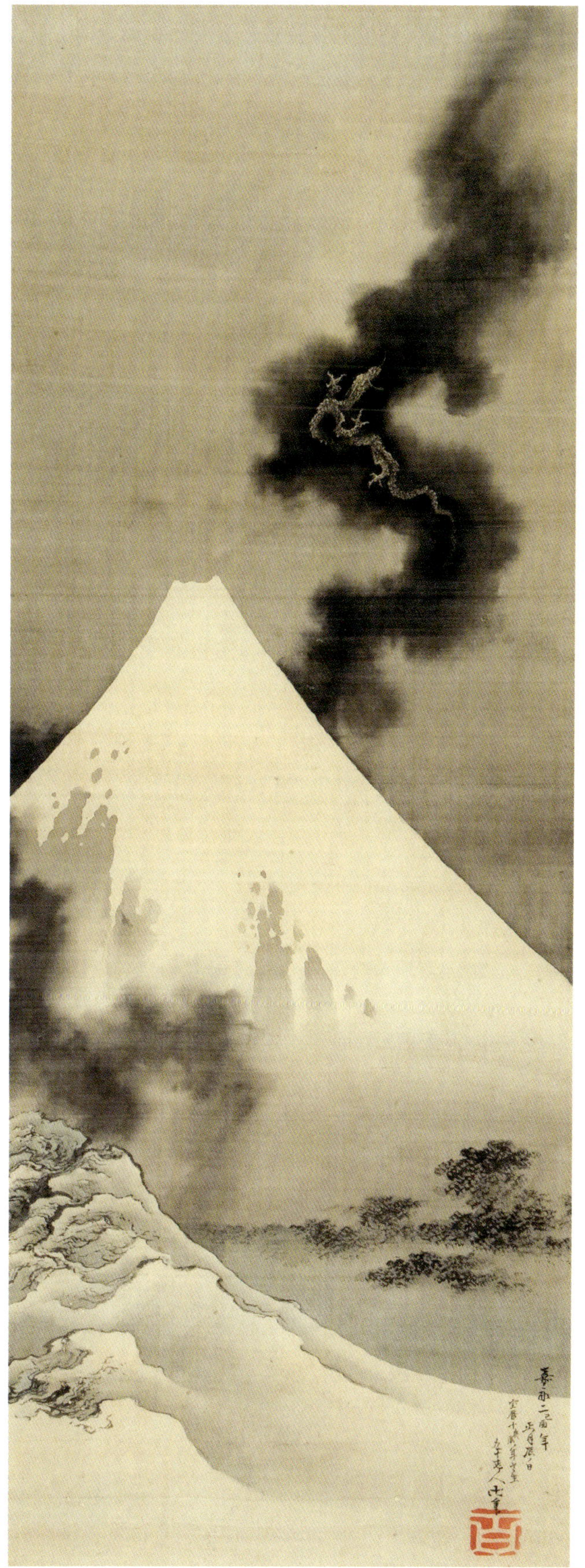

Nagata Seiji, "Hokusai's Artistic Career and Topics for Research", in: *Hokusai*, vol. 2, edited by Ann Yonemura, pp. 1–7

Sakai Nobuo, *Gakkyōjin Hokusai: Tanjō 250 ki'nen*, Rokusho vol. 2, Kyoto 2010

Schubert, Frank N. and Theresa L. Kraus, *The Whirlwind War: The United States Army in Operations Desert Shield and Desert Storm*, Washington, D.C., Center of Military History, United States Army, 1995

Smith, Henry, "Hokusai and the Blue Revolution in Edo Prints", in: *Hokusai and His Age*, edited by John T. Carpenter, pp. 234–269

Thompson, Sarah E., Joan Wright, and Philip Meredith, *Hokusai*, Boston 2015

Toby, Ronald, "The 'Indianness' of Iberia and Changing Japanese Iconographies of Prints", in: *Implicit Understandings: Observing, Reporting, and Reflecting on the Encounters Between Europeans and Other Peoples in the Early Modern Era*, edited by Stuart B. Schwartz, Cambridge 1994, pp. 323–352

Yip, Leo Shingchi, *China Reinterpreted: Staging the Other in Muromachi Noh Theater*, Lanham 2016

Yonemura, Ann, *Hokusai*, volumes one and two, exhibition catalogue, Washington, D.C., Freer Gallery of Art and Arthur M. Sackler Gallery, Smithsonian Institution, Washington 2006

Endnotes

1 Translation from Keyes 1987, p. 78.
2 Toby 1994, p. 342.
3 Translation from Yip 2016, p. 137.
4 Translation from Forrer 1991, cat. 64.
5 Translation from Mostow 1996, p. 158.
6 Ibid., p. 226.

Photo Credits

The publishers wish to thank the museums, private collections, archives, galleries and photographers who granted permission to reproduce works and gave support in the making of the book. In addition to the collections and museums named in the picture captions, we wish to credit the following:
© Baccarat: p. 83 b.; Bayerische Staatsbibliothek, Munich: p. 26 b.; Bibliothèque Nationale de France, Paris: p. 66 b.; bpk/The Art Institute of Chicago/Art Resource, NY: pp. 11, 37, 50; Collection Nationaal Museum van Wereldculturen, Leiden: pp. 45 t. [RV-5897-5], 52 [RV-1353-474], 53 [RV-1-4482k], 56 [RV-5897-6], 57 [RV-1-44820], 78 [RV-1-4448], 92 [RV 3513-1496]; Freer Gallery of Art and Arthur M. Sackler Gallery, Smithsonian Institute, Freer Study Collection, Washington, D.C.: pp. 24 [FSC-GR-780.4.1-3, vol 3, pp. 6–7], 28 [FSC-GR-780.230.1-3, vol 2, pp. 4–5], 29 [FSC-GR-780.230.1-3, vol 2, pp. 8–9]; Hagi Uragami Museum, Hagi: p. 22; Harvard Art Museums, Arthur M. Sackler Museum, Cambridge: Promised gift of Robert S. and Betsy G. Feinberg, Photograph: Imaging Department © President and Fellows of Harvard College: p. 80; Hokusai-kan Museum, Obuse: pp. 86–87, 95; Honolulu Museum of Art, Gift of James A. Michener, 1969: p. 74 [15495]; Gift of James A. Michener, 1991: pp. 13 [24616], 76 [21893], 84 [21912]; Keiō University Library, Tokyo: p. 2; Minneapolis Institute of Art, Minneapolis: Bequest of Richard P. Gale: Cover, pp. 64 [74.1.230], 68 [74.1.219]; Gift of Louis W. Hill Jr.: pp. 59 [P.70.148], 71 [56.52.3]; The John and Shirley Nilson Endowment for Art Acquisition: p. 47 b. [2014.66]; National Diet Library, Tokyo: pp. 8, 10, 93; National Museum, Tokyo/Photograph: TNM Image Archives, Tokyo: pp. 6, 7, 79; Osaka City Museum of Fine Arts, Important Cultural Property: p. 32; Photograph: Kobe City Museum/DNPartcom: p. 58; Photograph © 2018 Museum of Fine Arts, Boston: Gift of C. Adrian Rübel: p. 12; William S. and John T. Spaulding Collection: pp. 4, 31, 42/43, 55, 61 b., 62/63, 65, 66 t., 67, 69, 72 t., 77; William Sturgis Bigelow Collection: pp. 9 r., 30, 33, 41, 48, 60, 61 t., 70, 73, 89, 91; Private collection: pp. 21, 90; Property of the Japan Ukiyo-e Museum, Matsumoto: p. 15 b.; Shimane Art Museum, Matsue/Photograph: Arte Planning, Tokyo: p. 15 t.; The Cleveland Museum of Art, Kelvin Smith Fund: p. 49 [1998.178]; The Metropolitan Museum of Art, New York, Henry L. Phillips Collection, Bequest of Henry L. Phillips, 1939: p. 14; The Howard Mansfield Collection, Rogers Fund, 1936: p. 85; The Museum of the Imperial Collections, Sannomaru Shōzōkan, Tokyo: p. 88; © The Trustees of the British Museum, London: Back cover, pp. 1, 9 l., 16, 17, 23, 25, 26 t., 27, 34, 36, 38/39, 40, 44, 45 b., 46, 47 t. l., r., 51, 72 b., 75, 81, 82, 83 t., 94; © The Trustees of the Chester Beatty Library, Dublin: p. 18 [CBL J 2819]; Waseda University Library, Tokyo: p. 35.

The author

Rhiannon Paget studied at Tokyo University of the Arts and received her doctorate in Japanese Art History from the University of Sydney, Australia. The curator of Asian art at the John & Mable Ringling Museum of Art in Sarasota, Florida, she has published research on Japanese woodblock prints, textiles, board games and *nihonga*.

Imprint

EACH AND EVERY TASCHEN BOOK PLANTS A SEED!
Each year, we offset our annual carbon emissions with carbon credits at the Instituto Terra, a reforestation program in Minas Gerais, Brazil, founded by Lélia and Sebastião Salgado. To find out more about this ecological partnership, please check: www.taschen.com/institutoterra.
Inspiration: unlimited.
Carbon footprint: (almost) zero.

Want to see more? Visit *taschen.com* to view our current publications, browse our latest magazine, and subscribe to our newsletter.

© 2026 TASCHEN GmbH
Hohenzollernring 53, D–50672 Köln
www.taschen.com

Printed in Bosnia-Herzegovina
ISBN 978–3–8365–6337–6

FRONT COVER
Under the Wave off Kanagawa (detail), *c.* 1830/31
From the series *Thirty-six Views of Mount Fuji*
Published by Nishimuraya Yohachi
Colour woodblock print, *ōban*,
25.7 x 37.7 cm (10⅛ x 14⅞ in.)
Minneapolis Institute of Art,
Bequest of Richard P. Gale

BACK COVER
Tōru Daijin (detail), *c.* 1833/34
From the series *True Mirrors of Chinese and Japanese Poems*, published by Moriya Jihei
Colour woodblock print, *nagaban*,
49.8 x 23.1 cm (19⅝ x 9 in.)
London, British Museum